# a Jewish Understanding of the New Testament

# BOOKS BY SAMUEL SANDMEL

# a Jewish Understanding of the New Testament

Rabbi Samuel Sandmel

New Preface by Rabbi David Sandmel

*For People of All Faiths, All Backgrounds*
**JEWISH LIGHTS Publishing**
Woodstock, Vermont

*Walking Together, Finding the Way*
SKYLIGHT PATHS Publishing
Woodstock, Vermont

*A Jewish Understanding of the New Testament*

2008 Third Printing of the Third Edition
2005 Second Printing of the Third Edition
2005 First Printing of the Third Edition

Preface to the Third Edition © 2005 by David Sandmel

**Library of Congress Cataloging-in-Publication Data**
Sandmel, Samuel.
A Jewish understanding of the New Testament / Samuel Sandmel ; new preface by David Sandmel.
p. cm.
"Previously printed in the UK as A Jewish understanding of the New Testament, 1956, 1974."
Includes bibliographical references and index.
ISBN-13: 978-1-59473-048-1 (quality pbk.); ISBN-10: 1-59473-048-2 (quality pbk.)
1. Bible. N.T.—Criticism, interpretation, etc. 2. Judaism—Relations—Christianity. 3. Christianity and other religions—Judaism. I. Title.
BS2361.3.S36 2004
225.6—dc22
2004056570

10  9  8  7  6  5  4  3

Manufactured in Canada

Cover Design: Sara Dismukes
SkyLight Paths, *"Walking Together, Finding the Way"* and colophon are trademarks of LongHill Partners, Inc., registered in the U.S. Patent and Trademark Office.

*Walking Together, Finding the Way*
Published by SkyLight Paths Publishing
A Division of LongHill Partners, Inc.
Sunset Farm Offices, Route 4
P.O. Box 237
Woodstock, VT 05091
Tel: (802) 457-4000
Fax: (802) 457-4004
www.skylightpaths.com

*For People of All Faiths, All Backgrounds*
Jewish Lights Publishing
A Division of LongHill Partners, Inc.
Sunset Farm Offices, Route 4
P.O. Box 237
Woodstock, VT 05091
Tel: (802) 457-4000
Fax: (802) 457-4004
www.jewishlights.com

*To*

HARVIE BRANSCOMB

# Table of Contents

PART FOUR
OTHER WRITINGS

PART FIVE
THE SIGNIFICANCE OF THE NEW TESTAMENT

# Preface to the Third Edition

To the best of my knowledge, *A Jewish Understanding of the New Testament* remains the only book written by a Jew about the entire New Testament. This was true in 1956 when the book was first published, it was true in 1974 when my father noted this fact in the introduction to an augmented edition of the book, and it remains true today. Jews have written extensively on Jesus, Paul, Christianity, and on other various aspects of the New Testament, but no other Jew has written a book on the New Testament as a whole. Certainly, the interest in this subject remains high in the Jewish community and beyond. Current events, such as the Pope's visit to Jerusalem and the publication of "Dabru Emet: A Jewish Statement on Christians and Christianity,"[1] both in 2000, and the release of Mel Gibson's controversial movie *The Passion of the Christ* in 2004, regularly increase Jewish interest in Christianity and its foundational texts.

Born in Dayton, Ohio, in 1911, Samuel Sandmel was the child of Eastern European immigrants. His father escaped Tsarist Russia and the pogroms at the turn of the twentieth century. My father grew up in St. Louis and attended public

---

[1] "Dabru Emet" was written by Tikva Frymer-Kensky, David Novak, Peter Ochs, and Michael Signer. It was endorsed by over two hundred rabbis and Jewish academics from around the world. It begins with the premise that in parts of the Christian world there have been significant changes in the theology and attitudes toward Jews and Judaism since the Holocaust. In light of these changes, Jews can now reconsider how they think about Christians and Christianity. The text of "Dabru Emet" is included in a volume of essays published to accompany the statement, *Christianity in Jewish Terms*, edited by Tikva Frymer-Kensky, David Novak, Peter Ochs, David Sandmel, and Michael Signer (Boulder, CO: Westview Press, 2000).

PREFACE TO THE THIRD EDITION

schools. He graduated Phi Beta Kappa from the University of Missouri, where he studied philology. He entered Hebrew Union College in Cincinnati in 1932 and was ordained a rabbi in 1937. After a brief stint as a congregational rabbi, he became the director of the B'nai B'rith Hillel Foundations at the University of North Carolina and Duke University. There he met and married my mother, Frances Langsdorf Fox. He also met and came under the influence of Harvie Branscomb III, who was then the dean of Duke Divinity School. When Branscomb learned of my father's desire to pursue an advanced degree in "Old Testament,"[2] he urged him to focus instead on New Testament. Branscomb, who was well versed in the languages of the period and steeped in rabbinic literature and Jewish scholarship, understood that my father brought an expertise to the study of the New Testament that few Christian scholars at the time possessed.

In 1942 my father left Hillel to become a Navy chaplain in World War II. Following the war, he directed the Hillel Foundation at Yale where he also completed his doctorate under Erwin Goodenough, whose seminal work in Judaism in the Greco-Roman world greatly influenced not only my father but all subsequent scholarship on Judaism and Christianity in late antiquity. In 1949, Harvie Branscomb, who had become the chancellor of Vanderbilt University, appointed my father to the Hillel chair of Jewish religion

---

[2] "Old Testament" was the term of choice in academic circles at that time. More recently, it has been recognized that "Old Testament" is a Christian term with significant theological overtones, some of which denigrate Judaism. Jews refer to their sacred scripture as Tanakh (a Hebrew acronym for Torah, Nevi'im [Prophets] and Ketuvim [writings]). More recently, scholars have attempted to find a term, such as Hebrew Bible, which, though not entirely satisfactory, is more theologically neutral.

and thought, a position that Branscomb himself helped to create and that was, at that time, one of the few chairs in Jewish studies at any American university. In 1952, Nelson Glueck brought my father to Hebrew Union College–Jewish Institute of Religion[3] where he served as professor of Bible and Hellenistic literature as well as provost and dean of the Graduate School. He retired from HUC–JIR in 1978 to become the Helen A. Regenstein Professor of Religion at the University of Chicago. Shortly after moving to Chicago, my father became ill. He died on November 4, 1979.

During his career, my father wrote numerous books and articles for both scholarly and popular audiences.[4] His scholarship and, perhaps more important, his ability to speak honestly but without rancor, helped him become an internationally recognized pioneer in interreligious dialogue. Krister Stendahl, a Protestant scholar, former dean of the Harvard Divinity School, bishop of Stockholm, Sweden, and a pioneer of Jewish-Christian dialogue, wrote of him, "Samuel Sandmel was a gift of God to both Jews and Christians. It was given to him to help change the climate and even the agenda of Jewish-Christian conversations."[5]

---

[3] Hebrew Union College, founded by Isaac Mayer Wise in 1875, and the Jewish Institute of Religion, founded by Stephen S. Wise (no relation) in 1922, merged in 1950.

[4] In addition to his scholarship, he published a novel about Moses entitled *Alone Atop the Mountain* (Garden City, NY: Doubleday, 1973), and his short story "The Colleagues of Mr. Chips" was included in *The Best American Short Stories 1961*, edited by Martha Foley and David Burnett (Boston: Houghton Mifflin, 1961). The most complete bibliography of his work can be found in *Nourished with Peace: Studies in Hellenistic Judaism in Memory of Samuel Sandmel*, edited by Frederick E. Greenspahn, Earle Hilgert, and Burton L. Mack (Chico, CA: Scholars Press, 1984).

[5] "A Friend and his Philo-Connection," in *Nourished with Peace*, 13.

Many Jews involved in Jewish-Christian dialogue concentrate on pointing out those aspects of Christian texts and Christian theology that lie at the heart of the Jewish-Christian tragedy. My father did not shy away from this, but he was equally committed to teaching Jews how to approach Christianity with respect. This book, *A Jewish Understanding of the New Testament*, marks his first major effort in this regard, which along with *We Jews and Jesus* (1965, 1973) and *We Jews and You Christians* (1967) forms a kind of trilogy. *We Jews and Jesus* was written "for those thoughtful Jewish people who seek to arrive at a calm and balanced understanding of where Jews can reasonably stand with respect to Jesus."[6] This is not a book about the historical Jesus. Indeed, my father believed that it is impossible to recover the Jesus of history, because the Gospel accounts obscure him with layers of later legend and theology (see chapter XVI, "The Historical Jesus"). It is, rather, about what Jews have thought concerning Jesus throughout history and how contemporary Jews, with the benefit of historical and scriptural scholarship, might think of Jesus today. As the title suggests, *We Jews and You Christians* was written for a Christian audience in an effort "to give an answer to a question very often put to me by Christians: What is the attitude of you Jews to us?"[7] The book concludes with a remarkable, and I believe, largely overlooked "Proposed Declaration: 'The Synagogue and the Christian People'" that in many ways presages "Dabru Emet." That two of these books are written primarily for Jews and one primarily for Christians is a bit artificial. My father addresses both Jews and Christians in all three and,

---

[6] *We Jews and Jesus*, vii.

[7] *We Jews and You Christians*, 1.

indeed, both Jews and Christians have read all three books and learned from them. A fourth book, *The Genius of Paul*, though more academic than the other three, deserves mention because, unlike Jesus, some of Paul's own writings have survived; therefore, my father believed one could write about him.

One might well ask whether the fact that *A Jewish Understanding of the New Testament* is the only such book written by a Jew merits its republication a half century after its composition. One might also wonder whether it has become outdated because of advances in the field. To a great extent I think it is fair to say the work holds up quite well, especially for the purpose for which it was intended, namely, as an introduction for the uninitiated Jewish reader. Those who wish to go beyond an introduction will want to read more recent works or move on to more advanced study.[8]

If there is one area where contemporary scholars may take issue with my father's work, it is on the distinction he draws between Hellenistic and Palestinian Judaism.[9] My father believed, following the tradition of scholarship in

---

[8] To name but one option, see Bart Ehrman, *The New Testament: A Brief Introduction.* (New York: Oxford University Press, 2004).

[9] The contemporary reader who is not familiar with the history of scholarship may find the term "Palestinian" Judaism confusing. In today's political climate, "Palestinian" refers to Arabs living in the contested areas of the West Bank and the Gaza Strip, thus "Palestinian Judaism" seems like a contradiction in terms. In the context of antiquity, "Palestine" was the name the Romans used to refer to what Jews call the Land of Israel. Palestinian Judaism, then, signifies the religion and culture of Jews living in the Land of Israel in the Roman period and is often contrasted with Diaspora Judaism. At issue is the extent to which Judaism in the Diaspora was influenced by Hellenistic culture and Judaism in the Land of Israel was free from it.

which he was trained, that the New Testament documents were written in Greek, outside the Land of Israel. Though in their early stages some documents originated in Judea, in their final form the influence of Hellenism dominates. Between the first and second editions of the book, my father noted a trend in New Testament scholarship that "re-emphasized" the influence of Palestinian Judaism. In the introduction to the 1974 edition, he states that he considered this trend "unsound" and directed the reader to what is perhaps his most enduring contribution to scholarship, an article entitled "Parallelomania," his presidential address to the Society of Biblical Literature in 1961.[10] His adamancy on this subject can be attributed in part to his training with Goodenough and in part to the excesses that he addresses in "Parallelomania." The influence of Hellenism on Palestinian Judaism continues to be a significant focus of study and debate,[11] but I think that today he might moderate his stance and revise some of his conclusions.

Samuel Sandmel's scholarship and devotion to interreligious understanding touched the lives of rabbis, Christian clergy, scholars, and laypeople around the world. With republication of this, his first book, his life work will, I hope, continue to influence Jews and Christians who share his belief in the possibility of reconciliation.

---

[10] *Journal of Biblical Literature* 81 (1962): 1–13, reprinted in Sandmel, *Two Living Traditions: Essays on Religion and the Bible* (Detroit: Wayne University Press, 1972), 291–304.

[11] See, for example, Lee I. Levine, *Judaism and Hellenism in Antiquity: Conflict or Confluence?* (Seattle: University of Washington Press, 1998).

Aᴍᴇʀɪᴄᴀɴ ᴊᴇᴡs, by and large, know the New Testament today only from oblique and random contacts — a quotation here, a verse there, a chapter read in a literature course, a portion heard at a Christian wedding or funeral. With the physical isolation of the European ghetto far behind us, and with our intellectual homogeneity with fellow Americans taken for granted, our very modern generation of Jews is virtually as sealed off, whether through inertia or a vestigial sense of taboo, from a real knowledge of the New Testament as our forefathers traditionally have been. We are in constant contact with this great body of religious expression that has become a cultural force in our secular environment. Some of its frames of reference are part of the popular heritage, its echoes appear in our speech, and yet most of us have never equipped ourselves with a sound, necessarily rewarding understanding of it. Many average Jews certainly have not read it, and so its mysterious quality evokes Jewish judgments of an often strange and startling nature. Chauvinistic Jews dismiss it with derision. Unity seekers, on the basis of its parallels to Jewish teachings, extend to it an enthusiastic accolade that is often emotionally sound but unsupported by study. Still other American Jews, whose number makes them average, have neither preconceptions nor biases about the New Testament which they have not read, but only a thoughtful curiosity and an earnest desire for information; it is for such Jews that I have prepared this book.

In an earlier generation, even in the United States, such a book would have found few readers. Throughout the centuries leading up to our own it was customary, in fact commendable, for Jews to shun the New Testament. It was a book belonging in a context freighted with emotion. After all, it was the sacred scripture of the group that had proved itself to be the enemy and the persecutor. Indeed, some of its pages contained the theoretical justification of the actual, sad things which Christians did to Jews. It is only within the last century that there has been a shift in the basis of that irrational hatred of Jews, misnamed anti-Semitism, from a religious to a quasi-racial basis, and with this shift, a relaxation on the part of Jews of the intellectual barriers to inquiry about what at last must be acknowledged as a fellow religion. It is true that even within the last century crude traces of religious anti-Semitism have still made themselves manifest, and suspicion and antagonism on both sides still abide in varying localities and measures. But in a large sense, especially among enlightened Christians, religious anti-Jewishness has abated and often disappeared. Especially in the Western democracies, many Jews and Christians have been able to overcome the traditional animosity which is the heritage of almost twenty centuries, and have gone ahead in constructive fellowship.

Scholars have formed an important vanguard in this development. Both the readers and the author of this book can bear grateful witness to their pioneering efforts. Signally, during the past hundred years Jewish scholars have begun to join Christians in the field of New Testament study. The liberal scholarship of the nineteenth century transcended sectarian lines. Jewish historians and rabbinists have had frequent occasion to refer to passages in the New Testament, and more than one Jewish scholar has made substantial contributions to the general understanding of the New Testament. Indeed, such scholarly contributions by Jews have been sufficient in quantity to furnish the material for a lengthy book, written in German by a Swedish scholar, the translation of whose title is "The Question of Jesus in Present-Day Judaism" (*Die Jesusfrage im neuzeitlichen Judentum*), by Gösta Lindeskog, Uppsala, 1938); and a British scholar has written a small book summarizing the views of several Jewish scholars on Jesus (Thomas Walker, *Jewish Views on Jesus*, London, 1931).

This scholarly productivity has been for the most part highly technical, and has been published in the journals of the learned societies, which do not ordinarily come to the hand of the usual layman. The audience addressed in these writings has been the world of professors, regardless of religious affiliation.

In the United States several rabbis, of the Reform wing, have written "popular" accounts of Jesus for a Jewish audience. These have often been too superficial, or marked by a zeal for "re-claiming" Jesus for Judaism. Yet they have been useful and serviceable, despite the absence of a description of the New Testament writings, or an objective assessment of them.

The first Jewish scholar whose studies in the New Testament were directed towards the enlightenment of the Jewish laymen was Claude Goldsmid Montefiore. His two-volume work, *The Synoptic Gospels*, is a verse by verse commentary on the first three Gospels, Matthew, Mark, and Luke. Montefiore came from a famous Jewish family of position and wealth. He turned to scholarship in the field of religion as his hobby, and the liberal intellectual climate of Britain in his day was congenial to his pursuit of the study of Jesus in the Gospels.

A special interest of Montefiore was the relationship between the teachings of Jesus and the teachings of the rabbis of the period at the beginning of the Christian Era. The rabbinic literature, as we shall note, is difficult material to use properly, and Montefiore had the foresight to have associated with himself in the comparative studies two first-rate Jewish scholars: first, Israel Abrahams, and then Herbert Loewe. These partnerships were amazing affairs, in that neither subservience nor tyranny dictated the results of any difference of opinion; but both Abrahams and Loewe were cited constantly in Montefiore's writings in refutation of viewpoints which Montefiore expresses. The uniqueness of this relationship is the more discernible in the case of the collaboration with Loewe, for Loewe was a staunch Orthodox Jew, while Montefiore was a Reform, or Liberal, Jew.

Reform Judaism in England is a rather recent development, and Montefiore was one of its pioneers. In common with the early German Reformers of the first decade of the nineteenth century and the American Reformers of the 1850's, Montefiore frequently seemed to find that an espousal of Reform necessitated a criticism of Orthodoxy, contemporaneous or ancient, and some rather sharp and combative judgments of this sort are carried over into his New Testament studies in his comments about traditional Judaism. Moreover, in pursuit of his tendency to make evaluations, we get from Montefiore not only a comparison and contrast between the teachings of the rabbis and of Jesus, but also a judgment on the relative worth of these. In many instances, Montefiore expressed a greater admiration for certain teachings of Jesus than for the parallel but similar teachings of the rabbis of Jesus' time. Some of Montefiore's Jewish critics found such admiration distasteful, and accused him of truckling to Christians. Any fair-minded reader of Montefiore will recognize the absurdity and unfairness of this charge.

From an environment almost directly the antithesis of Montefiore's has come Joseph Klausner's *Jesus of Nazareth*, the best-known Jewish book on Jesus. Klausner, a staunch Zionist, is an East European by birth but is, by long residence, an Israeli.

This book was written in modern Hebrew; translated into English, it has become a standard reference in most liberal Protestant seminaries. While striving for objectivity, Klausner has been influenced by his Jewish nationalism, and he reads back into the time of Jesus many of the burning issues which have arisen in Jewish life in the modern period. I do not believe that his book is without some serious defects; but it is, nevertheless, a noteworthy achievement.

In part Klausner's book was a protest against Montefiore; yet, curiously, Klausner also evoked from some fellow Jews a hearty disapproval for venturing at all into what these critics regarded as forbidden or, at best, as distrusted territory. For a Jew to write on the New Testament has been a procedure not calculated to evoke universal approbation. Montefiore speaks — and here he might have spoken for Klausner, too — of the loneliness of the task.

The task is no longer quite so lonely as it used to be. In the present work, which may be presumptuously described as being in the tradition of both Montefiore and Klausner, I have found encouragement in abundance from many of my fellow Jews. Like my illustrious predecessors, I, too, am writing as a Jew. I, too, with all the fairness and balance at my command, attempt to present a lucid understanding of the New Testament to Jews. But the goal which I have set for myself is different from those which my Jewish predecessors have undertaken. Mainly they have written for persons with some technical competence. I have written for the average intelligent and educated American Jew. I have presupposed that his knowledge, whether of the New Testament or of the Jewish history of that period, is less than copious, and I have tried to supply what I have judged to be a usual lack.

That I am a Jew writing on the New Testament makes it

desirable that the reader be able to discount, in my case as in that of Montefiore and Klausner, any predisposition which my general background would occasion. I am writing on the significant religious content of the book, as a scholar of it, not as one religiously committed to it. In the sense that I am a Reform Jew it is undeniable that the modernism and rationalism of Reform Judaism shape my approach, as such factors shape the approach of anyone to a traditional literature. A Reform Jew is selective in what he accepts as valid in the ancient Jewish traditions; it is to be expected, then, that he will exercise similar selectivity in his approach to Christianity, and that an earnestly sympathetic understanding, therefore, of one facet or another of that tradition is not to be equated with a doctrinal acceptance of it.

But this volume is not entirely a Jewish, or Reform Jewish, approach to the New Testament. I express a good many judgments of my own, yet I am under heavy obligation to the Protestant scholarship under the aegis of which I studied the New Testament.

My own bias will be evident in that I find myself operating within the suppositions of the liberals. The liberal Protestant scholarship is free, objective, and rigidly honest. In it, predisposition and prejudgment are reduced to the vanishing point, and reverence for the New Testament has seemed to evoke as full and open-minded a study and investigation as fallible man can undertake. * The fair-mindedness of most liberal Christian scholars has been one of the delightful discoveries of my study of the New Testament.

The liberal or modernist mode, and the Fundamentalist mode,

---

*I shall speak later on of a recent Protestant development, Neo-Orthodoxy; for the moment I include it, for convenience, under liberal.

of interpreting either the Old or the New Testament abide in opposition, into our own day. The Fundamentalist regards Scripture as literally divine, and he is persuaded of its inerrancy and validity in every detail. The liberal regards Scripture as collected expressions of religious faith, and he seeks to understand the expressions as products of times and places and people; he does not attribute verbal accuracy or objective historical authenticity to every sentence, phrase, or syllable. For his own religious convictions he tries to winnow out of the transient and the local and the personal those religious insights which are abiding and universal.

Yet within this fair-mindedness liberal Christian scholarship is not of one piece. I doubt that diversity of opinion is as present in any other discipline as it is in New Testament study. There are differing schools of interpretation, as there have been different eras of interpretation. In paragraph after paragraph I have had to select my preference from among divergent and contradictory scholarly views; and at many points in what ensues I shall have to give summarily a view which I espouse, even without indicating at each point a different view found in an equally respectable Christian scholar.

It has not seemed useful to burden the new reader with this plethora of scholarly theories. Perhaps in many places I will have followed a view which may turn out to be erroneous. Certainly in one section, that on Paul, I have followed the minority opinion. I have done so, of course, through being persuaded that the opinion which I have adopted is the correct one. Though I have often indicated where opinions diverge, I have to rely on the indulgence of the scholars, who will, I trust, understand that in a work of this kind decisiveness, even when it is premature, is unavoidable.

To compress this material into one volume has meant perforce to gloss over some matters and to omit others entirely. My Jewish bias will be evident in what I select to include, and in the questions of proportion. Since I am writing for a Jewish audience, I advert primarily to those unquestionably basic matters about which I judge Jews will want to know. I try to present the New Testament material, not as our neighbors see it, but as it is studied by the scholars in our leading universities.

It is an avowed purpose that this volume shall serve as a solid medium for the better understanding of Christianity by Jews. A constant danger has been the pitfall which lies in words. What the author intends as description may appear to the reader as evaluation, and condescending evaluation at that. I have no fears about the scholarly content of what I have written. But an awareness, which I can immodestly call keen, of the dangers inherent in the area in which I am writing leads me to ask the indulgence of the reader. It is my earnest hope that he will take at face value the assertion that any derogatory nuances or overtones of this kind are completely inadvertent. For such possible inadvertencies I apologize. That they appear in the text, if at all, is only because eyes of Christian friends, in addition to mine, have somehow failed to note any latent connotation.

My greatest debt on the scholarly side is owed to my friend and teacher, Professor Erwin R. Goodenough of Yale University. An emphasis in the book, on the Judaism of the Greek dispersion, marks the divergence of my approach from that of the usual Christian introduction to the New Testament; scholars who note this difference should know that Professor Goodenough's influence is here to be discerned. Much of what I have written about Paul stems from Professor Goodenough; indeed, I am unable to say where his views leave off and where my own minor extensions begin. Moreover, if I have succeeded at all in fitting early Christianity into a broad setting of the Hellenistic-Roman world, then whatever breadth of outlook or width of horizon is revealed can again be traced to him. Perhaps it is unnecessary to add that the expression of gratitude to him should not include any responsibility on his part for any imperfections in my formulation.

If it should turn out that in my special studies I have sailed some useful course, then it is a course which Chancellor Harvie Branscomb of Vanderbilt University charted. My colleagues at the Vanderbilt School of Religion, Dean John K. Benton, J. Philip Hyatt, Kendrick Grobel, Robert M. Hawkins, Edward Ramsdell, Nels Ferre, the late J. Minton Batten, George Mayhew, and Samuel E. Stumpf, have seemed to me to embody in their personal convictions and actions the finest expressions of Christian idealism, and it is almost beyond expression to try to indicate the warmth and consideration so generously extended to me during the fruitful years of our fellowship.

Carl Kraeling, now of Chicago University, and Millar Burrows of Yale have both taught and steered me. My singling out of the late Dean Clarence T. Craig is to indicate a special debt of gratitude, since from him I received an awareness of the range and values in the accumulated New Testament scholarship. Again, my gratitude should not seem to attribute to them the responsibility for what I have written.

Less tangibly but equally persistently, I owe definite debts to Chaplain Harill S. Dyer, U. S. Navy Retired; to Albert Outler, Professor of Theology at Southern Methodist University; and to Sidney Lovett, Chaplain of Yale University. Similarly, I must not fail to mention Nelson Glueck, Julian Morgenstern, and Jacob R. Marcus of the Hebrew Union College-Jewish Institute of Religion. Professor James Harrell Cobb, of Yankton

Seminary, Yankton, South Dakota, and Rabbi Abraham I. Shinedling, of Beckley, West Virginia, have helped me enormously by their critical reading of the typescript. I am indebted to Rabbi Abraham J. Brachman and Rabbi Levi A. Olan, who headed the Alumni Publication Committee. To Rabbi Olan in particular I owe the initial suggestion which led the Alumni to make the publication possible. The solicitous interest of Rabbis Jacob P. Rudin, Ariel Goldburg, Ferdinand M. Isserman, and Albert M. Shulman has been most gratifying. Rabbi Herman Snyder has skillfully steered the course from typescript to a bound book. Dr. Maurice Jacobs has been to me, as to other authors whose works his firm has printed, a model of graciousness and solicitude. To Sylvia Dunsker and Helen Lederer I am indebted for invaluable stenographic help. Mr. Maxwell Whiteman of the American Jewish Archives helped me greatly in a variety of ways. Mr. Maurice Delegator's design for the dust jacket has been as pleasing as his solicitude has been friendly.

The quotations are principally from the Revised Standard Version of the Bible and are used by permission of the copyright owners, the National Council of the Churches of Christ in the U. S. A. Three selections from *Gospel Parallels* are used with the permission of the Thomas Nelson & Sons, who also publish the Revised Standard Version.

The indices, an addition to the second printing, are largely the work of Charles and Terry Kroloff.

My wife's part amounts virtually to collaboration in the preparation of this volume. If, as I fancy, the text often seems to flow along, and if complexities in the New Testament are presented with some reasonable clarity, then her gifts with the pen have borne fruit. Her labors on the manuscript, however, are only the crowning contribution. Without her there might well have been neither preparation nor determination and execution.

# NEW FOREWORD

## I

The direct purpose of this book, when I wrote it about twenty years ago, was to introduce the literature of the New Testament to Jews. I had in mind, in the word introduce, its basic meaning, to present to its intended audience something quite unknown to them. While very many Jews have written about Jesus, no other Jew, so far as I have been able to discover, has written a book on the New Testament. To write about literature almost two thousand years old, composed some five thousand miles away, seemed then (and still seems) to me to need the buttressing clarification which Christian scholars have provided. Hence, I attempted to reflect the general stream of what Christian scholars had thought and written about the New Testament writings. Where I expressed my own opinion this was almost entirely limited to selecting from a range of differing Christian opinions those that appealed to me as right. In later books and articles I have not hesitated to express independent judgments of my own, but in this book I usually tried to abstain from doing so.

The reception of the book was mostly gratifying. On one level, commercial publishers, while praising the manuscript, were unanimous in declaring there would be no market for it, and one leading firm returned the manuscript, including a reader's favorable report no less than glowing, with the assertion that a sale of more than two hundred copies was the verdict emerging from a survey which the firm had made. The book was published by the Hebrew Union College Press; six thousand copies were distributed within a year, and a first paperback edition of five thousand has become exhausted.

On a different level, the reviews have been cordial and laudable (though not without the disparagement from some few Christians that I, as a non-Christian, could simply not understand the Christian faith, and from some few Jews who felt that my goal should have been to denigrate, insult, and refute Christianity). Most of the reviewers had some sense of the acute problems of inclusion and omission entailed; some, to my regret, seemed unaware of the difficulty of putting complex matters into what I hoped was simple prose. A small minority responded, in typical pedantic fashion, to the absence of elaborate footnotes; I had omitted these deliberately on the premise that for the lay reader they would be deterring interruptions, and for scholars unnecessary, since the scholarship here reflected was in the common domain of New Testament researches.

At two points, despite considerable rewriting, I faced some problems for which I could not find solutions. I saw no way adequately to deal with Paul in such terms that a general reader could readily absorb the full nuances, but I felt that I had perhaps adequately suggested his contribution and influence. Second, the chapter on the Gospel According to John troubled me, for there too I could not come to a satisfying way of reflecting its full content and many subleties to the reader being introduced to it for the first time. I told myself that I did not, on first introduction, have to tell all that could be told. One does the best that one can, under the circumstances.

I am not sure, however, that I have in the book adequately made clear the difference between the Christian scholar and a Jewish family's friendly Christian neighbors who are not scholars. The New Testament is scarcely the same to the two, just as the Hebrew Bible of Jewish scholars is not the same as that of ordinary Jewish people. It is not alone that scholarship, broad and precise, is different from devoted piety, but rather that for our Christian neighbors Jesus is not a figure who has emerged from study but, instead, from agreeable associations: the home, the church, the religious school. This Jesus arises from Christmas carols and Christmas gifts, from Easter finery. He is found on the child's phonograph record:

Jesus loves me, that I know
'Cause my mother told me so.

To a sorrowing family at a funeral, in countless generations, the words "I am the Resurrection and the Life" have brought comfort. More than one person, confronting a moral dilemma, has found his sense of guidance by asking what Jesus would do in that situation. Men of undoubted integrity have felt that it was the example of Jesus which motivated them to deeds they have been proud of. Again, men of genuine depth have felt that through Jesus they have reached to the greatest profundity in grasping man's relationship with God. In such terms lies the range of meaning which Jesus has to our Christian neighbors.

Ordinary Christians are not deeply schooled in New Testament scholarship, so central in this book. Indeed they are usually unaware how profoundly Christian New Testament scholarship has challenged what is taught to children in Christian Sunday Schools. As in Jewish Sunday Schools, so in the Christian, a natural emphasis is put on the traditions a community has inherited; modern biblical scholarship, however, challenges the validity of a host of these traditions. Moreover, because Christian scholars encountered difficulties with church officials, endowed more with personal power and human authority than with learning, a tone of disrespect for popularly held traditions is a reality in the Christian scholarship I had been taught. This book is oriented to what learned Christians have come to think and to teach about the New Testament, rather than to the piety of one's admirable but not deeply learned Christian neighbor.

I tried to write with fullest respect about beliefs which I have not shared. In a word, I tried to write about Christian sacred literature in the way I would have wanted Christians to write about what is precious to us Jews.

Since my topic was the literature of the New Testament, and not Christian history, I think that I did not supply a certain aspect of the historical background which I make the effort to furnish here; I have in mind not so much details, as a more general statement:

Christianity arose within Judaism. Respecting time, there is a difference between the matters of dates (such as the last year of Herod's reign, 4 B.C., which is often taken as the year of Jesus' birth) and, without touching on calendar dates, the question of where Christianity believed it stood in relation to its past, its present, and its future. There lay behind Christianity, in its self-understanding, a world which had come into being with creation as described in Genesis Chapter I. Adam had been created, and Eve made from his rib, and *time* had moved on through ten generations to Noah. In Noah's day mankind had managed to become so corrupt that God had destroyed every living thing but the passengers on Noah's ark. From Noah's three sons there had arisen the populations of the three known parts of the world, Asia, Africa, and the Grecian lands and islands. In the tenth generation after Noah, there had emerged Abraham, the ancestor of God's people. (To interrupt here, *time* respecting this past was not so much a succession of dates as it was the record of the *progression* of mankind in past history.)

The Hebrews had originated in three solitary individuals, Abraham the father, Isaac his son, and Jacob his grandson. To Jacob there had been born twelve sons, the ancestors of the tribes which collectively constituted the Children of Israel. Two important events took place in close succession; one, the Children of Israel were enslaved in Egypt and redeemed from slavery under Moses. Second, at the sacred mountain, called both Sinai and Horeb, the Children of Israel had entered into a solemn covenant with the Deity. His obligation was to protect and defend Israel; their obligation was to be undeviatingly loyal to him and to obey his revealed laws.

The Israelites were destined to enter Canaan, to conquer it and settle in it. They already had, as tradition declared, a legacy from the previous times. Moses had been able, because of God's revelation of himself to him, to interpret for his generation what the will of God was now. In the future ages after Moses, there were to arise Moses' spiritual successors, the prophets, who, in their times, would be the means by which God would disclose his will to his people.

The covenant, dramatically entered into at Sinai, was remembered and, indeed, often renewed, so that loyalty to God and obedience to his laws were demanded of each generation. But the Israelites, being people, were incapable of fullest loyalty and obedience. Periodically they were scolded, indeed excoriated, by a succession of prophets (whose writings have in large measure survived). This disloyalty and disobedience meant the end of God's protection; the prophets interpreted natural catastrophies and political disasters as God's punishment on Israel for their disloyalty and disobedience. In 722/721 the Assyrians conquered the northern of the two related Israelite kingdoms; the people of these ten tribes were exiled eastward and they disappeared. In 596 the Babylonians conquered the remaining southern kingdom of Judas; in 586 the people were taken eastward into exile, but these people did not disappear. Persisting, they even managed, after the Persians had conquered the Babylonians, to return to Judah.

Up to this point, the dominant view of the prophets had been that a deserved punishment was coming upon the people. Now a new emphasis arose, this related to the past, the present, and the future. The past, it was now declared, was the time of when Israel had been formed; the present was its hazardous and uncertain recovery from the tribulations of exile and misery. Was there to be any future?

On the one hand, the immediate prospects seemed dismal. Judea ( a Greek form of *Judah*) was ruled by Persians, and neighboring nations had been, and still were, hostile. Judeans had been scattered into many lands. But, so ran a new prophetic message, beyond the dark immediate future, there were great and heartening events destined to ensue. On some future day God would arise in judgment, especially on the nations which had done evil things in general and which, in particular, had treated Judea cruelly. After that time of judgment, a new and better age would dawn. In that new age, destined for the end of time, war and threats of war would completely cease. Peacefully the nations of the world would stream to Mount Zion, and there, after being taught God's ways, they would become merged into a single humanity, secure and prosperous.

The two visions, of a near future with God's punishment, and the remote future with mankind's emergence into a new age, permeated the thought of the populace, and this thought grew and developed not over a period of decades but over a period of centuries.

When Christianity arose, its view was that its present was the time when God's punishment was about to be meted out; the next step was conceived as the arrival at last of that future that had once seemed so remote. To rephrase this, the wondrous things to happen *at the end of time* were now on the verge of happening, of happening immediately. It is in this sense that one allocates Christianity in time in terms of its view of itself.

This view of standing on the verge of the imminent arrival of the new age now needs to be understood against particular aspects of the period and of the developed thought. The idea of God's judgment had once been thought of solely in terms of *nations;* by the time early Christianity had emerged, it was thought of in terms of individuals too. In older thought, one needed to endure the pain of living under foreign domination, whether by the Persians, or later by the Syrian Greeks, and even later (as in early Christian times) by the Romans; the latter had ended the independence of Judea by a conquest in 63 B.C., and in 37 the Romans put Herod on the Judean throne, terminating the Maccabean dynasty.

The recurrent, almost continuous longing for political independence had come to be expressed in the hope that an independent

Jewish king, sent by God, would arise to rule over Judea. Because the ceremony which raised a commoner to a king was his anointment with oil, the word "anointed" denoted "king." The Hebrew for "anointed" is *Messiah*. Hence, the awaited Messiah was the king whom God would some day send to rule over his people, free of foreign domination.

This hope for a Messiah, arising many centuries before the time of Jesus, went through change, expansion, and subtle alterations in those centuries. Accordingly, the future dawn of a new age was associated with the hope of arrival of the Messiah, so that "new age" and "messianic age" now became synonymous. Also, it was to be at the coming of the Messiah that the awaited "judgment day" would come; since judgment day had become individual as well as national, the arrival of the Messiah came to be regarded as ushering in a judgment over all mankind. Resurrection, the belief that the dead would be restored to life, became conceived of as bound up with judgment day, so that those wicked people who had in this life gone unpunished, and the righteous as yet unrewarded, would be judged at judgment day. Some seemed to hold the view that all men would be resurrected and then judged, while others held that first would come judgment and, as a delayed reward, the righteous would be resurrected.

In short, the word "messiah" originally meant little more than a human king; by the age of Jesus it was a term with abundant associations: personal and national judgment; the ushering in of a new age; freedom from and independence of the foreign domination; the miraculous ingathering of Judeans scattered throughout the then known world.

At moments in Jewish history, when human suffering has been astute, the yearning for the coming of God's anointed increased in intensity. More than one person, both before and after Jesus, has emerged among Jews to be hailed by his followers as the long awaited Messiah.

Just as the term Messiah had changed and developed prior to

the time of Jesus, so, too, it became altered, certainly among his followers, after his time. Some, indeed, assert that it changed during his own lifetime. Two such changes are of surpassing significance.

The one change was to alter the *pattern* of the expectation. Before Jesus, the hope and expectation was that the coming of the Messiah would be a single event, a single action. The career of Jesus entailed a necessary alteration: he was believed by his followers to be the Messiah, but the Romans, interpreting him to be connected with the intermittent uprisings against the Roman occupiers of Judea, executed him by crucifixion. The belief arose among his followers that he had indeed died but had been granted a special resurrection, this in advance of the general resurrection so many Jews awaited. It was held that, on being resurrected, Jesus had appeared to his followers, and had been with them for a while. Then he had ascended, or re-ascended, to heaven (from where it was believed he had come), to await a future time, held to be near at hand, when he would return. The wondrous expectations revolving around the Messiah were associated with this "second coming"; the first appearance was regarded as preparatory for the new age and its miraculous benefits. That is, the older view expected the benefits to come in a single event; in the new movement a preparatory appearance was to be followed by a second event, the climactic return.

Inevitably, there were minds and hearts which embellished the meaning of the initial appearance, at the same time that these, and other minds, embellished what would take place at the second coming. The sense of time, that the world stood near the end of this age, abided. The judgment day was still in the future, though in the near future; the world, then, was for a short while still enmeshed in its wickedness. Some described this wickedness as the evil rule by Rome. Others gave as the explanation for the rule by Rome, and for other wickedness, that the earth had in some way become the domain of the devil, Satan. At an earlier time, Satan was viewed as part of the hosts of heaven, including the angels (who had become prominent in Jewish thought); now Satan had come to be viewed as a rebel against God. Because of Satan's rebellion, he had been cast out of heaven, and had managed to become the ruler on earth. Because of Satan's rule, wickedness of all kinds flourished, and, indeed, men were alienated from God through Satan's pervasive force and power. If the new age was to dawn, the power of Satan needed to be destroyed. The view arose, accordingly, that Jesus, at his first coming, had broken the power of Satan, so that the kingdom of God could soon replace the kingdom of Satan. At the second coming of Jesus, the power of Satan would be totally destroyed, and wickedness would cease, and man's alienation from God would come to an end. And the Second Coming was expected soon.

The second of the two alterations arose rather naturally. In Judea, the Messiah was conceived of as destined to destroy the power of Rome, and to inaugurate an independent kingdom (ruled over either by the Messiah, or by the person he might designate). Outside Judea, especially when non-Jews joined with adherents of the new movement in expecting the second coming to take place soon, the connection of Messiah and a Jewish king in Judea faded away, and minds now associated the Messiah with overcoming the universal alienation of men from God. In a phrase, earlier the Messiah was viewed as freeing the Jews from their untoward experience with Rome; now the Messiah was viewed as freeing mankind, Jew and Gentile, from its alienation from God.

The Second Coming was seemingly being delayed. The more it seemed delayed, the more adherents of the new movement centered their attention on the past, on the First Coming. Indeed, some, virtually abandoning the expectation of a Second Coming, now regarded the benefits of a new age as already at hand through the First Coming; that is, man's alienation from God was already ended; this, so it was contended, was the true significance of the First Coming.

Initially, Christendom was a movement supposed to last for the short time between the now and the Second Coming. As the Second Coming ceased to be a vivid expectation, Christendom became a movement to last for all ages. To last, it needed to develop. It needed organization, a way of worship, a set of officials, an explanation of its religious beliefs.

The literature of the New Testament is a series of documents which come out of Christian experience. The earliest writings, the Epistles of Paul, are from a time when the Second Coming was expected soon; Paul is a foremost witness to what I have described as "man's alienation." The four Gospels come from a time when the expectation of the Second Coming was still somewhat vivid, but the major interest has turned to what the First Coming had come to mean, and to what the career of Jesus had been.

The other writings reflect the variety of church interests and needs when it came to be conceived of as an entity destined to endure.

## II

When I wrote this book, it seemed to me that the dominating scholarship held that since the New Testament books were written in Greek, and outside Judea, a generous reflection of Greek notions and ideas had come to overlay the admittedly Judean origin of the movement. Some five years before then, the Dead Sea Scrolls had come to light, and when I was writing the book, there was taking place the earliest skirmishes in the "Battle of the Scrolls." Scholars in unequal division differed about their basic authenticity, for a few scholars regarded the Scrolls as medieval forgeries. There were some scholars who saw in the Scrolls a basis for attributing to Judea certain ideas and notions which earlier scholars had labeled Greek, "hellenistic." Some scholars believed they could see a direct, genetic connection between the community which had created the Scrolls and early Christianity. In a word, a general trend in New

Testament scholarship has been to re-emphasize Judea at the expense of the Greek world. I do not approve of this general trend, and consider it unsound.[1] It is part, so it seems to me, of a conservative bent in current scholarship which, instead of confronting the older, "radical" scholarship and of refuting it, has cavalierly ignored it; to give two examples, the Anchor Bible *Matthew* by William F. Albright and C. S. Mann, and the Anchor Bible *Epistle to the Hebrews* by George Wesley Buchanan.

A major motif in Gospel scholarship has been "Form Criticism." Its premises have gone along this line: the Gospels are products of the Greek world, written some forty or more years after the events which they describe. Behind the Gospels there were possibly some written sources, but also a period in which traditions about Jesus were transmitted orally. Is it possible to determine from the *form* of items in the Gospels (pithy sayings, short anecdotes, extended stories) how the material grew and was shaped from the time of Jesus in Judea until their appearance in the Gospels? If so, can the materials be stripped of the results of growth and transmission, and their original form within the age of Jesus determined?

Today, form criticism, though widely pursued by many scholars, is rejected by some conservatives because many of its results are negative in the sense of not taking us back to the time of Jesus, and by some (like me) who worry about the validity of the technique; I find it all too often subjective and even capricious.

In recent years, the view has arisen that to trace a Gospel item back as far as possible answers only part of the need. The more important task is to notice the use to which the author of a Gospel has put the developing or developed material. This pursuit is called "redaction criticism"; a synonym for redaction is "editing"; hence, the discipline asks, how did the writer of a Gospel "edit" for his use the materials he inherited?

---

[1] See my "Parallelomania," in *Journal of Biblical Literature*, 1961.

The new conservatism alluded to above has created a striking difference in current scholarship on Paul. Acts of the Apostles, which deals with the history of the Church after the ascension of Jesus, had long presented a great array of problems to scholars, especially in its treatment of Paul (as found in Chapter XXIII). Today these problems are very often bypassed, and as a result of taking Acts uncritically, a Paul emerges who is an ordinary Palestinian Jew, rather than the Grecian Jew of the older scholarship. On the other hand, there are some researchers who have now set forth some novel theories about gnosticism. The term is at once easy and hard to define. The root meaning of gnostic is "to know"; a gnostic was one who "knew" the way to God. The denotation of the word, though, is a bit different, for a gnostic's knowledge was not that which can be learned by study, but rather by an illumination that comes directly from God. In a sense, the word "gnostic" is not too distant from our word "mystic." Within an established religious tradition, with an array of officials and a way of worship, the gnostic emerges as if he needs none of these externals, for his sense of direct communication with God can persuade him that these are quite dispensable. It is a fact that in the second Christian century gnosticism emerged in various guises and forms.

In older scholarship, it was usually held that as Christianity became increasingly permeated by Greek philosophy and religion, these spurred the rise of gnosticism. Today, however, there are scholars who regard gnosticism as having roots older than Christianity, and as having existed outside it. Indeed, the background of Paul's work is seen by such scholars as one of intense and vivid currents and cross-currents, entailing even at that early time gnostic tendencies already so much at hand that, so it is held, it is not right to regard gnosticism as arising only in the second century. Other scholars have protested that such early gnosticism is only a scholarly hypothesis based on inferences, and that since no gnostic literary texts exist to buttress the hypothesis, it is quite unpersuasive.

The point is that scholarship in the humanities never stands still. One can question whether, in its moving, it always moves forward. I have not been always persuaded by much that is novel.

But even were this otherwise, I have not thought that a book of introduction should be encumbered by what could so easily become excessive. I have written a number of books and essays, and there, rather than here, I have expressed my opinions. On gnosticism, for example, one can see my introductory essay on Philo and gnosticism in *Philo's Place in Judaism* (second printing), KTAV Publishing House. My views on Paul are to be found in *The Genius of Paul: A Study in History* (Schocken paperback, 1970). Since in my view Paul is a Greek Jew, remote in thought and feeling from Palestinian Jews of his time, it has gone against the grain of those who seek for only Palestinian Judaism to explain the New Testament. One might consult also "Paul Reconsidered" in *Two Living Traditions: Essays in Bible and Religion,* and "Palestinian and Hellenistic Judaism and Christianity," in a presentation volume to Rabbi Levi Olan, scheduled for 1974 publication.

My *We Jews and Jesus* (Oxford paperback, 1972) is a more detailed statement of the conclusion found here on page 207. A chapter in that book, "Toward a Jewish Attitude to Christianity," is expanded in my *We Jews and You Christians* (Philadelphia, 1967). My *The First Christian Century in Judaism and Christianity: Certainties and Uncertainties* (New York, 1968) is directed to the scholar, and I fear it is beyond the usual lay person. It is written in opposition to the tacit assumption on the part of many about the character of our knowledge of this century; my contention is that there is much more that we do not know than that we do. I have written an essay, "The Trial of Jesus: Reservations" (*Judaism,* Vol. XX, No. 1, Winter, 1971). I set forth there the view found briefly here (pp. 128-129) that the "facts" cannot be recovered. I commend heartily, Gerald Sloyan, *Jesus on Trial* (Philadelphia, 1973) which responds, in a manner, to what the author calls my "historical agnosticism." I must plead guilty to the charge. My disposition is such that I prefer to say, "I do not know," rather than to suppose I know what I do not. The modern reader, approaching sacred books, whether the Tanach or the New Testament, naturally wonders if these books are "true." Ordinarily, the tacit assumption is that "true" is the same as "historically accurate." For over a century and a half modern people have viewed history as a discipline which can recover *exactly* what happened, when, and how. Books in the Tanach and the New Testament were not written in accordance with this definition, nor by men trained in modern universities. Precise history was the goal neither of the author of any of the Gospels nor of Genesis, I Kings, or Chronicles. To expect the ancient writer to conform to our modern standards of history writing is unrealistic and unreasonable. We ought not expect ancient writers to satisfy demands which are relatively new among us. I have no hesitation in describing biblical historical writings as generally reliable, but I cannot hold them to be accurate, and, indeed, not fully accurate. In context, my personal approach to the question of accurate history of the Gospels is no way different from my approach to accurate history in Genesis.

What they tell of history is, in a general way, sound. But history is not the pure science that, over-optimistically, modern historians believe their work is.

The matter really at stake, then, is not accurate history, but rather our ability to grasp the ideas, the conceptions, and the minds of ancient writers. Their world was much different from ours, and it can be hard for us to try to put ourselves into their frames of reference. But they were human beings, as we are, and perhaps the sense of a common humanity can lend some enlightenment to what we read.

January, 1974

# PART ONE

# *PRELIMINARIES*

# A Description of the New Testament

THE NEW TESTAMENT is a group of documents assembled about 175 A. D. in which the rising Christian church attests before the world to its conviction that in Jesus Christ it has uniquely received a revelation of God more recent and therefore more climactic than the revelation manifested in the Old Testament.

The word "Testament" is to be understood in the sense of covenant. The Old Testament, which Jews call the Bible, records a "covenant" between God and Abraham, and Abraham's favored descendants, the children of Israel. The New Covenant is the record of a similar compact between God and the new or "true" descendants of Abraham, the Christian church. The title page of a recent translation, the American Revised Standard Version, published in 1946, begins: "The New Covenant commonly called The New Testament . . .".

The *New* is to be understood as a contrast, though not quite in opposition, to the Old Testament. The New is more recent and, as we shall see, tends for Christians, in some but not in all ways, to supplant and supersede the Old. Just what the relationship of the Christian church was to the Old Testament was a matter of some differences of opinion in New Testament times, and we shall note some of the views.

A later chapter will concern itself with the compilation of the New Testament and the selection of its books from among numerous other books which were candidates for scripture.

Those books which stand as the completed New Testament represent four different types of writings. There are four Gospels, a group of letters called Epistles, a quasi-historical work known as Acts of the Apostles, and a book of revelation, the Apocalypse of John.

The word "gospel" means good tidings; in Old English it is "good spiel." It is used in a general sense among Christian writers as a term implying the entirety of the Christian message; Paul, speaking of "the Gospel," refers to his own teachings of the meaning of the Christ. More specifically, "gospel" is used to describe four books in the New Testament which deal with the career of Jesus. The Greek for gospel is *evangelion*, a word which is in turn the translation of a Hebrew phrase, *besura toba*, and the authors of the Gospels Matthew, Mark, Luke, and John are called evangelists. Each Gospel has the heading that it is the Gospel *according to* one of these.

The Gospels are often alluded to simply as Matthew, Mark, Luke, or John, it being cumbersome to repeat on each occasion "the Gospel According to . . .". Similarly, they are spoken of by their position in the New Testament (and this is not the order in which they were written): Matthew is the First Gospel, Mark the Second, Luke the Third, and John the Fourth Gospel.

The Gospels according to Matthew, Mark, and Luke have a close relationship to each other; they utilize similar material in much the same order. They are called the Synoptic Gospels; in editions for students it is a practice to print related segments of them on narrow, adjoining columns of the same page so that the eye can see quickly what each of them records about a given topic. The Gospel According to John does not readily lend itself to this arrangement, and in tenor and style stands quite far from the other three. In older times, the printing of the Gospels in such columns was called a "harmony"; the implicit notion

4

was that these versions of the life and teachings of Jesus supplemented each other and were in essential accord with each other. In our day scholarship does not essay to harmonize some patent difficulties and contradictions in Matthew, Mark, and Luke, but rather to assess the meaning of the differences. What used to be called a harmony is now called a synopsis. Of this, more later.

Within the group of writings called Epistles, several of the letters come from Paul, the second most significant figure in the history of Christianity. Modern scholarship does not credit Paul with the authorship of all the Epistles traditionally ascribed to him; and we shall see that some of the Epistles are as undoubtedly from Paul as others are undoubtedly not, while uncertainty abides regarding still others attributed to him.

The genuine Epistles are letters written by Paul in most cases to specific local churches which Paul himself had founded, and they were written to give his answer to questions or to express his opinion on certain matters. A second group of Epistles, on the other hand, were written not for specific addressees, but for the entire church, and are therefore called Catholic Epistles or sometimes General Epistles. (Catholic means "entire.") Four of these are ascribed to important leaders of the early church, James, Peter, and Jude; but modern scholarship has some serious doubts about the reliability of the ascription. A fourth Catholic Epistle, Hebrews, is held by church tradition to come from Paul, but the liberal Protestant scholarship does not accept this tradition.

A third group of Epistles bear the heading that they are by Paul, and they are addressed not to churches, but to individuals, Timothy and Titus. These men are mentioned in genuine letters as missionary companions of Paul. The contents of these Epistles have to do with the conduct of church affairs, and they are known as the "Pastoral" Epistles. The fourth group of Epistles

5

consist of three letters ostensibly by one "John," the author of the Fourth Gospel; these are known as the Johannine Epistles.

The Apocalypse of John also is attributed to the author of the Fourth Gospel. It is a book, peculiar by modern standards, which through obscure symbols and cryptic language reveals the future. While in form it is unique in the New Testament, it is of a type similar to Daniel in the Old Testament, and to other books which were admitted neither to the Old nor to the New. The Greek word for revelation is *apocalypse*; the work, often misnamed Revelation*s*, is called not only the Apocalypse of John, but also the Revelation of John, or simply Revelation.

Paul's Epistles, the Gospels, and Acts of the Apostles impinge considerably upon Judaism. The other writings come from a later time when the church had firmly established its independence from Judaism, and they reflect the various internal problems which confronted the church at this time of its early development.

Thus it can be seen that the New Testament cannot be taken as a whole, certainly not at the first glance, any more than the Old Testament. Each Testament is a collection of different books, and each book needs to be understood in its own light.

# II

# The Historian's Approach

PEOPLE CAN APPROACH the New Testament in different ways. A Christian sees in it the source of his faith. A person of Christian background, but with no religious affiliations, may enjoy the literary flavor, especially of the Gospels. The professional historian may use the documents for the light which they throw on the details of a complex period of human history.

It is difficult, to the point of impossibility, for anyone to approach the New Testament without some set of mind. The Bible, undergoing interpretation in every age, means different things in different ages, and often takes on, in the minds of readers, some associations that move it perhaps irretrievably from the original significance and purpose. Generation after generation of Christians has found the New Testament the fountainhead of its own religious convictions. In each generation, too, sincerely religious persons, following a particular bent of their own, have found in the New Testament passages aptly supporting their point of view. The advocates of slavery and the advocates of abolition, the proponents of temperance and the proponents of prohibition, have found their sanctions either in a direct statement or in the apparent implication of a passage of Scripture. An interpretation, now here and now there, has gained acceptance for its day and for succeeding years — even when the interpretation may seem, on new examination, to have little to do with the passage in question. For the modern age possesses not only the New Testament, but also a considerable heritage of variable meanings about it.

Predisposition, then, governs every approach to the New

Testament. The Christian Fundamentalist believes every word to be true. The agnostic brings his doubts, while the deist attempts to distinguish between the miraculous narratives which he cannot accept and ethical standards which he can.

Like any literature which is old, the New Testament is difficult to read. While its message deals with many universals, applicable to every age and situation, the New Testament was not expressly written for the ages. Indeed, the New Testament is a collection of some twenty-seven different books, selected by the church out of a larger number available, and most of these books were written for the specific need of a given moment.

Written for their own age, but exalted to a unique position throughout all succeeding ages, these books present certain problems for the general reader. First, it is to be seen that their writers naturally take for granted that the reader knows the political, social, and economic situations in the Graeco-Roman world of two thousand years ago. Accordingly, the New Testament often alludes to matters of its time as though they are crystal-clear; but many of these, despite our accumulated knowledge, are still beyond the recovery of our best scholarship. The ordinary reader is likely to lack the simple background information of the writings.

Second, for our day many passages in the New Testament suffer from a changed climate of religious expression, with the result that the full sympathetic response of the reader cannot be made. The outward forms of religious expression change, and the writer of a book in the New Testament relates a narrative such as that of an unclean spirit entering some swine, fully expecting to elicit a nodding head. Such a passage raised problems neither for the ancient writer nor for the ancient reader. But the modern man can readily have difficulty in attuning himself to such modes of expression.

8

Indeed, a variety of responses to such passages is bound to ensue, especially where belief rather than comprehension is the issue. The pious may accept such narratives without reservation and the skeptic may sneer at them, both not understanding. As another possibility, there exists a compromise mode or method of interpretation known as the allegorical, which ingeniously enables some readers to accept the general sense or significance of the passage without committing themselves to the actual wording of scripture.

A third problem which inheres for the general reader is that the New Testament is a religious book, the product of a religious community which believed that it had received a heritage of God's revelation. In this sense, it is not history, though history is in it; nor a story book, though stories are in it. Rather, it is a testimony to the assumption that all things are possible to God, and therefore it is also a record of those things which it believed happened. One who shares or participates literally in the New Testament faith finds the record of certain supernatural occurrences no problem at all; but difficulties loom for him in whom even the beginning of a doubt is born. For skeptics from within Christianity or for Jews from without, the rejection of a miracle story is not surprising. But the rejection of the details need not preclude an intelligent understanding of the aim of the writer. The modern reader, whether a Jew or a Christian, should understand why particular types of miracles are related, and out of what environment the type of miracle emerges. Moreover, he should recall that even though for the modern temper the miracle story by its very presence acts as a dissuader, that same miracle story was originally told with the express purpose of persuasion. Luke, who writes of the virgin birth of Jesus, believes in it, or else would not have written it; the miracle of the virgin birth is the proof which he offers of the unique nature of the

9

Christ in whom he believes God revealed Himself. This particular miracle raises for the modern mind problems which were not at all in the mind of Luke; and such matters are frequent in the New Testament, though of usually less miraculous proportions. They are, indeed, part of the fibre out of which the New Testament is made, since it is a book of supernatural belief.

The modern reader of the New Testament, of whatever background, will benefit by orienting himself to these initial problems. He will arrive more readily at an understanding of the New Testament if he keeps in mind that, whatever it may say for later days in matters of faith or reason, it is a series of voices which rise out of specific times of religious activity and direct their message to the people of their own times.

For the Jewish reader there are, in addition, some special problems. The tenor and tone of the New Testament are such that they put him immediately on the defensive. He reads what are no more and no less than direct or oblique attacks on Jews and on Judaism, for much of the New Testament was composed in a time of sharp conflict between Jews and Christians. As the Jewish reader identifies himself with his fellow Jews, he is apt to identify historical events, such as the Crusades, the Black Plague, the expulsion from Spain, Hitler, and the like, with sentiments to be found in the New Testament. Immediately an understandable bar to his sympathetic reading arises.

If he wants to understand the New Testament, he must, however, read with calmness and with an effort at comprehension. Since for the Jew this literature is not the literature of his personal piety, it is possible for him to read with an objectivity that is free from the traditional associations which often inevitably influence the reading by a Christian. For the Jew, the historical approach pursued in this volume should prove a good discipline and perhaps a helpful guide.

The historical approach can enable those attuned to it to find abiding religious truth in ancient scriptures, whether of their own group or of some other culture. An uncritical believer who attributes verbal accuracy to Scripture can have his faith shattered when modern scholarship invalidates a particular Biblical statement. The skeptic, quite similarly, does not go beyond the letter, and thereby he closes a door that could lead him to an understanding of how men long ago struggled with the deepest problems and mysteries of existence.

But the open-minded person can derive help and clarification for his own personal, present quest from the insight into the spiritual quests of ancient times to be learned from dispassionate study.

The solutions offered in ancient days are not necessarily the solutions for our day. Understanding does not always lead to agreement. A convinced Jew is not apt to share the sense of religious achievement or triumph which the Christian finds in the New Testament. But a Jew can see the road, though uncongenial to him, which other human beings took in trying to find answers to fundamental problems. A Jew will find some particular answers of the New Testament unsatisfying, but he can find that the questions asked are universal among men.

In pursuit of historical reconstruction, the student asks a set of questions about each book in the New Testament: When was this written? Why? Where? By whom? Some of these questions modern scholarship can answer with full confidence; some it answers in terms of probabilities; others evoke candid admission of not knowing.

The historian, confronted by these questions, is limited by the methods and results of research and inquiry. Respecting the virgin birth, for example, the secular historian is hardly able to affirm it as a fact or to deny it as a fiction. But he can note where in the New Testament the idea appears and where it fails to appear. The Epistles of Paul and the Gospel According to Mark do not mention the virgin birth. Subsequent writings do. Since the virgin birth is a relatively late doctrine, it can stem from pious meditation rather than from historical testimony. The historian can express the judgment that a doctrine so late in arising is probably unhistorical. Further than this he cannot go, except as his private disposition leads him, for faith in miracles is a matter of religious commitment, not of demonstrable historical research.

The historian of the New Testament works with specialized tools: languages, history, archeology, literary analysis, and additional non-Biblical literature — specific writings from specific times and places. It is with these tools, indeed, rather than with those of dogma or pietism, that the Protestant Biblical scholars of the past one hundred and seventy-five years have studied the New Testament.

The pages which follow attempt to mirror conscientiously the conclusions of the main lines of this liberal scholarship. The approach here, accordingly, is not that of the exhorter or of the apologist, or of the opponent. It is rather the reflection of a stringently honest scholarly tradition — the free pursuit of the truth. This liberal Protestant tradition has had among its purposes to portray the New Testament, as accurately as it is possible, in its own times and for its original meaning. This approach is surely the appropriate one for Jews who wish to understand the New Testament.

The historian, setting about his task of understanding the New Testament according to its original intent, must recover as clearly as possible, from the accretions of time and translations, the text as it was originally written.

For this task, he requires, initially, a knowledge of Greek and Aramaic. The New Testament, as we have it in its oldest preserved form, is in Greek, a later Greek, noticeably different from the ancient Homeric tongue. Known at first only from the New Testament and from the third-century B. C. translation of the Old, this form of Greek was at one time piously conceived of as a special holy language expressly designed to convey Christian revelation. The discoveries by archeology, however, have revealed to us that this New Testament Greek, known as *Koiné*, was the *common*, non-literary, uncultured language of the Mediterranean regions, used not only in Greece, but also in Asia Minor, Egypt, and Palestine, and even carried to Rome by colonists. An ability to use Koiné enabled one to be readily understood throughout the historically significant part of the world in New Testament times. In some places it replaced the native language, while in others it existed alongside the native tongue.

Christianity was born in Palestine, within Judaism. The language spoken by Jesus and his immediate followers was Aramaic, a language as closely related to Hebrew as, one might say, Portuguese is to Spanish.

The New Testament itself attests to the knowledge that the beginnings of the Christian movement were in a locale linguistically Aramaic, for it preserves within its Greek text Aramaic words in quotation. Somewhere in the line of development of Christianity, probably while its accumulating tradition was still being carried on orally, translation of some things from Aramaic into Greek took place.

Since translation did take place, various theories arise from time to time alleging that different books of the New Testament were composed originally in Aramaic and that what we have is the translation and not an original Greek composition. No such written documents in Aramaic have been preserved. While the earmarks of the results of translation are discernible in the four Gospels and are crystal-clear in Revelation, the main line of modern scholarship holds that the Gospels, as we have them, are not translations, but Greek compositions. No documents in Aramaic are preserved, it suggests, probably because none were written. The New Testament, it concludes, was not translated into Greek from an earlier writing, but was originally written in Greek.

Previous to the invention of printing in the fifteenth century, the New Testament, with other books, was published through succeeding generations by hand-copying. This "manuscript" method was a tedious and costly process; and no copyist was free from the possibility of copying incorrectly. Therefore the manuscripts of the New Testament exhibit minor variations resulting from inadvertent error. Additional factors contribute to the multiplication of these variations: a copyist working on Luke may have recalled from memory Mark's statement of the same matter, and in place of his following his manuscript of Luke, he could unconsciously have made his new copy conform instead to Mark. Indeed, even beyond such accidental accommodation, a copyist may have made the alteration deliberately. Likewise, a phrase or sentence may have been inserted to make a message more congenial to the copyist. For example, in the crucifixion narrative some rather late manuscripts of Luke contain a sentence not found in earlier manuscripts of Luke: "Forgive them, Father, for they know not what they do."

In view of the variations in manuscripts, a basic task of scholarship is so to study the manuscripts and the variations as to be able, if possible, to determine the correct reading. Such work is from many standpoints sheer drudgery, but it is the foundation out of which the nearest approach to certainty of the text is possible. Roman Catholic scholars have been of the greatest possible service in work on the text. Such study is called in scholarship "lower criticism" — a poorly conceived term, since it sounds like a lesser kind of work than the higher. The standard New Testament in the Greek has at the bottom of each page notations regarding the variations in the manuscripts.

The term "higher" criticism is reserved for a related but quite different mode of study. The lower criticism may show that a textual reading can be established at a given point; only then does the higher criticism begin. For example, when Jesus enters Jerusalem Mark portrays him as riding on an ass; in his description of the same incident, Matthew quotes from the Old Testament, from Zechariah 9:9, and states that this riding was in fulfillment of prophecy. Old Testament writings use a literary figure known as parallelism, such as, "What is man that Thou shalt be mindful of him, or the son of man that Thou shouldst remember him." "Man" and "son of man" here do not allude to two different individuals, but rather to a single "man." In the passage in Zechariah, the verse reads that the king is coming "mounted on an ass, on a colt, the foal of an ass." Zechariah surely did not have in mind two different animals. But where Mark portrays Jesus as sending two disciples to bring *a* colt to him, Matthew depicts him as charging them to bring *two* animals; Mark portrays Jesus as riding on *it*, but Matthew, in some manuscripts, portrays Jesus as riding on *them*; in other manuscripts of Matthew the *them* is found as *it*; in still others, the reading is *on the colt*; and one manuscript omits the incongruous phrase entirely.

The lower criticism establishes that the most reliable manuscripts of Matthew read "riding on *them*"; it explains that the variations are due to the effort of copyists to eliminate the troublesome phrase. Noting the variations and the reason for them, we can be satisfied that the acceptable reading is *them*. It is at this point, when the text is already established, that the higher criticism begins. It notes, first, that Matthew records a notion only implied in Mark at this point, that the riding was in fulfillment of Old Testament prophecy; it finds that in other places Matthew similarly supplies Old Testament verses along with the formula "to fulfill what is written in the prophets." It finds that the motif of the fulfillment of prophecy is a characteristic of Matthew. It notes that Matthew apparently misunderstood the parallelism in Zechariah, even to the point of portraying an individual riding on two animals simultaneously.

That is to say, the higher criticism addresses itself to the task of the minute analysis of the established text, for the sake of the original and intended meaning which often must be sought beyond the actual, existing letter. Its tools are rigid logic, dictionaries and lexicons, and the comparison of one passage with other related passages both within and outside of the New Testament. The higher criticism would not hesitate to regard Matthew's account of the two animals as an unhistorical item, supplied by the author to support his own message.

But for those believers for whom the very words of each evangelist have been literally dictated by God, the view that a statement is unhistorical is most unpalatable. Fundamentalist Christians therefore reject the "higher criticism" *in toto*, as presumption and heresy. Conservatives do not reject it as a discipline, but often ignore its suggestions. Liberals in general accept the results.

If one may for a moment distinguish between higher criticism and the higher critics, there is this to be said. Individual critics have sometimes carried ingenuity to farcical lengths, and the formulation of a theory, both radical and untenable, in the interest of sensationalism, or some individual bent, has seduced more than one scholar. It has to be conceded that higher critics have occasionally distinguished themselves through inanity and nonsense. Pet theories have been ridden by some, especially along those paths where the Fundamentalist or the Conservative could be shocked or dismayed; and, while the purpose has been ostensibly scholarship, its basic exhibitionism has not been undiscernible.

But the products of scholarship, and of higher criticism, as soon as they are published, come into an arena of public notice and evaluation where the fantastic and the unsubstantial cannot long survive. Once a theory is formulated, it is discussed in books and journals by others and measured against the background of what has remained and what has proved transient. Theories gain acceptance through their own persuasive powers, not because of flamboyance or the iconoclasm of the author. The higher criticism carries within its own best intentions a check against the farfetched and the unlikely, as free scholarship examines the opinions and the arguments which scholars advance.

# III

# The Jewish Background

To UNDERSTAND the New Testament as it was understood in its own time, the historian must understand the circumstances and concerns of that time, as well as the languages which voiced its history. We have seen that the minimum equipment for the purpose of establishing the New Testament text is a knowledge of Greek, Aramaic, and Hebrew. In order to examine that text more deeply and analytically, even beneath the level of the words themselves, further specialized tools are essential. Jewish history and religion, rabbinic literature, Greek philosophy and popular religion, and the social and political conditions of the Graeco-Roman world — all must be known to the scholar, to supply him with the content out of which the New Testament arose.

In this list, the subjects of Jewish religion and Greek philosophy and religion seem unrelated and antithetical; but it is indeed the confluence of the two, preceding the time of Jesus, that makes their study essential to begin an orientation in New Testament times.

Palestine had been conquered, about 325 B. C., by Macedonian Greeks under Alexander the Great, whose empire, after his death, split into three parts. Palestine, a part of the empire of Seleucus, contained many Greek colonists who had brought their language and institutions into Palestine, and a good many Jews abandoned their ancestral religion, with its distinctive practices, and became devotees of the Greek religions. This Grecianizing (known also as Hellenizing) made steady inroads, particularly among the wealthy urbanites in contrast to the poor and the rural. At one juncture, the ruler, Antiochus Epiphanes, wanted to hasten this process. His motive was to strengthen his empire through universal conformity to Hellenism. He apparently misunderstood or recklessly ignored the prospective reception in Palestine of his design. In 168 B. C. the Maccabean revolt against Antiochus broke out, touched off by the resentment of a heavy-handed desecration of the Temple in Jerusalem. A serious miscalculation of the magnitude of the rebellion, and the ineptness of the insufficient troops dispatched against the intrepid and zealous Maccabees, coincided with other imperial difficulties to nullify the effort to destroy the Jewish patriots; and the Maccabean revolt was successful.

The Temple was restored to purity, the restoration being commemorated in an institution known as Hanukka, which means Dedication, a festival mentioned in the Gospel According to John 10:22. The Maccabean warfare was directed against both the Seleucidian Greeks and against Hellenizing. As a by-product Palestinian Judaism thereafter deliberately shunned Greek ways and practices and enhanced all the more the significance of its own religion and of its group solidarity.

Outside of Palestine, Jews were already to be found in ever-growing number throughout the eastern and central Mediterranean. In Alexandria in Egypt, the Old Testament had already been rendered into Greek to serve initially the vast Jewish community there. This Greek translation, known as the Septuagint ("seventy," from a legend that seventy, or seventy-two, men had translated it), spread beyond Egypt to become a standard version of the Old Testament for the Greek-speaking Jews, replacing, for them, the Hebrew text, or the Palestinian translation into Aramaic.

In the time of Jesus these Jews in the Mediterranean world

outnumbered the Jews in Palestine considerably; the estimates vary from five through ten to one. It became customary to speak of the non-Palestinian scene as the Dispersion, or Diaspora. These words describe, but with a somewhat different effect, the Hebrew word which they render: Golah, the Exile. The difference is that Exile seems to imply a temporary state of affairs, and it stresses the absence from Palestine, while Diaspora stresses the widespread scattering of the Jews, without suggesting an inherently temporary situation.

There were, indeed, two (or even more) quite dissimilar diasporas. East of Palestine, Babylonia was already the haven of a flourishing Jewish settlement, destined several centuries later to be the hub of the Jewish world. Aramaic, though in slightly differing dialects, was the language of the Jews both in Palestine and in Babylonia; and within a framework of minor variation, a Judaism developed that was common to both, with a maximum of intercommunication.

But in the western Diaspora the adoption of the Greek language by Jews was only the beginning of a division from Palestinian Judaism in sentiment and in values. Communication with Palestine by no means ceased. But the Greek Jews were confronted with the challenges of Greek religion and philosophy in a measure so formidable that they could not fall back on ignoring their existence; and the Greek Jews, perforce, came to terms with Greek culture. Specifically, we know that Jews wrote in the Greek style such things as histories, epic poems, and tragedies; and the writings of an Alexandrian Jew, Philo (20 B. C. to 40 A. D.), who dealt with Jewish matters in the mode of a Greek philosopher, are preserved in almost their entirety, filling, in the modern Loeb Classics Edition, eleven volumes.

It was Greek Jews in the Diaspora who first felt the growing power of Rome. Then, in 63 B. C., Pompey subjected Palestine to Roman rule, bringing to an end the independence enjoyed under the Maccabean family, the Hasmoneans, and making Palestine in fact as well as simply in time a suffering part of the Graeco-Roman world. The period from 162 to 63 B. C. was marked by internal disorders and ugly rivalries, so that the successors of the Hasmonean rebels are remembered in Jewish history with a shame which is as deep as the praises for their forebears are high. This shame centers around the fact that the office of the king and that of the high priest were held by the same man. Old Testament requirements made it urgent that the high priest, who was to preside at the Temple in Jerusalem, be above all reproach. But fratricidal struggles for the kingship involved equally disreputable struggles for the high priesthood, and all that was unseemly in the temporal realm was duplicated in connection with the Temple. It was a period of unrest, disorder, and violence. The connection of the king with the Temple led to the natural creation around it of a small body of the nobility, the priesthood, and the wealthy and ambitious. Their primary concerns were dictated by the narrowness of their interest, and the power and munificence inherent in royalty and in an official priesthood forged this group into a party, the Sadducees.

By this time the study of the Old Testament had become widespread among Jewry throughout the known world. Though Jews then would not have recognized it, a kind of rivalry became implicit between two institutions, the Temple at Jerusalem and the Bible itself. The Bible was read to Jews in their local assembly, for which the Greek word is *Synagogue*. The distinction between the Synagogue and the Temple, and the unique importance of each in the Jewish history and religion of New Testament times, are basic necessities to an understanding of the New Testament.

The origin of the synagogue is obscure, but in all probability it arose as a center where Jews gathered during the Babylonian Exile (586–520 B. C.). At first the synagogue was primarily a place of study, a school, as witnessed by the fact that European and some American Jews still today use the Germanic word Shul (*Schule*), or school, to name it. Study and prayer in Jewish tradition, however, are akin to each other, and where the one existed the other quite naturally arose. At synagogues both in Palestine and in the Diaspora, it became the practice that prayers were held thrice daily, and also on Sabbaths and the festivals; while the Bible, especially the Five Books of Moses, was read and expounded on every Saturday, and, at least in Palestine, on Mondays and Thursdays. The more remote a Jew was from Jerusalem and the Temple, the more completely his religious life tended to center in the synagogue. For most Jews, indeed, the Temple served in no direct or vivid way, though a tax to maintain it was paid voluntarily by Jews the world over. Also, Jews from all over Palestine and the Diaspora made pilgrimages there on the three festivals: Passover, Pentecost, and Tabernacles, for the purpose of bringing sacrifices of thanksgiving, which could be offered only at the Temple and only by Temple priests. The poor, however, could hardly make such journeys, and most Jews had to content themselves with the wish to visit the Temple rather than with the visit itself.

The Temple was administered by a hereditary priesthood. The synagogue, however, could be served by any Jew, whatever his birth; and the historical distinctiveness of the synagogue was its lay character. The man who expounded Scripture had no ecclesiastical office, but only an acknowledged great measure of learning; the expounder and the one to whom matters were expounded were equal in religious rank.

The manner of expounding a section of Scripture was determined, of course, by the contents. Genesis is primarily a series of narratives; the exposition of Genesis took the form of expanding the incidents mentioned in the Bible somewhat in the way in which a terse short story can be turned into a lengthy novel. In an age before widespread literacy and inexpensive printing, memories were relied on heavily, and the apt exposition of some gifted expositor was handed down from mind to mind, ultimately to be written down in a collection of such expositions, called the *Midrash*.

As an example of such expansion, Gen. 22 tells that God tested Abraham in ordering him to offer Isaac as a sacrifice at Moriah. Synagogue exposition inferred that other things which Abraham was bidden to do, such as to depart from home, in Gen. 12, were likewise tests. The Bible mentions only one test, but Midrash expands and gives a list of ten. The Bible does not mention Sarah in Gen. 22; but Midrash wonders how Abraham could have left home for three days without telling his wife, and it resolves the issue by portraying Abraham as telling Sarah that he is to take Isaac on the morrow to a school conducted by two characters of Gen. 11, Shem and Eber, to enroll him.

Such exposition was often fanciful and only ingenious. But often, too, it was deeply perceptive and incisive in its analysis of religious issues. Above all, it had to be crystal-clear to those who gathered in the synagogue to listen and learn. The expositor had frequent recourse to anecdotes which clarified his intention; and the relevance of an anecdote was its usefulness in making a point. Such an anecdote, called a Parable, became a familiar device in synagogue exposition.

The exposition of a book like Genesis was an enlargement on narratives, and it was itself narrative in form. Such narrative passages in Midrash are called by Jews the *haggada*, or narration. But the expositor in the synagogue was not only a storyteller. Biblical narrative gives way in the twentieth chapter of Exodus to a law code, the Ten Commandments; and, similarly, Leviticus, Numbers, and Deuteronomy deal with statutes and ordinances, and not primarily with incidents. Accordingly, the exposition turns to the expounding of law.

The Bible is less than systematic in its legislation. Occasionally it presents a general principle, but no specific applications; occasionally it presents a series of specific ordinances, but no general principle. The work of the synagogue fills in these discrepancies. Furthermore, the legislation in the Bible does not cover every single aspect of legislative possibility. The synagogue exposition points the way from the intent of the Bible to new laws covering what was not in the Bible. This legalistic aspect of Midrash is called *halaka; the* halaka is the Jewish post-Biblical expansion of Biblical law.

The wish to live in full accord with the Bible and the biblically-based halaka produced a group of persons whose urgent concern was to make of the Bible and especially of its legislation a living, contemporaneous institution. These persons were laymen, not priests; they centered not in the Temple, but in the synagogue, the common man's house of prayer and study. They were "separatists," that is to say, they separated themselves from iniquity and transgression; the Hebrew word for Separatists yields their name, the Pharisees.

No group in history has had a greater injustice done to its fine qualities and positive virtues than have the Pharisees through parts of the Gospels. Western tradition, taking its cue from the New Testament, has accorded the word "Pharisee" with the connotation of one satisfied with the mere externals of religion, or else a hypocrite. That Pharisaism was not immune from the possibility of such aberration is attested by the Pharisaic writings themselves, which warn against it by depicting caustically the Pharisee who has gone astray. The denunciations in the New

Testament, however, are not limited to potential aberrations, but to all of Pharisaism and to all Pharisees. And earlier generations of Christian scholarship, going on from these denunciations, have tended to label all of Judaism as no more than the hollow shell of religious observance, or as pure and simple hypocrisy.

Modern Christian scholarship has been able to assess the Pharisees more justly, and hence much more favorably. The foremost writing on the Pharisees is a three-volume work, *Judaism in the First Centuries of the Christian Era*, by a Christian, George Foot Moore of Harvard (Harvard University Press, 1927–30). We shall speak of this again when we speak of the historical Jesus.

The Pharisees, then, were the party of the synagogue and of the Bible. The Sadducees were the party of the Temple and of the court. On a number of scores tensions arose between the two parties. In general matters the Sadducees, content with the Temple ritual, had little need for the midrashic exposition of Scripture developed in synagogue teaching. A more specific grievance was that the Pharisees espoused the non-Biblical doctrine (for which they sought Biblical proof-texts) of resurrection; while the Sadducees rejected both the argument of the proof-texting and of the doctrine. (Matthew 22: 23–33; Mark 12: 18–27; and Luke 20: 27–40 tell of an exchange between the Sadducees and Jesus on the question of resurrection.)

The chief issue, however, between the Pharisees and the Sadducees was the non-Biblical, midrashic legislation. Because it was not in the Bible, the Sadducees rejected it. The Pharisees considered this fruit of their study to be the logical and unbroken extension of the Torah, the Law of Moses. The Pharisees, indeed, spoke of two Torahs. The written Torah was the product of Moses; the non-Biblical laws were an oral Torah, resting, they averred, on a continuous line of succession through which the Torah passed, from Moses to Joshua, to the Judges, and down to the Pharisaic sages. As a derivative of the Bible, the oral law was for the Pharisees already implicit in God's revelation to Moses, and its authenticity in this regard was vouched for by the chain of continuity.

The tradition of the elders, as the New Testament calls the oral law, became binding on the Pharisees. Ultimately the Pharisaic party triumphed, and Pharisaism became interchangeable with Judaism after 70 A. D. But at the time of the subjection to Rome in 63 B. C. the issue between the Pharisees and the Sadducees was still unresolved. There were, in addition, a number of marginal groups, such as the Essenes, a perhaps ascetic, monkish group, of whom we know relatively little. Of other groups we have little more information than scanty knowledge that they existed. The Dead Sea Scrolls have so far added no great, significant knowledge, despite claims which are made to the contrary, especially in popular writings.

Sharply contrasted to the legalistic atmosphere of the issue between the Pharisees and the Sadducees, and to the stress upon careful observance, in this life, of what either side construed to be God's Law, was the tone of the "apocalypses," being written with fresh fervor in the tension of these late pre-Christian times. In obscure and flamboyant language, these apocalypses revealed what was to happen in the end of time, and what the coming of God's judgment would mean to Israel and to mankind. Some of these Jewish books have been preserved into our own day, not by Judaism, but by the Christian church. From the standpoint of Judaism, they represent an uncongenial extreme, a bypassing of man's time on earth when religious laws can be observed for a conjectural time after the world will have ended. Christianity found them concerned with events at the crucial end of the age, and somewhat less than wholeheartedly preserved them, but kept them outside of Scripture.

The capitulation to Rome, which was the circumstance that agitated the writers of the apocalypses, added, or rather revived, a strong factor in Jewish thought, the resentment of foreign domination. The highhanded Roman administrators of the province of Palestine did little to abate such sentiment. The political head of the Jews (the ethnarch) was both "king" and high priest, but his sovereignty was limited to what Rome permitted him; and his subjection to Rome commended him to many Jews as though he were Rome itself. What national pride in or support for their Jewish "rulers" may have survived Pompey's conquest, diminished greatly in 40 B. C., when the unstable, ruthless, but gifted Herod came to the throne. Herod was not of pure Jewish extraction. His father, Antipater, was an Idumean, a related tribe descended, according to tradition, from Edom, also named Esau, the son of Isaac and the brother of Jacob. Antipater had manipulated himself into a position equivalent to that of prime minister to the tottering Hasmonean kings in the year 47 B. C., and he had managed through crafty dealings to seat his son on the throne. Herod made more than one gesture to establish his legitimacy; he married the Hasmonean princess Mariamne (whom he later murdered); and he managed to evoke some national approval by a judicious refurbishing of the Temple in Jerusalem; but his Idumean extraction plagued him from time to time. He could maintain his power only by tyrannical means, buttressed by Roman authority, and anti-Roman sentiment abided among Jews even in the relatively high domestic tranquillity of his reign, which terminated in 4 B. C.

This sentiment was most marked in a group of zealots known to us by the peculiar name, the Fourth Philosophy. Josephus is the source for this inept description; in writing for the Romans he portrayed the Jews as consisting of four classes of *philosophers*. For three of these he could find some suitable philosophic trappings: Sadducees, Pharisees, and Essenes. Our knowledge of the Fourth Philosophy is most uncertain, respecting both its origin and its antecedents. The Fourth Philosophy can be characterized with some security as favoring violence as a means of breaking the hold of Rome, and under various leaders it resorted from time to time to guerrilla warfare. It was this group — to move ahead in the account — which plunged Jewish Palestine into unsuccessful rebellion against Rome, first in 66 A. D. and again in 132–135.

There was less than a unanimous sentiment among the Jews for such rebellions. Part of the population was eager for peace, despite the subjection to Rome. To a large segment of the population overt rebellion was not an attractive instrument, nor were any human devices or agencies considered the effective medium. Many Jews believed that the release from Roman oppression would come ultimately when God would send a leader to accomplish the task. This man, a divinely-sent messenger, would become the freely acknowledged ruler of the Jews, and as such he would have his kingship symbolized by a traditional ceremony in which his head would be anointed with oil. The Hebrew word for "anointed one" is *Messiah;* the Greek translation of Messiah is *Christ*.

It is difficult to be precise and accurate about the much discussed Jewish conception of the Messiah, even though the greatest possible precision is important to an understanding of the New Testament. The term Messiah is not often used in the Old Testament in the sense of the agent of God destined to bring release from foreign domination; rather, the doctrine is largely post-Biblical.

It is, in fact, a composite doctrine in Judaism, contributed by

28

various persons, known and unknown. Actually, there were several Jewish notions of the Messiah which overlapped and which later on were merged into a more or less unified conception. For our purposes, it can suffice to say that resentment of Rome, speculation on the incidents of the coming day of God's judgment, and belief in a resurrection were the several streams that flowed together to form the messianic doctrine.

The Jewish Messiah was expected to accomplish specific aims. He would destroy the sovereignty of Rome; he would set up a legitimate Jewish kingdom, not of the hated Hasmonean or Herodian stock, but of the genuine Jewish royalty, the stock of King David; he would gather in the exiles from all over the Diaspora; his coming would usher in the judgment day, and there would ensue a resurrection of at least the righteous dead.

Such, in fact, is the mission of the Messiah still awaited today among strictly Orthodox Jews. The agency of God in the messianic goal is so stressed that ultra-Orthodox Jews have opposed the Zionist movement, which achieved the re-establishment of the state of Israel, as a bit of presumption on the part of mere humans, arrogantly usurping God's prerogative.

We do not know the precise dates of the origins of this or that phase of the complex Jewish messianic doctrine. We do know that the increasing pressure inflicted directly by the Romans, or indirectly through the Jewish kingly vassals, evoked ever-increasing messianic longings.

For Jews, the test of the Messiah was the effectiveness of his accomplishing the messianic missions. The initial reception of one who might claim to be the Messiah was hardly apt to be universal, and the continued belief in a claimant would rest on his capacity to disarm incredulity. For the complacent, or the economically well-placed, the disorders which a would-be Messiah could stir up by armed rebellion discouraged any tendency to believe or to accept the claims. Still others, more willing to believe, needed the confirmation of convincing proof; and, accordingly, some of these accepted the proffered evidence as persuasive, while others abstained. The greater the zeal to overthrow Rome, the more ready were extreme "nationalists" to accept and embrace a messianic claimant.

The efficient Roman authorities were alert to the dangers of rebellious movements, and it is understandable that their ruthless provincial policies hardly moved them to patience or temperance towards dissidents. The minor religious sectaries, such as groups of the Essenes, or followers of a prophetlike person such as John the Baptizer, were difficult for the Romans to distinguish from political rebels; indeed, the religious basis of messianic rebellion made such a distinction well-nigh undiscernible. The Romans looked to some Jews, the royalty or the priesthood or the advantageously placed, for information and assistance in determining the character of a minor movement; and it is natural that those Jews who would lose a favored position by a rebellion, whether it could have been successful or not, were moved by considerations of self-interest to preserve the surface tranquillity.

The king of Judea ruled through the grace of Rome, and hence his interests were hardly diverse from Roman interests. Similarly, the Assembly, which had certain judicial and legislative powers, derived some of its strength from Roman support. The Greek word for Assembly is *synhedrion*, which the Jews Aramaized into *Sanhedrin*. (The Sanhedrin was invested by later Jewish tradition with an antiquity which it probably never possessed; but certainly by 4 B. C. it was a relatively old institution.) It was often controlled by the Sadducees, but its legislative program required the special knowledge of experts in the Bible and Biblical Law. These experts, both within and without the Sanhedrin, were known initially as Scribes; shortly after the time of Jesus they were called Rabbis.

To certain Jews, such as those in high places whose position hinged on Roman favor, as well as to the Roman officials themselves, the prevention of rebellion against Rome was a vivid concern, as rebellious movements were directed not only against Rome, but also against these Jewish collaborators.

Such was the temper of the times when, on the death of Herod in 4 B. C., the "kingdom" was divided among his children into smaller units. Herod Antipas became the "Tetrarch" of Galilee in the north and Perea in the northeast; Archelaus became the king of central Judea, Samaria just to its north and Idumea just to its southeast; Philip received the northeast regions beyond those given to Herod Antipas, and was likewise called a "Tetrarch." The Roman official to whom the king of Judea was subject was called the procurator; among a succession of these, it was one Pontius Pilate who was the procurator when Jesus came to Jerusalem.

# IV

# From Judaism into Christianity

THE THOUGHTFUL READER will inevitably raise the
question of where in the New Testament Judaism definitely
leaves off and Christianity begins. He reads in it of Jesus, a Jew
in a Jewish setting, quoting from the Jewish law and prophets,
and claiming a large Jewish following, and yet throughout his
reading the implication in the New Testament seems everywhere clear that Jesus is of course not a Jew, but already a
"Christian."

To determine when the transition was made, and in what
way it was made, and what was the nature of earliest Christianity
which evolved from Judaism, is one of the most delicate tasks
which confronts a New Testament scholar, and one most baffling
to exactness. The reason for this lies in the New Testament
itself. For every fact which it permits us to know about early
Christianity, there are dozens which we wish to know. The
historian must reconstruct a kind of jigsaw puzzle, many significant pieces of which are lost or were never made.

The Gospels, which discuss the earliest events in the history
of Christianity, were written, modern scholarship has determined, in a time much later than Jesus' own. Paul's Epistles,
the earliest writings, give us only fragmentary information on
the Christianity that had developed before Paul's own time, and
a later work, the Acts of the Apostles, even were it regarded as
reliable, gives only meager information about the pre-Pauline
period. The historian is required to fill in blank places at frequent
junctures, and to make perilous deductions from hazy clues.

32

He must be stringent in distinguishing between what he knows to be a fact and what he only believes to be one.

Certain bare facts are historically not to be doubted. Jesus, who emerged into public notice in Galilee when Herod Antipas was its Tetrarch, was a real person, the leader of a movement. He had followers, called disciples. The claim was made, either by or for him, that he was the long-awaited Jewish Messiah. He journeyed from Galilee to Jerusalem, possibly in 29 or 30, and there he was executed, crucified by the Romans as a political rebel. After his death, his disciples believed that he was resurrected, and had gone to heaven, but would return to earth at the appointed time for the final divine judgment of mankind.

All this knowledge is later recorded in the Gospels, which cite words some of which, in my opinion, Jesus unquestionably said, and record deeds that he undoubtedly did. The primary interest of Jesus' followers, however, writing their Testament long after the death of Jesus in order to draw others to their belief, was not in what Jesus said or did, but rather in what he was.

Any claims made, during the lifetime of Jesus, that he was the Messiah whom the Jews had awaited, were rendered poorly defensible by his crucifixion and by the collapse of any political aspect of his movement, and by the sad actuality that Palestine was still not liberated from Roman domination. Also, the belief in his resurrection made the usual quasi-political idea of Messiahship relatively inconsequential. In the perspective of these facts and of the time that had passed since his death, the career of Jesus was interpreted by New Testament writers as of more than human significance. It is in this interpreting, done after his lifetime for the purpose of spreading a fervent faith, that the turning point between Judaism and Christianity lies.

Interpretation of the role of Jesus developed in an ever-expanding way. The various books of the New Testament can

33

be regarded as a series of milestones at which we can view the development of the expanding significance seen by Christians, consolidating their special faith, in the career of Jesus.

We have the milestones, but not the full account of the road traveled. As persons at a wayside inn often mention things which they have seen on the way, so the New Testament writings often give us glimpses of the past. More often, however, we are left to infer from the location of the inn which of a variety of roads may have been followed by the guests. And as some travelers prefer only the roads, while others incline to the lanes, we cannot be sure which was the route followed.

There is reliable evidence, however, that no one route was followed. Christianity, emerging as a "Church" from the development of views on the significance of Jesus, did not possess an orderly and uniform belief. Certain views clashed with each other, and one man's opinion seemed to another person error, or, more technically, heresy. We know from I Corinthians 1:12 that various men, of different backgrounds, spread Christianity in varying forms. A basic unity of religious appraisal should not hide the divergence of viewpoints in the New Testament. We shall see, for example, that the Epistle of James expresses reservations about the doctrine of faith taught by Paul. And it cannot be expected that Christianity rising in Rome would be identically the same as Christianity in Alexandria, Egypt; the Christianity of Palestine Jews would not coincide exactly with that of Gentiles of Athens.

It is impossible to view Christianity, then, as an orderly and concerted crusade for a well-defined cause. Rather, we should be moved to see in the books of the New Testament a variety of pioneer ventures into a heterogeneous realm of faith, but having in common, as a certainty amid a wealth of yet unrecovered fact and as the source of their inspiration, Jesus, and the need to interpret him as in some sense divine.

# PART TWO

## *PAUL AND THE PAULINE EPISTLES*

# V

# The Background of Paulinism

THOUGH BORN in Palestinian Judaism as a movement for Jews, Christianity soon spread throughout the Greek world as a movement for Gentiles. The most important figure in effecting the transition was the Greek Jew Paul, the foremost missionary of Christian history. Some, indeed, regard him as considerably more than a missionary, and they would credit Paul rather than Jesus with being the founder of Christianity.

When Paul first heard of the new movement, he opposed it. Later, after an experience of the spirit almost ineffable in its magnitude, he firmly believed that the Christ, risen after resurrection, had appeared to him. Opposition gave way to espousal, and a driving impetus within Paul led him to travel about the Greek world, to tell other people the overwhelming revelation that had come to him. As he traveled, he founded churches; later on he had occasion to write letters to the churches which he had founded. These letters are the Epistles of Paul, the oldest writings in the New Testament, dating from some two or three decades after the death of Jesus.

The message of Paul is a complicated one, and the complexity is increased for modern Jews because Paul not only writes from a world signally different from the world of today, but also his religious point of departure is one which neither an Orthodox nor a Reform Jew of today would accept. He was deeply meditative, and his viewpoints about the nature of man and the nature of sin, and an impending end of the world which, mistakenly, he thought was soon to come, are based on assumptions which are diametrically opposed to the views which traditional Judaism has bequeathed to us. Indeed, to move from the rabbinic Jewish mode of thought to Paul's requires a radical shift.

Perhaps briefly to notice these contrasting assumptions may be the best preface to understanding Paul. Rabbinic Jews and modern Jews believe that man is by nature good; Paul, that he is by nature bad. Jews hold that a man may commit sins and by repentance re-establish himself in God's grace; Paul, that man, in possessing a physical body, is gripped by inherited sinfulness from which he himself cannot extricate himself. Jews believe that each person, through repentance and good deeds, works out his own personal atonement; Paul, that helpless man requires atonement to be made for him, and that the death of Jesus was this atonement.

It should follow from these contrasts that when we deal with Paul we are confronted by a person caught in a "predicament" which is not shared by Jews, rabbinic or modern. Both his predicament and his solution of it rest on basic assumptions that a rabbinic Jew would not make. Accordingly, Paul's religious concerns are so strange to Jews that it is often difficult for them even to recognize the nature of his spiritual unrest.

The Epistles of Paul are not easy reading; the New Testament itself contains the view that they are difficult. The Jewish reader, in crossing over from the Old Testament directly to the Epistles, must make an abrupt transition from the familiar simplicity of Palestinian Judaism to a complex Graeco-Jewish doctrine. He will encounter an exposition of an abstruse theological viewpoint and a metaphysical explanation of Jesus as the Christ rather than attractive Gospel narratives, partly familiar to him, of Jesus as a personality.

However, it will not do, as some Jews have attempted, to begin with the Gospels, for the Gospels were written later than Paul's time. Yet if the reader finds the material on Paul too difficult initially, he might turn ahead to the chapters on the

Gospels and Jesus, and after them revert to Paul. No honest presentation of Pauline thought can be truly simple.

What was the specific importance of Paul to emerging Christianity? What is the substance of his message? The answers to these questions form the necessary prelude to any understanding of any one Epistle and its particular doctrine. An over-all view of Paulinism is the most clarifying approach to the doctrine of any single letter, and inseparable from this doctrinal understanding is a clear conception of the extent to which the Christian movement had developed between the time of Jesus and that of Paul.

The spirit of ferment out of which the primitive Christian Church had begun to emerge and to take form is reflected in the very nature and tone of Paul's writings, and the temper of the times can be recognized in the spirited counsel of the genuine Pauline Epistles.* It is a regrettable fact, however, that specific information relating to the church before Paul does not exist in the New Testament in any satisfactory abundance. The most trustworthy though fragmentary picture of the early church

---

*It is customary to refer to the Epistles of Paul by the name of the church or community to which each is addressed. Modern scholarship uniformly accepts Galatians, Romans, First and Second Corinthians, First Thessalonians, Philippians, and Philemon as having actually been written by Paul. Second Thessalonians is not uniformly accepted. Colossians and Ephesians seem related to each other; most scholars who accept Colossians as genuine likewise accept Ephesians, but the doubt as to the authenticity of Pauline authorship is more abundant regarding Ephesians than Colossians. The Pauline authorship claimed for First and Second Timothy and Titus is not accepted by modern scholars, though there are some verses which are believed by a few scholars to be authentic. Unlike these "Pastoral Epistles," the Epistle to the Hebrews makes no claim to be by Paul, but Christian tradition ascribes it to him; while some Roman Catholic scholars accept the validity, liberal Protestant scholarship does not. (For Roman Catholics, a papal Bible commission issued authoritative decisions in such matters in the Council of Trent; no such authoritative body exists for Protestants, for whom, indeed, such authority would be inconsistent with the premises of Protestantism.)

must be reconstructed, in the end, from those scattered facts which Paul himself, in his Epistles, has to offer.

It is certain from the text that a "mother church" existed at Jerusalem and was supported at least in part by contributions made throughout the Diaspora (Romans 16:25–27; I Cor. 16:1–3). Some of the leaders in Paul's time are mentioned by name — the brother of Jesus, James, and Cephas and John (Gal. 1:18 to 2:9). But the actual history of the early Jerusalem Church is obscure, both as to origin and its end, for after Paul's time it fades from view. We do not know how it came into being in the earliest days when a group within Judaism became distinguished by its belief in the resurrection of its crucified leader; we know only that it existed.

The primitive Christian church at Jerusalem conformed to the Law of Moses, by which man's conduct was guided and even prescribed in every sacred and secular avenue of living, from the requirements of ritual worship to the acceptable mores of sex and marriage, from the eventuality of murder to the obligation of philanthropy. This system of all-inclusive law, as we have seen, was developed and expanded by the Pharisees from the Biblical revelation, and was Judaism's distinguishing and exalted possession.

The early Jerusalem church added to this Law its convictions about Jesus, without in any sense detracting from its essential Jewishness. Precisely what these convictions were we do not know. But the possibility of a distinction between Judaism and the Church had at most only dawned at that time; and with emergent Christianity still a part of Judaism, there was as yet no compulsion to examine the relationship of the respective religions. The new movement was a Jewish movement, for Jews; and its missionary activity, until Paul, was directed primarily to converting fellow Jews to a special phase of Judaism.

But Paul was not the first missionary in the early Christian movement, and certainly not the first or only missionary among Jews scattered throughout the Greek world. Others, not he, founded the churches at Rome, Damascus, and Alexandria. What distinguishes Paul is that he made, or at least was decisive in, the crucial change. Himself a missionary, he was faced with the question as to whether, in order to be a follower of Jesus, one had to be a Jew first. Paul's answer, cleaving the history yet to come, was "No."

Judaism in Paul's time was a missionary religion. Such missionary activity has now been dormant in Judaism for almost seventeen hundred years, and this long dormancy has led to the incorrect assumption that Judaism never sought out followers. Certain commentators have drawn the contrast between the supposed universalism of Christianity and the alleged tribalism of Judaism in such a way as to preclude even the possibility that Judaism at any time ever welcomed in an outsider. The picture is wrong, and the alleged contrast unsound; for the Pharisees to compass earth and sea to make one proselyte (Mt. 23:15) is intelligible only against a background in which Pharisees were involved in missionary activities.

The missionary activity of Jews among their pagan neighbors in the Greek Diaspora was by no means unsuccessful. The unfavorable comments of Greek and Roman writers attest to the notice which such activity elicited. The literature speaks of "God-fearers," semi-proselytes who were disposed towards Judaism but who did not take the final step of conversion. Unverifiable traditions point to an abundance of women who became converts to Judaism; that fewer of the converts were men is explainable, at least in part, by the disinclination of men to undergo circumcision at a mature age. Men, nevertheless, visited synagogues and listened to expositions of the Bible.

41

What had Judaism and the Bible to offer to troubled pagans? The Jewish Bible was offered as testimony that the one true God of the universe had revealed Himself to His people. Judaism not only asserted this claim, but also denied the claims of other religions. While the ancient cults offered themselves confusingly as alternatives to each other, so that one could, as it were, select, in those days, Orphism, Isisism, Mithraism, or some local cult, Judaism offered itself as the only true, lasting faith. The Scripture of the Jews, persistently held to be sacred, was constantly expounded to this end in the synagogues in sermons of a common-sense or quasi-philosophic nature. The wooden or stone idols which men could see were less likely to remain enshrined as gods in a time of continual war and turmoil than the invisible God with whom they were contrasted. The religious response of the Greek-Gentile world was not an unwillingness to listen, but a readiness. In an era of uncertainty, of poverty, of physical insecurity which the universal ruthlessness of the Roman occupation provided, Judaism offered man the secure haven of God. To the troubled and the philosophically unsettled it offered religious certainty.

The Greeks and Romans who sneered at the faith which Judaism offered were primarily those intellectuals whose failure to believe the first premise, that the Bible was divine in origin, led them to reject the detailed Jewish claims. Especially was this true in Egypt. The accounts in Genesis and Exodus of the discomfiture of their ancestors at the hands of the Jewish God did not predispose the Egyptians towards a friendly view either of Judaism or of the Jews. The Egyptians replied to the Bible, which derogated them, by derogating the Jews both of their day and of the day of Moses; the truth, they said, was not that God had through Moses led the Jews out of Egypt in the great Exodus, but that the early Jews were lepers whom the Egyptians had expelled. A noteworthy pogrom against Jews took place in Alexandria in 38 or 39 A. D.; it was accomplished not by the Greek or Roman colonists of Alexandria, but by the native Egyptians. The anti-Jewish writings evoked replies from Jews — replies which preserved the Egyptian assertions, and thereby bequeathed them to the church to preserve, in tenor and in usefulness, for enemies of Jews throughout the ages, up to Hitler himself.

Such Jewish literary activity and the attention paid to it are understandable only against a background of fluid communication between Jews and Gentiles. Along with the intellectuals who scorned and the Egyptians who defamed, there were women who became converted and men who became almost converted. Their converters were emissaries sent out for that very purpose. The Greek word "Apostle" translates a Hebrew term for "one who is sent" (m'shullach).

Paul was an apostle, not of the usual form of Judaism, but of the newer movement within Judaism. His work was within the same intermingled Jewish-Gentile setting which any Jewish missionary would have found: a small, local synagogue, meeting either in a special building or, more probably, in someone's home; interested Gentiles, especially among the women; and unpersuaded and unfriendly Gentiles, particularly those with some philosophic training or knowledge.

The missionary, or apostolic message, needed to be couched in such terms as would be both understood and accepted in such a milieu. The language used in the Greek Diaspora had to be Koiné. The references, allusions, and suppositions had to be those quickly identifiable by the auditors. And the contents of that message had to deal with matters of vivid relevance to those who would listen.

We shall see that for a missionary task of this kind Paul was admirably suited.

# VI
# Paul

Who was this Paul? Three main influences shape his historical individuality as it is revealed through his Epistles, unadorned and free from the romanticizing of later Christian tradition.

First, he was a product of Greek civilization, at home in it, and sensitive to its subtlest nuances. Second, he was a Jew; he was at home in the Bible and in the practice of expounding it; he shared the group-feeling of Jews, and he was, from his own standpoint, unreservedly loyal to Judaism. Third, his Epistles were written *after* he became a "Christian," and his "conversion" is the most significant influence of his life. The Greek and Jewish influences are for him general qualities; his Christian faith is his specific character.

Paul's Greek reveals a fluency possible only to one immersed, as it were, in the language. His quotations from the Bible demonstrate that it was the Greek version, and not the Hebrew Old Testament, which he knew; in passages where the Septuagint diverges sharply from the Hebrew text, his interpretation is uniformly one that could be derived only from the Greek translation. His knowledge of Hebrew was either small or totally lacking.

He asserts that he was of the tribe of Benjamin (Romans 11:1; Phil. 3:5; and II Cor. 11:22 ff.); and his being Jewish is always mentioned in support of the validity of his labors. His claim to have excelled his fellow students in the study of Judaism need not be doubted (Gal. 1:14), for his knowledge of the Old

Testament is so keen that he quotes from it effortlessly and spontaneously; he shows knowledge of traditional Midrash (Gal. 5:14), and has no difficulty in utilizing the somewhat stereotyped modes of exegesis of the time, especially that of allegory (I Cor. 5:6–8; 9:8 ff.; Gal. 4:24).

Although Paul quotes from only one classical author, Menander (I Cor. 15:33), he probably was well-versed in the rudiments of secular education. He is to be thought of as a bright and logical reasoner, but not as a formal philosopher. He knew philosophy in much the same way that many persons of our day know Freud, from the atmosphere, and not from careful reading and study. He was distinctly not an intellectual; he was a man of action, quick of mind, and aggressive in temper.

In personality he reveals a combativeness attested to by the fact that of all his Epistles only that to Philemon is free from the mention of opponents. Contemplative calmness is not his chief characteristic.

He was subject to the most intense feelings: anger, scorn, disgust, joy, and hatred. In these he knew no moderation. He did extreme things — such as disdaining financial support from his churches — and he said extreme things. His report of receiving the thirty-nine lashes from his fellow Jews on five occasions is quite believable. Jews had such autonomy in the Roman empire, and there is no reason to doubt that Paul's personality and actions evoked such sentences.

He was single — we do not know whether a bachelor or a widower. He describes his appearance as unimpressive, and he speaks of his oratorical gifts as small ones. But his manner was undoubtedly arresting, and he seems to have known neither discouragement nor fear. Only his physical malady sometimes halted him, a malady the exact nature of which scholars have not discovered. In the nineteenth century, when Paulinism was unfashionable among "enlightened" religionists, an amazing perspicacity diagnosed his malady as epilepsy — a convenient term of opprobrium for which there is no shred of evidence.

The pitfalls which Paul's literary style presents for the unwary are occasioned largely by these personality traits just mentioned. For example, as an extremist, Paul is prone to make sweeping statements and to develop them in a manner that would seem to preclude any modification. As instances, he so treats the Law of Moses and the Jews. Yet the sweeping statement is often followed by a reservation which logicians would appraise as destructive or in refutation of the main statement. But in such cases it is Paul's manner which is difficult, and not the import of what he is saying.

More difficult to resolve are his frequent pursuits of secondary matters, to the complete abandonment of initial themes already presented. Paul often announces that he will pursue some line of thought, and frequently begins it, but interrupts himself, and then fails to return to his starting point. His doctrines are thus made particularly difficult for systematizers to catalogue.

Also, it is difficult, and sometimes impossible, for the conscientious student to find in the Old Testament the meaning that Paul derives from a specific passage which he may mention. Paul argues from the Bible, but he quotes selectively, and assigns significance to what he quotes in a manner which modern persons may find arbitrary and unconvincing, but which is not without parallel in his time.

Another obstacle for systematizers is Paul's seeming inconsistency. Though he may speak of the same thing in different Epistles, he does not say it in the same way each time. The very fact that Paul's writings are epistolary in form — that they are business letters written as specific answers to urgent matters — almost necessarily gives rise to this and other kinds of normal irregularities. Those of us who write letters for the business of the day, however important, do not prepare them for publication or strive for perfect textual consistency, especially when the probable scrutiny of our letters by pedantic scholars two thousand years later is a factor as far from our minds as it was from Paul's own. When content rather than phraseology is made the standard of judgment, it can be seen that the supposed inconsistencies in Paul's Epistles are either surface ones or minor in import.

Further, it must be considered that most of Paul's letters were dictated; they were not written essays constructed from an outline. Those of us who have found our intentions betrayed by a dictaphone can be sympathetic to Paul, whose speed of thought exceeded his speech by a notable margin.

In addition, the full meaning of Paul's doctrine suffers because the Epistles which have come down to us are a random collection. Paul wrote other letters; but those canonized have alone survived. Therefore, we have only such views as these chance Epistles bequeath to us. We know a great deal; but there is also a great deal which we do not know.

Finally, it is possible that Paul's Epistles may have been edited when they ultimately became a part of Scripture and were copied by the early church. There is some evidence of such editing in the letters, provided both by the lower and by the higher criticism. The extent and purpose of such editing are not agreed upon by scholars, and some ultra-conservatives deny it entirely.

The Epistles come from Paul after he has become a follower of Jesus. They are an inspired example of the traditional zeal of the new convert, yet nowhere do the Epistles set forth the specific facts of when Paul became a "Christian," or precisely where, * or, most important, what was the sequence of his reasons

---

*In Acts the conversion experience of Paul is described romantically as occurring on the Road to Damascus.

why. It is important to gauge those reasons, for in the measure that they are typical of the state of mind of persons whom he in turn converted, they are a key to the successful appeal of the new Christian movement. A study of Paul's distinctive doctrine, seen in the context of contemporary Judaism and of the Greek world, leads to a probable reconstruction of the main lines along which Paul reasoned.

For Paul, as for other Greek Jews whom history records, Judaism in its usual form had become inadequate. Fidelity to legal prescriptions, believed to have come long ago from God, did not provide that spiritual security for which both Gentiles and many Jews of that tumultuous time were seeking. The need of the imperilled individual was not for the symbol representing God, not for His codified word, but for direct communion with God Himself.

We can understand the Greek Jew Paul better when we understand also the Greek Jew Philo who lived in Alexandria about the same time. The abundance of knowledge which we have about Philo enables us to see what another Greek Jew faced as religious challenges in the same age as Paul and in a comparable environment, for Philo, although his individual contribution was outstanding, was representative of an entire segment of Diaspora Judaism. Both Philo and Paul are to be understood in contrast to the Judaism of Palestine.

Rabbinic Judaism found the primary expression of its relationship to God in an exaltedly careful observance of the Divine Law. It held that God had spoken through Moses and other prophets; and that His words, recorded in the Bible, were available to any Jew to know in any age. But prophecy, the Palestinian Jews held, had ceased at the time of Ezra. Newer midrashic explanations supplanted the simplicity of Biblical passages with complexities. If one read in the Bible that "God appeared to Abraham," the later midrash considered the appearance in the light of how God manifested Himself, and how Abraham was able to perceive this manifestation. As complexity increased, the appearance of God was supplanted by the appearance of divine agents, such as angels. The "Holy Spirit" is a late device, needed or used in explanation of the manner in which God had revealed Himself to man: not God, but the holy spirit spoke to the prophet; or, the prophet spoke, as rabbinic spokesmen have put it, in the "Holy Spirit." Thus while the "Shekina" or the "holy spirit" by which the divine presence came before man provided an abundant and frequent medium of communion to Palestinian Judaism, there was no possibility that God Himself would come face to face with man in this religious system for which prophecy was a thing of the blessed past.

But for Philo, a Greek Jew, "prophecy" had not ceased at all. Direct communion with God, he believed, was still possible and was, indeed, the true goal of religion, therefore the goal of Judaism. All the legalism of Judaism and all its accumulated commandments were for Philo but steps towards the one true purpose of Judaism: the direct communion of the individual with God. Yet for Philo, too, prophecy was not the simple formula of "God appeared to Abraham." Hellenistic midrash, like the Palestinian, had changed the older simplicity of communion into something complex and elaborate. God, in Philonic terms, derived from the Platonic, was the True Being. In the Old Testament view God was simply not visible. In Greek terms He was not visible to the eyes, though He might be contemplated through the mind. The senses of the body could teach one that God existed, but one could not discern God through the senses. Indeed, only as one through one's higher mind controlled one's senses and one's passions and rose above them could one conceive God. To achieve freedom from the senses and the passions was to achieve a "spiritual" state. The body was the prison-house of the "higher mind," of man's "spiritual" soul. The soul was a divine part of man incarcerated in the body, and constantly seeking release from it. The body, being material, bound one to the material world, and, being mortal, obligated one to die. In its fullest sense "salvation" meant the escape from the world and from death.

Complete release from the material world, however, was too great a perfection to be attained by man unaided. For the gifted contemplator actually to arrive at the goal through his own efforts would have compromised the Godhood of God. But God, in Philo's thought, responded to the earnest striving of man and "appeared" to the spiritually gifted, even though their inevitable degree of imperfection necessitated a communion that was also less than absolute. Philo borrowed a term — Logos* — and a conception from the Greeks, to define and describe such a communion in which the individual was face to face, not with actual deity, but with some more attainable godly aspect. As it was man's mind which apprehended God, so, in Greek thought, it was God's mind, the Logos, which man apprehended; and it was the Logos which performed in the material universe the divine functions of immaterial True Being. In Philo's scheme of things, as for other Diaspora Jews, the motivating idea of Logos was synthesized into the moral aspirations of Judaism.

For Philo, observance of the laws of Judaism was the soul's path to salvation. The essential difference between this point of view and that of Palestinian Judaism is that Palestinian Judaism

---

*Logos is often translated "Word," as at the beginning of the Fourth Gospel. This is a most unhappy translation, and has contributed to widespread misunderstanding, as scholars have struggled vainly to make "Word" fit into the context in the Gospel According to John.

never conceived of man as requiring such salvation. Traditional Judaism to this day has no such doctrine, since it never accepted the Greek premise that the material world is evil, but insisted that it is good. But for Philo and for Paul, who were Jews inclined by the Greek atmosphere towards the goal of transcending physical nature, salvation from the material world was the very focus of religious aspiration. Philo paved his road to salvation with an allegorical midrash on the meaning of Jewish Law. Paul found salvation in his interpretation of the meaning of the career of Jesus.

To Paul, Jesus was God's Logos. The Christ was that aspect of deity which could be apprehended by man. It miraculously had come to earth in human form and had graciously gone through the experience of crucifixion, death, and resurrection. Christ Jesus, in dying, had left his human form to ascend to heaven; and he had provided an example and a means for men to do the same. God had graciously provided man with salvation, Paul insisted, if man would believe and identify himself with the Logos.

The older Jewish term, Christ (Messiah), was used by Paul in a new sense as the designation for this ultimate Logos, in whom the earlier Jewish idea of the Shekina, transmuted into the Greek concept of the divine mind, now lost its philosophical abstractness to become dramatically epitomized in one individual. The force of personalities — Jesus, the inspiration, and Paul, the inspired — thus brought to birth out of Greek-oriented Judaism and its search for salvation a new religion, a religion clearly the product of its ancestry and yet uniquely itself.

# VII

## Paul's Doctrine of Christ

In Paul's new-found way of salvation the conception of God, of His nature and of His medium of revelation, contains both that which is traditional and that which distinctively departs from tradition. The God of Judaism and of the Bible is affirmed by Paul; he speaks of His eternal power and of His Godhood which has been known since the creation of the world (Romans 1:19 ff.). Not God, therefore, but the means of knowing Him has changed. In the remote past, Paul says, God revealed Himself to Israel through the Law and the Prophets. Now, more recently, God has revealed Himself in Jesus Christ (Romans 3:21–22). Here is at once the continuity with Judaism and the difference.

It is not Jesus, the man, who might conceivably have been accepted as the Jewish Messiah, but the divine Christ whom Paul encountered in a revelation who fills Paul's concern and to whom Paul is dedicated. He is determined not to know Christ "from the human point of view" (II Cor. 5:16); his interest in the significance of Jesus' career completely overshadows the details of the career, and his writings give few data about Jesus. He shows knowledge of the Davidic descent (Romans 1:3); he speaks of God's son born of a woman without specifically mentioning the virgin birth. Of John the Baptizer, or of the baptism of Jesus, or of the transfiguration, motifs prominent in the Gospels, Paul gives no word. He quotes only one teaching of Jesus (I Cor. 7:10 ff.), relative to divorce, and even this differs, in a significantly varying form, from the teachings to be found in the Gospels.

52

The charge that Jesus was betrayed by the Jews and that they were responsible for his death is notably absent from Paul's detailed discussions of Judaism. The notion of a betrayal by Judas receives no specific mention; the passage in Paul which might be taken to allude to the betrayal reads: "For I received of the Lord what I also delivered to you, that the Lord Jesus on the night when he was handed over. . . ." While some translations render the Greek word for "handed over" as "betrayed," it is likely that this meaning is influenced by the Gospel narratives and does not at all represent Paul's intent. From Paul's standpoint, the death of Jesus was part of the working of divine providence, and to have ascribed it to Jewish malevolence would have made it the result of a human action.

The man Jesus, then, has little relevance to Paul's thought. He does not often use the name of Jesus alone, but uses Jesus Christ or Christ Jesus. Yet he does not use "Christ" in the usual connotation of Messiah, a term which would be unintelligible to the Greeks. Rather, Paul keeps the importance of the name without its original meaning. For him, the Christ is the "son" of God. He is an offshoot of God, not identical with Him, but subject to the Father (I Cor. 15:28), just as the Logos was a manifestation of God's mind, not identical with God. But whereas for Philo the Logos was a metaphysical abstraction, in Paul's thought it is no abstraction but a reality, which, Paul says, on the historic occasion took on human, though exceptional, flesh. Not flesh, however, but spirit, was the true nature of Christ (Phil. 3:20); and in Paul's figure of speech, Christ, though rich, or spiritual, became poor, fleshly, so that by his poverty believers could become rich (II Cor. 8:9 ff.).

The Pauline distinction between God and the Christ is emphasized in the word Lord (*Kyrios*), which in literal Greek meant *master*, *ruler*, or simply, *sir*. Hebrew usually used two different words for God, *Elohim* and *Adonoi*. The Septuagint renders

*Elohim* by *Theos* (God) and *Adonoi* by *Kyrios* (Lord); in the Old Testament the words are as interchangeable as God and Lord in our English speech. But Paul designates separate meanings; he consistently reserves "God" for God, and never alludes to God as "Lord." Lord, somewhat as in Philo, is an attribute, or facet, of God, but not God Himself. Christ, then, is an aspect of God; godly, yet not God. "Though he was in the form of God (he) did not count equality with God as something to be grasped, but emptied himself, taking the form of a servant, being born in the likeness of man" (Phil. 2:6-7). Christ, in this likeness, was the form in which the God of Israel, having appeared preliminarily to Moses and to the prophets of the Old Testament, now revealed Himself decisively and crucially. To put it perhaps more simply, though the Christ had taken on human form, he was not a mere human, but rather an aspect of God. God Himself was beyond man's reach; the Christ, though, was available to man. The Christ was the vehicle through which man could reach the otherwise unattainable God of Israel.

But we must look at an even more difficult bit of complex thought. We must try to understand that the Christ became Jesus, that is, took on human form on an occasion, but in Paul's view the Christ was a spiritual being both before and after the incarnation. As a spiritual being, the Christ could enter into even other men, such as Paul himself; or the figure can shift so as to describe a man who is "in Christ." Perhaps it may be clearer to oversimplify and to suggest that the Christ, as distinct from the Christ Jesus, is in Paul's mind the equivalent of a divine spirit. Paul offers us no clarifying definition, and we need to be instructed by his intent rather than by his direct words. In summary, the Christ to Paul is a divine spirit; the Christ Jesus is the interval in which the Christ became transformed into the man Jesus.

The Christ, either in the Christ Jesus or apart from that interval, is in Paul's view the means of continuing revelations from God.

To Paul himself, revelations were abundant (II Cor. 12:1–7), and his Epistles contain frequent mention of such experiences. God has revealed Christ to him (Gal. 1:16); he did not "receive the gospel" from any man, but by a revelation of Jesus Christ (Gal. 1:12); a trip to Jerusalem was not in compliance with orders from the Jerusalem Church, but because of a revelation (Gal. 2:2). More specifically, Paul insists that he has seen Christ (I Cor. 9:1); that the Christ appeared to more than five hundred brethren at one time, then to James, then to Paul (I Cor. 15:5–9).

The chief passage, however, is an autobiographical account worth quoting: "I must boast, . . . I will go on to visions and revelations of the Lord. I know a man in Christ who fourteen years ago was caught up in the third heaven — whether in the body or out of the body I do not know, God knows. And I know that this man was caught up into Paradise — whether in the body or out of the body I do not know, God knows — and he heard things that man cannot be told, which man may not utter. On behalf of this man I will boast, but on my own behalf I will not boast, except of my weaknesses" (II Cor. 12:1–5). This, indeed, may have been the climactic vision which transformed him from an opponent of the church into an adherent; this may well have been his "conversion" experience.

But this conversion was preceded by a period of profound, inner unrest. The tone of Paul's writings reveals his emotional depths. He records in his Epistles that he has previously persecuted the "Church" (I Cor. 15:9; Gal. 1:23), but he does not specify what form the persecution took. He was undoubtedly violently opposed to the new movement, but then espoused it completely. Such religious uncertainty, precipitating Paul from one extreme to the other, stemmed from problems which were environmental, and which were at least a common symptom of the times, however unique Paul's response to them may have been.

The religious dilemma which confronted Paul, both a Jew and a Greek, was that Judaism, premised on the Law of Moses, was alien to the more mystical religious approach of his familiar Greek world. The writings of Philo make it clear that many Jews were torn by this same conflict. Scoffers at the Bible and apostates from Judaism were numerous enough in the Alexandrian Jewish community to elicit from Philo both stirring denunciations and ingenious efforts to try to silence the Jewish skeptics. Philo uniformly answered these young Jews who challenged their Judaism with Greek thought by asserting that worthy Greek ideas were really Jewish ones: true, man was an unhappy mixture of the immaterial soul and the material, evil body, but Judaism taught one how to rise above the body; true, Plato and Aristotle were great intellects, but they were latter-day plagiarists and imitators of Moses, whose Scripture anticipated all that philosophy; true, there was a life higher than the letter of the Law, but that higher life, too, was prescribed by Judaism and was symbolized by the Law itself; it could be achieved only through the sum of the Law. The questions which Philo answered about Judaism would have had no reality in the Palestinian scene, but were of pressing importance in the Greek Dispersion, where other basic approaches invited comparison.

It was the mysticism in Greek thought that ultimately drew Paul, in his religious seeking, beyond the bounds of Judaism. For him the Law of Moses was an inadequate religious totality; and he required a conviction of actual personal communion with God to satisfy himself. The complex philosophy of the time, depicting True Reality and Logos, determined Paul's form of communion; not with God Himself in His essence, but with God as revealed in Christ. Thereafter the persecutor became a convert; the convert became a missionary.

Yet there is a certain sense in which it is not quite correct to speak of Paul as a convert, certainly not *from* Judaism. To Paul, the newer convictions are the essence of the true Judaism, and Christ is not a nullification of Judaism or of the Old Testament, but actually crowns them.

Paul, accordingly, never rejects the Old Testament. Though his attitude towards the Law of Moses is distinctly at variance with the prevalent line of Jewish thought, his Christianity intensifies rather than lessens his devotion to the Scripture in which he was reared. He sees in it the corroboration of what has been newly revealed to him. The death and resurrection of Christ by crucifixion were in accord with the Scriptures (I Cor. 15:3–4). Christ crucified, he says, became a "curse"; and in explanation (in Gal. 3:13) he cites Deuteronomy 21:23, "cursed be every one who hangs on a tree." Christ, Paul says, is our paschal lamb (I Cor. 5:7), a figurative allusion to the Jewish Passover sacrifice. (Christ as the Lamb figures prominently in later writings.) Thus Paul, in his discovery of salvation and communion with God through Christ, is still deeply rooted, from his standpoint, in the faith of his fathers. He often finds himself in keen conflict with Jews, but never with his own view of Judaism — "He is not a real Jew who is one outwardly. . . . He is a Jew who is one inwardly" (Romans 2:28–29).

In this Christ-centered "Judaism" the crucifixion and, following from it, the resurrection, form the strong double keystone of Paul's conviction of salvation. Though the resurrection is the most significant item in his mind, it is the death of the Christ which claims his major attention. The burden of all his preachment, Paul says, is "Jesus Christ and him crucified" (I Cor.

57

2:2; see Gal. 3:1). That Christ was crucified was in part a difficult problem for Church apologetics, "a stumbling block to Jews and a folly to Gentiles" (I Cor. 1:23). But Paul argues that it attests to the "power of God and the wisdom of God" (I Cor. 1:24).

By that death, in which Christ died for all, symbolically all men have died as far as their bodies are concerned, and they now live for Christ (II Cor. 5:14–15). As a result of the crucifixion and its "atonement" men are reconciled to God (II Cor. 5:18–21). Christ loved Paul, gave himself for Paul (Gal. 2:20). Mankind's salvation was bought with a price (I Cor. 6:20; 7:23).

Crucifixion thus was not a defeat for Christ, but necessarily paved the way to the triumph of resurrection. Resurrection, then as now, evoked no universal assent; some of Paul's hearers at Corinth denied that any resurrection was possible. Paul's refutation of them is based solely on the specific case of Christ; "He was raised on the third day in accordance with the Scriptures"; moreover, he was seen by Cephas, the twelve, and five hundred "brethren" at one time, "most of whom are still alive." If Paul and these others have seen him, surely Christ must have been resurrected (I Cor. 15:3–10).

The special resurrection of Christ, moreover, was both proof and prophecy that the dead can be resurrected. Christ is the first instance, "the first fruits of those who have fallen asleep" (I Cor. 15:20), but others, Paul says, will undoubtedly rise from death if they have believed in Christ.

"Belief" is in Paul called "faith." It is not faith in the sense of a set of credos, but a dynamic inner experience. Faith in the Christ means belief that as Christ had died for man's bodily, sinful nature, so man was now free from that sinfulness, and therefore saved, or "righteous." This salvation for all was available through the redeeming acts of Christ, death on the Cross and resurrection. One was required to "believe" implicitly, profoundly, and without reservation that the events took place and had saving power, in order to benefit from them.

There is at this point a sharp contrast between Paul's view of sin and that which we Jews have inherited from the ancient rabbis. For us, a sin is an act of commission or omission which is wrong. For Paul, sin is a state of being; it is man's normal condition, because man is a bodily creature. But in the view of the rabbis, a person who sinned could, and should, regret it and make suitable amends. The Yom Kippur is the occasion par excellence in the year when man makes atonement for his misdeeds.

But when sin is thought of as a state of being, and not as individual acts, and when it is deemed to be man's usual condition, then man's departure from sin is not the result of any remorseful actions, but is possible only if man's essential nature is changed.

In the Jewish tradition, man atones and, it is believed, God graciously pardons him. In Paul's view, man cannot atone, but needs to have his nature changed from the bodily to the spiritual. The death of the Christ was interpreted by Paul as the atonement made on behalf of man. By symbolically dying as the Christ had died, man abandoned his bodily nature.

The contrasts, then, are between sins and sin, between the atonement which man makes and that which is made for him, and between man forgiven for sins and man transformed from one state of being into another. In Judaism the pardoned sinner remains a man; in Paul's view, man becomes transformed from a bodily being into a spiritual one.

Belief of this sort — acceptance of the acts of Christ and their saving effects — exalted the purified believer. He had been "dead," in sin, in body; through faith he lived again in sinlessness, in spirit. Thus he was identifiable with Christ and with the two-part drama of salvation in which Christ had anticipated him. Baptism, a "sacrament of regeneration," enabled the saved individual actually to enact this identification. The person entering the water symbolically died as Christ had died, and, emerging, rose again, as Christ rose at the resurrection into newness of life (Romans 6:4–11). Baptism, in Paul, is descended from an ancient Jewish ceremonial of cleansing one's body from dirt and from the yield of the pores and organs of the body — though some scholars would trace church baptism to pagan cults. The old Jewish rite was an actual washing; the new church ceremony was not, but extended its meaning of death and resurrection over and beyond the ceremonial act.

Another rite, also of Jewish derivation, and expressing the same symbolism, is mentioned by Paul. On the eve of Jewish festivals and the Sabbath, it is the custom to partake, before the meal, of wine and of bread broken from a whole loaf, while giving thanks to God for the gifts of drink and food. The church utilized both the wine and the bread, which later was used in wafer form. The technical name for the ceremony is "eucharist," or "thanksgiving," but this term is not found in the New Testament. Paul declares that the meaning of the ceremony was given him by Christ. The bread is broken as Christ's body was broken on the cross, and the wine symbolizes the shedding there of Christ's blood (I Cor. 11:23–26); although the resurrection aspect is not overt, it is implied in the "death." The ceremony is a sacrament, an outer form with an inner "grace"; again it enables the participant to identify himself with Christ.

Paul not only found for himself a mode of communion with God, but he provided the interpretation whereby two traditional Jewish ceremonies were invested with the capacity of providing communion. As God had revealed Himself in Christ, so the believer, by baptism, imitated the experience of Christ, or by the eucharist shared it; and he thus communed with God.

# VIII

# The Church and the Law of Moses

Paul's epistles are answers to questions or comments on situations that are arising without precedent in the new churches. All the churches to which he wrote, except those at Rome and Colossae, address their questions to him as their founder. They deal with new problems in a new context; the answers which he gives are invariably direct replies to inquiries or comments elicited by reports which come to Paul.

The Church of Paul's day was as yet hardly an organized institution, and the lack of the order of a stabilized system made the questions and the answering Epistles necessary. Paul speaks of church officials variously as those "who labor among you and are over you" (I Thess. 5:12) and as teachers (Gal. 6:6); in another passage he says: "God has appointed in the church first apostles, second prophets, third teachers, then workers, then helpers, administrators, speakers in various kinds of tongues" (I Cor. 12:28). "Speaking in tongues" is the literal translation of a Greek word, which might be better rendered for our day as "speaking in ecstasy"; Paul boasts that his ability here exceeds everyone else's (I Cor. 14:18). Elsewhere he speaks of an unnamed brother, "famous among all the church for his preaching the Gospel" (II Cor. 8:18).

There was apparently no uniformity in church support. Mention is frequently made of alms for the church in Jerusalem (I Cor. 16:1–4 and elsewhere). Paul insists that he received no support for his livelihood from the church at Corinth, but that this support came from other churches (II Cor. 11:8 ff.). He declares that though "they that serve the altar partake of the altar," he has not exercised that right to food and drink (I Cor. 9:2–14). From examples such as these it is apparent that tradition in this relatively new church has not had time to become established practice. Paul exhorts the Corinthians to be faithful to traditions handed down, an exhortation needless unless the practices varied (I Cor. 11:2).

Paul speaks of the Church in terms of a mystical or metaphysical entity, transcending mundane membership. (Jews often fail to note that when a Christian today speaks of the "Church," he does not mean an edifice or a congregation or a union of congregations.) An allegory, greatly developed later on from Paul's laconic statement, speaks of the Church as the pure Bride of Christ (II Cor. 11:2). The singleness of this concept, however, is challenged by the presence of a diversity of ministries within the Church; and, in a long passage beginning in the twelfth chapter of First Corinthians, Paul seeks to explain this and to assure his correspondent that each functionary is a necessary part of the Church's unified whole. These functionaries differ: "There are varieties of gifts . . . inspired by one and the same spirit who apportions to each one individually as he will. For just as the body is one and has many members, all the members of the body, though many, are one body, so it is with Christ." (Therefore, there should be harmony among the functionaries.) Again, Paul says, stressing the unity of the Church, "We, though many, are one body in Christ" (Romans 12:5).

Though Paul knows the Church as an entity, and even gives injunctions to expel a wayward member (I Cor. 5:2, 12–13), the Church, in his time, is not so well developed as to have a thorough sense of its individuality. Its separation from Judaism, therefore, although well defined, is not complete. It may be put this way, that when one tears a paper in two, one first creases and then tears; in Paul's day the crease has been made, and the paper is divided by the crease — but the tearing is only commencing. For Paul, the Church is the people of Israel, the true Israel, divided by a crease from the "false" Israel, the Jews. Regrettably, the Jews have been blind to God's crowning revelation in the Christ, and therefore have been set aside, perhaps folded under, but only temporarily; their rejection is a providential opportunity for God to turn for the moment to the Gentiles, but afterward He will turn back to the Jews. Paul realizes that the Church and the Jewish people have been drifting apart, and are perhaps being severed from each other, but he insists that the Jews, not the Church, have moved away; the Church is still Judaism. It is the false which has moved away — or, rather, has been pushed away by God.

Though Paul clearly indicates his discernment that Judaism and the Church have moved along the road to separation, it seems to me likely that he would have repudiated the drastic political, economic, and social use which subsequent church writers make of his doctrine of God's rejection of the Jews. He insists that for the Church there is no distinction between Greek and Jew (Romans 10:12; Gal. 3:28); and in another passage he speaks laconically of Jews, Greeks, and the Church of God (I Cor. 10:32), revealing his awareness that the Church is different from both pagan and Jew. Paul is a Jew who finds in his own Judaism a plan of salvation, for Jew and Gentile alike; but what is to him a Jewish plan of salvation gains adherents primarily among Gentiles, to the unexpected point of their constituting a group. Paul can become profoundly immersed in the new group, but he cannot cut the silver cord that has bound him to Judaism. He can turn on Jews, and even speak vulgarly of them (Phil. 3:2; also Gal. 5:12; in this latter passage read "castrate" in place of "mutilate"), but he cannot forget that he is a Jew.

Did one have to be a Jew first, before one could be a member of the Church? The question faced the early church, as soon as it moved into the Gentile, Greek environment. Arising in Paul's time, the issue was of great concern to Paul, and his own thought on it matures in him as a result of the deep and unsettling religious crisis through which he has had to struggle. Paul's view that to be a Jew first was not prerequisite to becoming a Christian became the dominant and, in time, the only view of the church.

The distinguishing feature of being Jewish, apart from being born of Jewish stock and belonging to a synagogue, is the carrying out of observances explicitly commanded in the Old Testament, and in their midrashic expansions. These include the mandate of the circumcision of males, and the prohibition against eating certain foods, such as swine, rabbit, and birds of prey. The primary source of these laws, it will be recalled, is the Five Books of Moses.

Palestinian Jews, as we have said, observed these laws as literally commanded by God; within an all-Jewish environment, there was neither propriety in questioning the divine nature of the Law, nor occasion to do so. But in the Greek world, the situation was different.

The Greeks, too, had their laws, and in the arena of reciprocal notice, Jew and Greek had opportunity for comparing each other's legislation. The Greeks, in the Platonic tradition, and later under Stoic influence, conceived of law on two levels. The lower level was that of the laws actually enacted in the various city states; these laws were the imitation of the metaphysical ideal law, the law of nature. This higher law was faultless, immutable and eternal, and never made manifest among men. The written laws were often marred by injustice, they were altered from time to time; and when a tyrant arose, his introduction of substitute laws demonstrated the transient nature of the written code.

To Greeks, the Laws of Moses constituted a written code; to them the claim made by Jews that the laws were divine was refutable on the simple basis that they were written down. Greek Jews, such as those in Alexandria, who accepted the prevailing contrast between the enacted laws and the higher law of nature, struggled to find some solution for the pressing problem. The author of a work called Fourth Maccabees, a Jew probably of Alexandria, showed the direction in which a possible solution might go by asserting that the faithful observance of the Laws of Moses would lead one to possess the four Greek cardinal virtues: justice, courage, prudence, and temperance. The Law, he argued, enabled one to triumph over one's body, and thus be virtuous; and he illustrated his thesis by a legend of the Maccabean period which told of Hannah and her seven sons who died martyr deaths at the stake, rather than comply with the heathen demands. Their control over their senses and passions through the Law was such that they were impervious to the flames and the wracking pains. Implicitly in Fourth Maccabees, the justification for the Law is not primarily its divine origin, but its utility.

Philo goes in the same direction, but considerably farther. He accepts as axiomatic the view that there are the two levels of law, the unwritten law of nature and the written Laws. He makes the concession that the Law of Moses belongs on the level of the written Laws. But within the framework of that concession, he advances several arguments. Greek law, he says, differs from place to place; Sparta, Athens, and Alexandria have different laws, but Jewish Law is everywhere the same. Greek law is variable, but Jewish Law is constant. Greek law is the product of unholy tyrants, but Jewish Law is the work of the priest-prophet Moses. And, finally, the Law of Moses is in complete conformity with the law of nature, and the best possible approximation to it.

Furthermore, Philo argues, the Laws of Moses are actually symbols of the natural Law. Circumcision is the pruning away of the passions from the body; Jews abstain from pork, not because it is (as the uninformed often contend today) bad or unhealthful, but precisely for the reason that pork is the sweetest and best meat, and the prohibition is merely a device for teaching self-control, a cardinal virtue.

Thus, with a conception parallel to the Greek idea of law on two levels, Philo explains that there were two levels of Biblical law. The literal law is the statement as found in the Bible in legislation stemming from Moses. But there is a higher law, stemming from God, and God's Law is the Law of Nature. The patriarchs Abraham, Isaac, and Jacob who lived before the Law was revealed to Moses conformed to this higher Law, and those of their descendants who emulated their examples could similarly rise to God and to natural Law. For those Jews who know and observe only the literal Law of Moses, Philo has a feeling of condescension, bordering on contempt. He himself knows the higher as well as the lower level.

An altered attitude towards practice was the inevitable result of this dividing of the law into two levels. Philo takes to task a group of Alexandrian Jews. They were "spirituals" and they read the Torah for the knowledge of natural Law, but they abstained from observing the literal Law of Moses. Philo's reproof of them is only mild, and there is marked similarity between his own conception and that of the group whose negligence distresses him. Both he and the "spirituals" have found the higher Law. For both, the Law of Moses, which Philo retained and the "spirituals" ignored, was only a secondary concern.

Paul, a Greek Jew, has similar views on the two levels of law. He speaks, for example, of Gentile believers, who do not have the Law of Moses, yet do by nature what the Law requires (Romans 2:14–16). Paul's profound religious upheaval was due to the fact that for him, too, the Law of Moses was of secondary importance, and his religious yearning could not be satisfied by a commandment once sprung from the divine source but now for long the property of man. He required not a divine Law, but God. And he found God in the Christ.

This conviction raised for Paul the question of the maintenance of the Law of Moses. Now that he had the higher Law, did he still require the written Laws? His belief that they could be passed over brought him into a secondary dilemma. The Bible was valid and true for Paul. The Law was in the Bible. How could these opposing thoughts be harmonized?

Paul, like Philo, discovered a solution from the Pentateuch itself. Genesis is virtually without laws; these begin with Moses in Exodus. Yet, Abraham, Isaac, and Jacob are extolled in Genesis as great and holy men; how could they, living before the time of Moses, have achieved this goodness without knowledge of his Laws? Philo, as we indicated, explains that these patriarchs were eminent in that they lived by the Law of Nature; and thereafter the Laws of Moses were written down as records of what these men did, so that the Law conforms to "nature."

Paul's solution also is inspired by the example of Abraham. The first patriarch did not observe the Law of Moses; nevertheless, he was reckoned as righteous because of his faith (Gen. 15:6). From this Paul argues that the Law was not always in existence as a means of salvation, nor need it remain so. It was only a finite thing with limits set in time; it began with the revelation of God to Moses, and was superseded by the revelation in Christ. Moreover, the revelation of the Law of Moses was not of the first rank, Paul avers, for it was mediated by angels, not vouchsafed directly by God. (The Old Testament lacks confirmation of this unusual view.) Hence the Law of Moses is supplanted, for Paul, by reason of the quality of the final revelation of God Himself in Christ.

As a product of revelation, even a second-rank one, Paul must concede some positive qualities to the Law; it cannot be evil, it cannot be sin. The Law was preparatory, the custodian of a child, a jailer, and hence good. But it was temporary. What were its deficiencies?

All the anguish of his religious crisis is poured out in Paul's lament: the Law should have made him good, but it did not. Although it prohibited evils, its mention of what it prohibited stirred Paul not to obey, but to disobey. Indeed, the enumeration of sins inclined him towards sin as though he would never have thought of transgressions had the Law not prompted him. Intellectually he knew what was right, but since he did not have control over his senses and passions, his body did not respond obediently to his mind. What he willed to do, he failed to do, and he acted, rather, along lines which he had not willed.

Commentators have frequently explained Paul's negative attitude towards the Law as stemming from the difficulties and inconvenience of the Orthodox Jewish regimen. Paul has not one word to say of such difficulty; indeed, this commentary must be ascribed to a mixture of condescension towards Judaism and of unfamiliarity with it. Moreover, this explanation deprives Paul of any profundity, for it would mean that principle was not at stake for him, but only ease and convenience.

Other scholars, especially Jews, have explained Paul's turning from the Law as stemming from his lack of success with Jews and his persuasiveness with Gentiles. This explanation confuses a cause and a result. It was Paul's defection from the Law which failed to win him Jews; it was not his failure here that produced his defection. This explanation, too, reduces Paul to a status of superficiality, for it would make his religious crisis dependent only on expediency and fortuitous circumstances.

Paul's crisis, it must be emphasized, antedated his joining the church, and it was precipitated by his governing conviction that the Law was not the ultimate which he sought. "Wretched man that I am! Who will deliver me from this body of death?" (Romans 7:24) is an echo of his unhappiness before conversion. The Law implied that it was the ultimate, and that man, in using it, could help himself. For Paul, however, the clue to man's true nature was the helplessness that he himself felt, and the inevitable need of God was Paul's own need. The rabbis, who urged reliance on God, did not deny large areas of man's self-dependence. Paul sees man as completely dependent on God.

God, through Christ, provided Paul with the salvation which the Law could not provide. A prerequisite for that salvation was the possession of Abraham's unique quality, faith. Faith and works of the Law are, for Paul, a set of contradictory and opposing principles.

"Works of the Law" means the scrupulous execution of written enactments; faith means the attainment of that spiritual level at which one lives in accord with the unwritten Law of Nature. (The later church fathers, indeed, readily combine Philo's exposition of the Patriarchs with Paul's doctrine of Abraham's faith; Eusebius, in the *Preparation for the Gospel*, gives us such a stock combination.) When Paul tells us that he died to the Law (Gal. 2:19), he means that through faith in Christ

69

he has gone beyond the validity which the Law once had for him. The Law, dealing with subspiritual matters, comes ultimately to be described by Paul as a law of death, while faith in the Christ is the law of life.

Once personally convinced, Paul makes this belief a part of his teaching. In Galatian churches which he had founded, consisting of Gentiles, the Law of Moses had never been practiced. Paul learns, however, that other apostles, visiting Galatia, have asserted the necessity of observing the Law. This insistence on the validity of the Law, coming from contemporaries of Paul in the church, indicates that Paul in abrogating the Law was drastically altering the earliest church practice.

For Paul's Jerusalem predecessors, the Christ was an addition to their Judaism. For Paul, the Christ is a replacement of that which was central in Judaism. Paul is not content that a person should both observe the Law and have "faith in Christ"; the choice, he insists, is exclusive; "if you receive circumcision, Christ will be of no advantage to you" (Gal. 5:2). The Law, in sum, must not be observed.

Paul's way eventually became the way of all the church; not immediately, but surely within a century. It was Paul who made the "ideological" pattern for the separation of the church from Judaism.

"Antinomianism," as Paul's opposition to the Law is called, leads to the doctrine of Christian "freedom," in contrast to Jewish "slavery." It was Paul's intention, by means of this doctrine, to nullify only the Law of Moses, and not to preach lawlessness. Faith, he insists, makes the believer a spiritual person; and love, joy, and peace are the fruits of possessing the spirit; therefore, the right attitude automatically achieves that which legislation elicits only through enforcement. Paul's doctrine of freedom is one which invites misunderstanding. Paul and the later church have to contend with those who confuse freedom with license (Gal. 5:13). Far from being license, Paul's special kind of freedom is ascetic in nature. Those persons, Paul believes, who belong to Christ Jesus have crucified the flesh (Gal. 5:24) with its passions and desires, and as they "die to the body" they become spirit and are no longer subject to the material universe.

They have received the Spirit of God (I Cor. 2:14). Though they live in this world, they are not of it (II Cor. 10:3 ff.); "For me to live is Christ, and to die is gain. If it is to be life in the flesh, that means fruitful labor for me. Yet which I shall choose I cannot tell. I am hard pressed between the two. My desire is to depart and be with Christ, for that is far better." Again, "Our commonwealth is in heaven, and from it we await a Savior, the Lord Jesus Christ who will change our lowly body to be like his glorious body" (Phil. 1:23 ff.; 3:20).

This view of the imperfect body and its lowly limitation is like the view of the Greek pessimist, the dualist. This life is bad; it must be escaped, Paul says. Not only is individual man himself bad, but the whole world is evil. Not only must the righteous rise above this earthly life, but they must save themselves in the impending general destruction, when the whole evil world will come to its End.

Christ is not the escape itself, but he is the means. The initial coming of Christ provided the faithful with the preparation; their sin had died, and they were in the "spirit." But the crucial moment was to be his return, when the universal judgment would fall upon all creation.

This future judgment was a doctrine explicit even in the Old Testament. It is found in traditional Judaism, a matter bound up with the future Messiah who was connected by varying formulas to Judgment and Resurrection. The Greeks, too, had notions of eons or cycles of time, culminating in world-wide destruction.

But in both the Jewish view and the Greek, the coming event was a matter of a remote day, to come "at the end of time." The concept is given pressing immediacy in Paul's thinking; it is thought of as an event for the nearest future. "The appointed time," he writes, "is growing short . . . ." "The form of this world is passing away" (I Cor. 7:29, 31). "Salvation is nearer to us now than when we first believed; the night is far gone, the day is at hand" (Romans 13:11–12).

Back of Paul's thought lay a mythological drama, which was part of the common folk knowledge of Near Eastern peoples. A rebellion against God had taken place in heaven, and certain fallen angels, under the leadership of Satan, were in defiance of God. Until the Satanic power of evil was broken, the Day of Judgment could not come. Once this power was destroyed, and Satan was no longer a factor, God's reign would be universal and unlimited; His kingdom would come. Paul uses this phrase, which is so strongly associated with Jesus in the Lord's Prayer, several times: I Cor. 4:20; 6:9; 15:50.

The initial coming of Christ had already partly broken the power of Satan, Paul assured the faithful. The believer, through faith in Christ, was no longer subject to Satan's rule of the body and its evil, and in Christ he was now free from subjection to the "elements of the world" (Gal. 4:3). The second, and climactic, coming of Christ, known technically as the *parousia*, would take place on Judgment Day, at the End. As yet the very last bit of destruction of Satan's broken power was not accomplished; and it was this small margin which kept the Second Coming a matter for the nearest future, rather than a realized present. On the Judgment Day, a day of God's wrath, the Christ would return; believers, prepared through being already spiritual, would be saved, and would enjoy great glories. The unspiritual, however, would be subject to the ire of the last day.

Accordingly, since the time left was short, Paul said, man should not make those arrangements which are sensible only on a basis of permanency. To Paul, as to Philo, the sex relation was a matter of passion alone, unredeemed by higher emotions; Philo reluctantly approved of sex relations only as the necessary means of procreation. Moreover, to both of them marriage implied succumbing to the body. Paul, notably, could not actively countenance marriage, since it was a relationship usually of permanence but now destined for only a short time. Marriage, indeed, was no sin; but it was not only the impending end of the world which made it something preferable to avoid; in Paul's thought it is "well for a man not to touch a woman." Yet marriage is better "than to be aflame with passion" (I Cor. 7:1-8). Paul does not urge marriage as in itself a good thing, but only as a legitimizing of an otherwise illegitimate status. Within marriage, the conjugal rights may be bestowed: "Do not refuse one another except by agreement for a season, that you may devote yourselves to prayer, but then come together again, lest Satan tempt you through lack of self-control. I say this by way of concession, not of command" (I Cor. 7:5-6). Again: "If anyone thinks that he is not behaving properly toward his betrothed, if his passions are strong, and if it has to be, let him do what he will, he does not sin; let them marry. But whoever . . . has determined . . . to keep her as his betrothed, he will do well" (I Cor. 7:36-37).

Paul affirms strongly again and again that the End is near, and he gives his advice accordingly, but he cannot say, with certainty, when the time will be. In the Epistles to the Thessalonians he faces up to the questions: When? How soon will that which is imminent manifest itself? What will take place? And what about those who have died in advance of Judgment Day? Paul replies as best he can. "We who are alive, who are left until the coming of the Lord, shall not precede those who have fallen asleep. For the Lord himself will descend from heaven with a cry of command, with the archangel's clarion call, and with the sound of the trumpet of God" (I Thess. 4:15–16). "But as to the times and seasons, brethren, you have no need to have anything written to you. For you yourselves know well that the day of the Lord will come like a thief in the night" (I Thess. 5:1–2).

The question by the Thessalonians takes its point of departure from the fact that for many members of the church, the parousia was already long expected; and an acute awareness of delay had developed. The church, as we shall see, had to deal initially with the problem of delay and then with the fact that the Judgment Day did not arrive, and doctrine had to be adjusted to reality. Paul, however, is concerned only with the delay, and not, like the later church, with the failure of the predictions to materialize.

On the coming day, which the church will greet triumphantly, vengeance will be inflicted "upon those who do not know God. And upon those who do not obey the Gospel of our Lord Jesus. They shall suffer the punishment of eternal destruction and exclusion from the presence of the Lord and the glory of his might when he comes on that day to be glorified in his saints and to be marveled at in all who have believed" (II Thess. 1:8–10). This passage shows clearly that Paul conceived of the Church alone as enjoying the Grace of God. Much argument has been advanced to the effect that Paul broke the shackles of narrowness of Jewish "racism," for by admitting Jew and Greek alike to the Church, he had founded a universal religion. But though Paul admitted the erstwhile Jew and Greek within the faith, the attitude of the "new Israel," the Church, was neither more universalistic nor less particularistic than that of Judaism. Ultimately the Church was to assert that there was no salvation outside of it, a view which is still offered in only slightly modified form by the Church of Rome and which frequently annoys the Protestants thereby excluded.

Paul's activity, reduced to simplest terms, was to bring to people, Jew or Greek, the good tidings that through identification with Christ a man could escape the destruction to come. His message is based on views of man, of life, and of the shortness of time left to this world — views which are poles apart from the views of rabbinic Judaism. The rabbis conceived of man, essentially noble and free, serenely doing God's will in a world destined permanently to endure. Paul, on the other hand, exhibits not serenity, but charged emotion; the world is about to be destroyed, and helpless, sinful man needs to escape the destruction. God has made eligible for that escape those who believe that the death and resurrection of Jesus, the Christ, transformed them from evil, bodily persons into good, spiritual beings.

A summary may here be useful of the distance which early Christianity has traveled from its inherited Judaism even in the early age of Paul, as led by him. What it has carried over is the Jewish Scripture, though interpreted now in a new and unique way. It has a continued belief in the God of Israel and a sense of a special place in the divine scheme of things for Israel — except that Israel is no longer the Jewish people, but is instead the emerging Christian church.

The rejection of the law of Moses implies an end to those two items most readily characterizing the usual Judaism. One of these is the dietary laws. The second is the religious calendar, with the New Year and the Day of Atonement in the fall, Tabernacles in the fall, Passover in the spring, and Pentecost in the early summer.

Passover in a sense becomes the Christian Easter — the New Testament does not use the word Easter; Pentecost abides in Christianity, but as the anniversary of a particular Christian occasion mentioned in Acts 2. Passover and Pentecost, though retained, become radically altered, Passover to the point of a lack of recognition; all the other events in the Jewish calendar disappear from Christian usage and practice. It is uncertain just when the Sabbath was altered from Saturday to Sunday.

Paul is the author of most of the elimination. But along with what was eliminated, notice must be taken of what has been added. We are still before the time of a stabilized observance of Holy Week with its Good Friday and Easter; we are still centuries before the time of the observance of the unknown day of Jesus' birth. But the two ceremonies, baptism and the eucharist, have become in Paul's own time focal in the Christian observance.

The Gospels indicate by specific mention the observance of some of the days in the Jewish calendar by Jesus. This observance disappears in Paul. It is a notice of this phenomenon that has in part led to the frequent judgment that Paul substituted a religion about Jesus for the religion of Jesus.

In Paul's time officialdom was still in a fluid stage; the liturgy was only in its formative period. While it must be conceded that Paul did not go the entire distance which the Church after his time went, it is a reasonable conclusion that the task of the Church was less to extend the road which Paul had traveled than to broaden it, pave it, and maintain it. Paul's elimination of Jewish items carried him to the outer borders of Judaism; his innovations carried beyond the border and into the new entity.

As Paul brought his message to a group, he formed it into a church, and thereafter he departed to found or visit some other church. Problems arose after his departure; inquiries were made of him, sometimes by letter and sometimes by some convenient messenger. The difficulty in his answering Epistles is that both Paul and the addressees of his letters knew what the questions were, but we do not.

The Epistles are enormously difficult to read in their own light. Once they became Scripture, they were regarded as shedding light on matters which had arisen to concern the later readers. Our age inherits both the Epistles and a stupendously large body of interpretations of that material. Since the Epistles are only random correspondence, they are often terse, allusive rather than expository, and less than fully clear. The interpretative literature is, accordingly, not all of a piece. Paul's writings are such that the literature which explains them is often more difficult than Paul himself.

# IX

# The Epistles of Paul

LIKE A FORMAL LETTER in our day, the epistle in the Graeco-Roman world followed a set pattern. It began with a statement of the name of the writer and that of the addressee, followed immediately by a complimentary paragraph. Then came the body of the letter, after which there was a closing greeting, including some words of regards, and often the name of the scribe who recorded the dictation. All Paul's genuine Epistles fit into this pattern except Galatians, and in the case of Galatians there is ample reason for the departure from the form.

The order of the Pauline Epistles in the New Testament is by length. We do not know the order in which they were written. The traditional scholarship usually tried to fit the Epistles into the framework of Paul's missionary journeys as these are recorded in Acts. The failure of the Epistles and Acts to àccord on Paul's movements led the older scholarship into ingenious but unpersuasive solutions of formidable problems. The more recent scholarship does not try at all to make the Epistles and Acts so accord.

For the novice, it can be advantageous to read the Epistles as they are here considered, by beginning with the easiest to understand and proceeding to the more difficult ones.

### PHILEMON

Paul wrote this Epistle while he was a prisoner. The older scholarship held the imprisonment to have been in Rome; more recently, the statement in I Cor. 15:32, "I fought with beasts at

Ephesus," is taken to be a reference to an obscure imprisonment, and modern scholarship is inclined to regard Ephesus in Asia Minor as the place from which Paul wrote the "prison epistles."

The Epistle is a note written by Paul to Philemon, a man otherwise unknown. It is to be delivered by one Onesimus, on whose behalf the letter is written. Onesimus was a slave of Philemon, but had escaped; while in jail with Paul, Onesimus had become converted. Paul now writes to his old friend Philemon that Onesimus is on his way back, and would Philemon therefore receive him "no longer as a slave, but more than a slave, as a beloved brother" (Philemon 16)?

The Epistle to Philemon contains no doctrine, nor are its contents of any striking importance to the church at large; therefore its presence in the New Testament has been questioned. The obvious reason for its inclusion is that it is by Paul; it is a purely personal note which was by chance preserved. Some modern scholars who have sought for even more significant reasons than the obvious one have conjectured that no one would preserve a personal letter but a person to whom it was precious, and the presence of such a letter in the collection reveals Onesimus as the hitherto unknown person who first assembled the Epistles of Paul.

### PHILIPPIANS

Paul wrote a second letter from prison, again probably in Ephesus. This cheerful letter is in essence a note of thanks to the church at Philippi, a city in what is today Greece, which had sent some presents to Paul.

Along with his words of thanks, Paul sends some words of advice. He urges the Philippians to cultivate humility as Paul does. This will insure blamelessness, so that he can be proud of them on the coming Judgment Day. Other apostles do not possess humility, and are not only pretentious, but even deal in falsehood. But Paul himself imitates the Christ, who underwent the extremes in self-abasement, as a result of which God exalted him.

Himself unable to come to the Philippians, Paul is sending Epaphroditus to visit them, and hopes in the near future to send Timothy, apparently Paul's chief co-worker. For what purpose? Paul launches into an attack on "dogs and evil-workers" who practice circumcision — a bitter bit of invective against Paul's opponents, Jews or Jewish-Christians faithful to the Law of Moses. One can be a faithful Jew, Paul insists, without observing the Law; Paul himself is a full-blooded Jew, he had never broken the Law, indeed, he inclined to the Pharisaic approach. Therefore Paul can personally attest that observance of the Law is not the true means of salvation, but rather faith in Christ is the means. Indeed, since circumcision is a matter of the flesh, Paul thinks little of it, for though he has not yet attained perfection, he is on the way to being transformed into a spiritual being like Christ. Indeed, the Lord is at hand.

Despite his attack on Judaizers, the tone of Philippians is pleasant and rather unruffled, and it is quite easy to read.

Twice in the letter Paul says, "and finally." Some scholars have believed that the second "and finally" introduces a fragment from a now lost letter. But it is likely that as Paul is dictating the letter, he has forgotten that he has already said, "and finally," and goes on to repeat the phrase.

## First and Second Thessalonians

A crucial and very practical problem, already mentioned, is at the heart of the first Epistle to the church at what is today Salonica. Paul had told the Thessalonians that the return of

Christ was imminent, and for many Thessalonians the emphatic matter was not that Christ would return, but that his return was very near at hand. But since the time when Paul had been with them, some believers had died; would these, who "have fallen asleep," be deprived of the rewards awaiting the righteous at the Second Coming? Moreover, what sense was there in busying oneself on earth for the short time remaining? And exactly when will the End come? These questions have come to Paul, and First Thessalonians is his answer.

As for those who have died, Paul comforts the Thessalonians, these will precede the living in the coming kingdom of God. "The dead in Christ will rise first; then we who are alive, who are left, shall be caught up together with them in the clouds to meet the Lord in the air" (I Thess. 4:16–17).

As for their question, "When will the event take place?" he answers that the Thessalonians really have no need to know. It will come suddenly, therefore "let us keep awake and be sober." Let the idlers be told that they must work, and let the fainthearted and the weak be encouraged.

These matters are preceded, in the Epistle, by several chapters filled with references to things lost to us, but known to those to whom Paul writes. Paul speaks of his affection for the Thessalonians and of his hope that they will not be dismayed by certain persecutions. But all this is but the prelude to his direct answers to their questions.

\* \* \*

Second Thessalonians also deals with the coming Judgment Day, but in a slightly different way. From time to time the rumor gets out that the day has already arrived, and excitement and enthusiasm have been frequent, only to turn into dismay.

And in the light of Paul's insistence that the End was near, what is the reason that it has not come?

The delay, answers the Epistle, is occasioned by the fact that a prescribed pattern of events has not been followed through completely: "That day will not come unless the rebellion comes first, the man of lawlessness is revealed, the son of perdition who opposes and exalts himself against every God or object of worship." That is, before the Christ can return, first the "anti-Christ" must come. Something, unhappily lost to our knowledge, is said to be restraining the anti-Christ. When the restraint is withdrawn, the anti-Christ will come, and Christ will slay him, and come then.

The delay, then, is not to be wondered at, either for existing or for being protracted. And since it is known now that there is a series of intervening events, the Thessalonians should not believe the various rumors that arise, even when they are ascribed to Paul as the source.

More clearly than in First Thessalonians, the idlers are told, and quite plainly: "If any one will not work, let him not eat."

* * *

Why should there be two Epistles, so nearly alike and yet in part so strikingly different? Scholars have offered an abundance of answers to the question, because no single, completely persuasive answer is to be found. It has been suggested that there were, in fact, two churches at Thessalonica, one Jewish and one Gentile, hence the two letters; it has been suggested that the Second Epistle is in reply to questions raised by certain vaguenesses in the First Epistle.

A substantial number of scholars believe, however, that Second Thessalonians is not really by Paul, but was written at a later time in his name; such a practice was quite common in the

Graeco-Roman world. On this theory, the differences between the Epistles arise from the desire or need at a later time to explain the delay of the Coming; the similarities stem from a deliberate imitation of the First Epistle in the Second. While this theory is not completely satisfying in all respects, it is the one with the least amount of objections.

Scholarship has questioned the passage I Thessalonians 2:15, "For you, brethren, became imitators of the churches in Christ Jesus which are in Judea; for you suffered the same things from your own countrymen as they did from the Jews, who killed both the Lord Jesus and the prophets, and drove us out . . . ." Nowhere else does Paul speak in such bitter accusation about Jews. His tone elsewhere, as in Romans, is one of regret that the Jews have failed to see what they might have seen. Nowhere else does he charge them with responsibility for the Crucifixion; indeed, from Paul's standpoint the Crucifixion was something chosen by the Christ, and not forced on him. Moreover, the notion that the church was driven out of Judaism is in flat contradiction with the basic reason for the conflict which we shall see recorded in Galatians, where Paul's view is that the church, hitherto confined to Jews, must on its own go out to Gentiles. Not only does this passage fail to accord with Paul's other views, but also it fits in completely with sentiments found in the later writers, Acts 7:52; Matthew 23:31. Many scholars, therefore, regard this passage as the result of editing and interpolation by the later church, in the interest of an accrued bitterness which had developed between Jews and Christians.

## CORINTHIANS

Corinth was an important city, located at the southern end of the isthmus which connected the district known as the Peloponnesus with the rest of Greece. Commercial trade preferred to use the narrow land crossing instead of the stormy sea route around the Peloponnesus, in much the same way in which, before there was a Panama Canal, the isthmus at Panama was crossed by land, avoiding the long trip around Cape Horn. Commerce made Corinth a cosmopolitan city, and in ancient times it had some notoriety for its vice.

Paul had founded the church among Gentiles. A number of internal difficulties quickly arose, which Paul deplored. Later Paul's own authority was questioned. His letters deal with the difficulties, and with the question of his authority. They have aptly been called the history of a quarrel.

The New Testament gives us two Epistles, First and Second Corinthians. Modern scholarship believes that Second Corinthians is in reality fragments of three different letters, so that in all Paul wrote not two, but four letters, to the church at Corinth. Morever, a fragment of Second Corinthians was written actually before what we call First Corinthians. Scholars list the four letters in this order of composition: a. II Cor. 6:14 to 7:1; b. I Corinthians; c. II Cor. 10 to 13:10; and d. II Cor. 1 to 6:13; 7:2 to 9; and 13:11–13. (The bases for this conclusion are available in the standard introductions.)

Letter A, in the fragment preserved, tells us little more than that Paul gave injunctions against too free association with unbelievers. Letter B, a very long Epistle, falls into several natural divisions: Paul comments on improper conduct at Corinth involving factionalism, immorality, and litigation in the secular courts by believers. Next, he gives corrective instruction, on such matters as marriage and mixed marriage, the eating of meats offered to idols, conduct in church worship, and the tenability of the doctrine of resurrection. Letter C is almost entirely a defense by Paul of the legitimacy of his personal claims to apostleship. Letter D records Paul's joy that the difficulties between him and the Corinthians have been smoothed over.

There are a number of matters of significance in the Corinthian correspondence. There is revealed to us the diversity in the early church; and while we do not learn what the basis of the factionalism was, we are made acutely aware that it was quite extensive. We see also that the early church more nearly resembled the contemporary rural, enthusiastic churches than our sedate and decorous city institutions. The relative novelty of the Christian movement among Gentiles is clear from the fact that Paul is answering questions which have never come up before. He gives them his judgment to avoid mixed marriages. His advice, in view of the impending Day and his aversion to sex relations, is to avoid marriage, if possible. He steers the church to a seemly form of church worship. He tells the rival functionaries (prophets, ecstatics, and the like) that they can reduce and eliminate their frictions if they will love each other. The correspondence is important, then, for our understanding of the church in its earliest Gentile manifestations.

We get the beginnings of church doctrine, much later to become dogma, for example, in Paul's explanation of the nature of the body at the time of resurrection. The issue before Paul here is that, differing from Pharisaic Judaism, he denies the physical resurrection. But the denial of the physical raises the problem as to what form of resurrection there can be. Paul therefore speaks of a "spiritual body," a term which seems to describe a paradox, but which may be taken to mean that the individual, though without his body, remains an entity at resurrection. What Paul is doing here is rejecting both the physical resurrection and also certain Greek notions, known from the Stoics and Philo, that the immaterial part of man loses its identity, and is simply reabsorbed into the immaterial source out of which man's soul came prior to union with the body. Rather, Paul is insisting that the spiritual entity abides in its individuality.

It is in Corinthians, also, that we read the earliest written accounts of the institution of the "eucharist" (I Cor. 11:23). "For I received from the Lord what I also delivered to you, that the Lord Jesus on the night when he was handed over took bread, and when he had given thanks, he broke it, and said, 'This is my body which is broken for you. Do this in remembrance of me.' In the same way also the cup, after supper, saying, 'This cup is the new covenant in my blood. Do this, as often as you drink it, in remembrance of me.' "

A sacramental import has been here attributed to the bread and the wine which they lack in the traditional Jewish practice of giving thanks over the broken loaf and the cup. The simple Jewish grace has been transformed into a ceremony of the most intense Christological significance. Two sharply divergent interpretations have developed regarding the origin of this transformation. One view holds that the eucharist is older than Paul, and that he is giving the Corinthians material, already traditional, about which he learned from those who were in the church before him. The other interpretation, and the one which I prefer, is that Paul, in saying, "I received from the Lord," is speaking of a revelation which he believes he has had, rather than a church tradition, and thus is himself the first to ascribe to the traditional bread and the wine the novel sacramental meaning which Christianity has thereafter accepted for them.

The most striking passage in First Corinthians is the poetic praise of love, in Chapter 13. Old English versions of the New Testament have accustomed many to an exaltation of faith, hope, and "charity," but the strong connotation of philanthropy, rather than forbearance in the word, has made it seem commendable for the most recent English translations to use the word "love" in order to preserve the intended meaning of the chapter. Those who have ever heard the setting composed for it by Brahms have experienced its majesty under the most favorable circumstances. However, the passage is usually quoted without its context. Great as its poetry may be, it is not intended by Paul as a poem, but rather as something more modest, and eminently practical: a rule of thumb method for the promotion of tranquillity and cooperation in the church. Speaking in tongues, prophecy, and self-immolation mentioned here are not abstractions, but the specific exhibitions by which various church leaders tried to prove their superior faith. Paul had learned that rivalry existed among these people for the unnamed prerogatives to which their talents made them think they were entitled. It is against the sad by-products of discord and envy that Paul directs his argument. Prophecy and knowledge will pass away, he says, tongues will cease, but love never ends. There can be peace in the church, if people will not insist on their own way, but will espouse the greatest virtue, love.

The exhortation to love is part of Paul's appeal to the Corinthians which stems from his dissatisfaction with their conduct. But after he had written to them so solicitously, and appeasingly, something unknown to us transpired, involved in which was Paul's right to be an apostle. Letter C is a fragment in defense of his right; the sincerity and charged emotion give the passage a great impact.

In Letter D the quarrel is over, and the tone is one of relief that the storm has passed away. Paul appears to have visited Corinth between the time of the writing of Letter C and the present letter (such is the implication of II Cor. 2:1).

The Corinthian correspondence, then, is the greatest source of our knowledge of early Christian practices, and our clearest view of what kind of intensely ardent and volatile man the apostle to the Gentiles was.

## GALATIANS

In parts of the Corinthian correspondence, Paul is on the defensive, upset, and hurt. In Galatians he is the angry aggressor in the argument. This Epistle alone lacks a complimentary paragraph, for Paul begins promptly in a combative manner which he retains throughout the Epistle.

What has distressed him so? According to Paul's instructions, the church which he founded in an area of Asia Minor in which West European Gauls had settled (hence Galatia) had followed the practices of Gentiles in not observing the Jewish Law. But now word has come to Paul that "judaizers" have been turning the Galatians towards the observance of the Jewish Law, and his anger knows no bounds.

In part Paul's wrath stems from his believing that the issue had already been settled in an incident at the neighboring city of Antioch. Cephas, a fellow apostle, had joined with Paul in the non-observance of the Jewish Law. But when certain emissaries came from Jerusalem, Cephas had ceased to eat forbidden foods. Paul had accused Cephas, publicly, of insincerity, both in changing his own way and in requiring persons born Gentiles to observe the Laws which Cephas had formerly disregarded.

Even before this, Paul had straightened out with the leaders of the Jerusalem church that as Peter was to go to Jews, so Paul was to go to Gentiles. With the matter apparently settled, Paul feels betrayed that the Galatians have turned towards Jewish observances. The gist of the Epistle is Paul's effort to demonstrate by the Old Testament itself that the Mosaic Law of the Old Testament need no longer be observed and, indeed, ought not to be observed. The part of the Old Testament which Paul is declaring obsolete is only the Mosaic Law; the rest is still valid for him.

His proof is based on the example of Abraham, who lived before there was a Mosaic Law, and therefore, in Paul's view, gained salvation without it. (The rabbis, from their standpoint, aver, to the contrary, that Abraham observed the Law even before it was given.) Paul argues from the Bible, contrasting works (of the Law) with faith, slavery (to the Law) with freedom; and by allegory he contrasts the bodily (and inferior) descendants of Abraham with the spiritual descendants, the church.

A more significant aspect of Galatians can be easily overlooked in unreflective reading. Paul insists over and over again that his version of the Christian message is unique and different from that of other apostles. In the opening verse he describes himself as an apostle, not from man but from God. He was not preached to by any man, nor was he taught the gospel, but he was set apart for it before he was born, and it came to him as though a revelation of Jesus Christ. After this revelation he did not confer with any man, nor did he go to Jerusalem to consult the members of the church there. When, later, he did go to Jerusalem, he points out that this, too, was by a revelation, not as a result of receiving instructions. He conferred with the leaders there, privately, but not in a subservient way; and when they perceived the divine grace which was given to him, they conceded that Paul had the right to go to Gentiles. Paul did not need them to empower him to go; indeed, he consulted them only to ward off any possible interference with his missions.

Paul's claim to direct revelation, and his assertion of his independence of the Jerusalem church, conflict with the idealized picture in Acts which hopefully ascribes harmony to the apostles and uniformity in the early church practices. Most Pauline scholarship seems not to take this portion of Galatians seriously, discounting Paul's claims to uniqueness as statements exaggerated by anger, and preferring to envisage all those inspired of Christ as working in concord. Other scholars, with whose views I concur, find the account of apostolic harmony in Acts to be excessively editorialized, and see in the passionate tone of Galatians its authenticizing factor. Paul would not have so hotly defended the uniqueness of his message, they believe, if it had not been strongly contested by other factions of belief within the church. Thus Paul's painstaking declaration of the source and the strength of his message must not be taken, in my opinion, merely as an offended outburst of personal vanity, but as a true reflection of the conflicts and rivalries which must have existed not alone among lower church officials (as in Corinthians), but also on the highest level of church leadership.

## Romans

The Epistle to the Romans rehearses much of the argument found in Galatians, but more calmly and at considerably greater length. It is a rather well-organized succession of arguments, though considerably less than a systematic exposition of Pauline thought.

Externally, the lower criticism raises two matters worth attention. In some manuscripts the Epistle lacks the words that it was written to Rome; and it circulated at one time without the 15th and 16th chapters. An attractive theory has been offered that the Epistle was written originally without a specific addressee in mind, but was intended for all the churches; subsequently, substantially the same version was prepared for the specific church at Rome. The argument in favor of this theory is that if the Epistle was written originally only for the church at Rome, which Paul never visited, it is hard to understand why he picks these particular matters to write about; but if it is a general Epistle, then we can infer that its purpose was to give a more orderly statement of Paul's views on what to him were major matters.

The major interest in the Epistle is Paul's explanation of the relationship of the church to the Law of Moses, and to Judaism. The problem which faces Paul, as we have mentioned, is that in denying the validity of the Law of Moses, he is aware that he is negating what is central in Judaism; at the same time, he insists that that which he is preaching is the true Judaism. He must therefore explain what the Law means to him and why he must reject it, and demonstrate the power of faith which for him replaces the Law.

Paul begins first with the assertion that the Gospel which he preaches is a living power of God to bring man to salvation. One receives this salvation through believing in it; faith, indeed, is the only way to righteousness and salvation. Gentile and Jew alike have pursued the wrong way, the Gentile pursuing "wisdom," and the Jew the Law of Moses. What God truly requires is obedience to His higher Law, the Law of nature, yet neither the wisdom of the Gentiles nor the Jewish Law of Moses reaches the level of the higher Law. Indeed, he contends, Jews do not fully observe the Law of Moses; obviously, then, they are not at all obeying the higher Law. Moreover, says Paul, the true Jew is not the man who tries, unsuccessfully, to obey the Law of Moses outwardly, but the one who inwardly obeys the higher Law.

If even Jews, then, possessing the Law, are unrighteous and are under the power of sin, the Law surely does not bring salvation. Salvation comes apart from the Law, in the gift of the Christ. And man, whether Jew or Gentile, believing in the Christ, attains salvation.

Accordingly, says Paul, his principle of faith is not really in opposition to the Law of Moses; but, rather, faith is the means by which one lives up to what that Law requires, and faith therefore upholds the intent and basic purpose of the Law.

The proof, again, is Abraham, who lived before the Law was given; Genesis says (15:6) that Abraham had faith and Abraham attained righteousness. Clearly, then, it is possible to attain that righteousness without observing the Law of Moses.

But Genesis 17:10 declares that Abraham was circumcised, and circumcision is one of the requirements of that Law. Did Abraham, then, obey the Law? No, replies Paul; it is to be noticed that first Abraham attained righteousness, and only thereafter was he circumcised. In his case circumcision was not an act of obedience to the Law, but rather a sign or seal of that faith which he had had prior to circumcision.

God, according to Genesis, had made promises to Abraham before the circumcision. Jews who insist that works of the Law are the means to salvation are descendants of the circumcised Abraham, while Christians can claim as their spiritual ancestor the uncircumcised Abraham. Indeed, since the promises in Genesis were made prior to the circumcision, the true heirs of the promises to Abraham are not the circumcised, but the church.

Judaism, through this latter line of descent, is still the valid religion, although the Law of Moses is no longer, as formerly, its central aspect. Instead, attainment of righteousness through redemption in the Christ makes it possible for one to live one's Judaism as Abraham did, without recourse to the Law of Moses. In a striking simile, Paul seeks to make it clear that there is no infidelity to Judaism involved in this change of emphasis. The

Law is binding on a person only during his life, he says, just as a married woman is bound by law to her husband. If her husband dies, she is free from that law, and if she marries another, she is not an adulteress. Just so, the faithful have died to the Law so that they may belong to another who has been raised from the dead.

For, Paul goes on, while the Law itself was not sin, its list of specific sins, by the mere mention, made Paul aware of sins and impelled him to them. This impulse to sin warred inside him with his desire not to sin. Passions tended to rule his body, even while his mind tried in vain to control them. His release from the domination of his body came when through Christ he found the medium of rising above it.

The Law of Moses, then, had brought Paul only tension. God through Christ had set him free from this tension and had put him beyond encountering such tension again. Such freedom, or salvation, was given by God to His elect church through love, and "neither death, nor life, nor angels, nor principalities, nor things present, nor things to come" can separate the elect from the love of God in Christ.

Jews do have certain advantages: first, their past history in which Scripture was entrusted to them; second, Christ, of the flesh, was a Jew. Nevertheless, Jews pursued salvation as though it could come from the Law of Moses, and therefore, despite commendable zeal, it was a human righteousness which they were pursuing, not a divine one, for "Christ is the God of living law." God has therefore temporarily turned from them to Gentiles, who, through Paul's ministry, are offered a more recent revelation and superior salvation. Not, indeed, that God has rejected the Jews, for Paul himself is a Jew; but only a few Jews, such as Paul, have become God's elect, like the saving remnant of which Isaiah spoke.

Indeed, Paul hopes by his turning to the Gentiles to awaken among the Jews a jealousy for salvation. The opaqueness of the Jews resulted in Paul's turning to the Gentiles; thereby there was effected a reconciliation of the Gentiles to God. How great and good it would be if Jews, too, in time, shared in this reconciliation!

Gentiles are not to vaunt themselves over Jews, however, because Gentiles are only branches grafted onto the tree of Judaism. After the period of the hardening of the hearts of the Jews has passed, God will revert to Israel and save them. Israel's blindness was an opportunity for the eyes of Gentiles to be opened.

Thus Paul salvages some integrity for the Judaism which he cannot bear to reject entirely, by establishing it at least as a point of departure. The church is to regard its faith as the new, fulfilled Judaism; its followers are the true Israel. His Epistle to the Romans makes clear the religious argument which gives these names their validity.

### COLOSSIANS AND EPHESIANS

Quite a few modern scholars doubt that Colossians is by Paul, and even more do not regard Ephesians as genuine. Colossians, it is argued, gives a view of Christ far more complex and developed than the view found in the other Epistles, and it contains denunciations of teachers of false doctrine, who could hardly have arisen at a period in church history when doctrine was as yet only loosely defined. Those who hold that Colossians is genuine deny that the presence of these errorists is surprising; and they see no marked difference between the Christ of Colossians and the Christ of the other Epistles. Ephesians, however, reads more like a tract than a letter, and it is a hymn on the mystical meaning of the church; the indications of later speculation are much more evident than is the case with Colossians. Ephesians lacks for most modern scholars the personal touch of Paul found so abundantly in the other Epistles.

Colossians is a warning against becoming a prey to "philosophy and empty deceit, according to the elemental spirits of the universe, and not according to Christ." It appears to have been written in opposition to an obscure type of speculation and ritual practice which, from the point of view of the author, is inconsistent with the doctrine of the Christ. A rhapsodical interpretation of Christ as the revelation of the fullness of God is given: "He is the image of the invisible God, the first-born of all creation; for in him all things are created, in heaven and on earth, visible and invisible . . . all things were created through him and for him." While this passage is not in any way inconsistent with Paul's view elsewhere, it extends considerably beyond it, and seems to be rather an elaboration upon what Paul has taught than Paul's own more restrained view. Colossians refutes certain heresies, in which the significance and power of Christ are declared to be limited, by insisting on the unlimited nature of Christ as the Logos of God.

Ephesians is directed also at some unknown heresy, but only obliquely. It is primarily a statement of the basic mystical unity of the church. Society had become divided, and discord reigned in the world; now, however, through Christ, mankind is unified. Jew and Gentile are united in the church; harmony has supplanted the earlier divisiveness. All this has been part of a divine plan, which, as a secret in God's mind, was a "mystery." The mystery, however, has come to light in the unifying power of Christ.

\* \* \*

In the case of Second Thessalonians, which some scholars believe was not written by Paul, the explanation for its carrying Paul's name was the desire to use Paul's authority to explain the delay in the coming of Judgment Day. Ephesians similarly leans upon the authority of Paul's name. But what is the basic purpose of a treatise which is so abstract? The most likely explanation offered is that Ephesians was written as an introduction to the gathered Epistles of Paul by an unknown author who assembled the extant letters. The writer was a Paulinian, of course, and he built his essay on Paul's doctrine. But he wrote from a later time, when the conflicts with Judaism were long settled, and when the threat to the unity of the church came, not from Jews, but from Gentile speculators, known as gnostics. Thus Ephesians presents the developed view of the later church, as a preface to the reading of the collected letters of Paul.

# X

## Pauline Christianity and Greek Religion

So FAR we have looked at Paul's message and contribution from the standpoint of the Judaism from which he was departing. It is well, for the sake of perspective, to look at it now from the Graeco-Roman Gentile world into which it was moving.

The debt which the Western world owes to Greek philosophy, especially to Plato and to Aristotle, is a great one. The Greek inquiry into the nature of the world and of man has bequeathed to us a tremendous legacy of intellectual achievement.

Frequently, indeed all too frequently, it is assumed that Greek philosophy was a disinterested pursuit for the sake simply of knowledge, and that its attainments were the result of clear but cold logic, detached from any profound, human need. Or, at best, it is often interpreted that the Greek study of ethics was motivated by no more than a desire to find in human terms an appropriate guide for human beings.

On the contrary, the motivation for Greek philosophy was the desire to achieve standards beyond human levels and to ascertain norms of conduct more reliable than the usual fallible, human norms. Philosophy believed that the human intellect, when it could be purified from the dross of human deficiency, could glimpse ultimate reality, a reality which lay in the realm of the mind and in its capacity to distinguish between mundane manifestations and spiritual, imperishable values. Greek philosophy was in this sense a handmaiden of religion. However objective and introspective it became, it was motivated by a glowing ardor and purpose quite akin to religious impulses.

Greek religion, too, was an effort to rise above the level of human existence. Its rites and ceremonies were symbolic devices through which the initiate achieved the capacity to raise himself. Philosophy explained the transformations which could occur; popular religion provided the means for the transformation. Pure philosophy — if such a thing ever existed — was speculative and theoretical; popular philosophy was eminently practical.

The popular religions were organized into cults; they had rites and ceremonies, such as ablutions and animal sacrifices; they had more or less elaborate legends and myths associated with the divine-human figure central to the particular cult. To the philosophic mind such legends seem often to be either crude or untenable, and one of two procedures lay at the philosopher's choice. He could either reject the crude and the untenable as inconsistent with rationalism; or else he could apply the ingenuity of "allegorical" interpretation to the traditional myths, simultaneously rejecting a coarse literalism and at the same time espousing a symbolic truth. The philosophically minded person could deny the literal existence of the gods of Olympus and, by ascribing only symbolic value to the tales about them, could proceed in the direction of monotheism. Within a cult a "philosopher" could participate in rituals and repeat legends, and yet could abstain from committing himself to a literal belief in what his intellect might have told him were absurdities. Such was the nature of the interweaving of religion and philosophy.

Many Greek cults went beyond the merely ceremonial and the rationalistic explanation. With only these alone, they would have lacked any compelling justification for their existence, for a man would not need to join a cult or submit himself to the activities of priests if outside of the cult he could practice similar rites and offer similar explanations. The cult needed for its existence a capacity beyond that of any isolated individual; the cult had to be able to claim that it was offering something which was not available outside of it, something which was the private possession of the cult and the possession of which was limited to cult members. Such private possession was usually some secret doctrine, a "mystery" disclosed only to those who would undergo initiation into the cult. The mystery religions were those ancient cults which utilized rites and ceremonies, offered "philosophical" explanations of the ceremonies, and gave the initiate his salvation from the world and from death.

By our standards, the rites of the mystery religions were often hideous and orgiastic, but to cult members they were the means of rising out of troubled human existence. The array of rites and ceremonies was wide enough to include in some of the mystery religions such things as "baptism" and a type of the "eucharist"; indeed, one of the church fathers complains bitterly about the "theft" of such Christian rites by a cult.

Most of our information about the mystery religions comes from the denunciation of them in the church fathers and in occasional Jewish writings of the period. An appreciation of the strivings and aspirations of the cults is possible only when one rises above these traditional denunciations. The mystery religions, paralleling Christianity and Philo's version of Judaism, were man's effort to escape from this world to the deity.

The similarities between Pauline Christianity and the mystery religions need to be recognized, for only then can one glimpse that what Paul was offering his hearers was not a new purpose or a new vision, but a new form of a familiar need and goal. He was teaching, not a different salvation, but a newer version, and, as he insisted, the only form of salvation; not a strange or recondite religious goal, but what he considered to be the sure and sole means of achieving the commonly recognized goal of religion.

Modern scholarship has often labeled early Christianity a "mystery religion"; the label has been deeply resented by many Christian historians. The resentment is in part justified, for the label has been often applied by secular scholars to disparage Christianity. But, on the other hand, much of Christian historical scholarship, based on presumptions of total uniqueness in both time and form in Christianity, has rejected the label along with the appropriateness of the ascription.

If one will use the term "mystery religion" as a description rather than as a derogation, it is as apt for Paul's Christianity as it is for Philo's Judaism. Both Paul and Philo believed that there existed in their versions of Judaism cult rites and ceremonies with symbolic force, buttressed by "mysterious" doctrine, out of which the initiated achieved salvation. Both Paul and Philo used abundantly the usual terminologies of the mysteries, such as "initiation" and "perfection" — some of the respective Christian and Jewish scholarship is grotesque in the effort to empty these terms as used by both writers of their mystery religion meaning and significance.

For Philo, in his version of "mystery," Passover was not merely the anniversary of the freeing of the Jews from Egyptian bondage; it was a ceremony which enabled the soul of the participant to be freed from bondage to the body.

The similarity of Pauline Christianity to the mystery religions in externals explains its capacity to gain a hearing and to elicit response. The particular distinctions from the other mysteries are even more important to notice, however, because these explain the triumph of Christianity.

The pagan religions were organized into local groups, *thiasoi*;

Christianity had a wider unity, stemming from Judaism, which the cults apparently did not pursue, at least not in the same measure. The dying and rising Lord-Savior was not unique to Christianity. But in the pagan cults, the Lord was a man who became God, while in Pauline Christianity it was the divine being which became man. In the pagan cults the transformation had taken place ages and ages ago; in Christianity it had the powerful appeal of utmost recency — within the lifetime both of the apostles and of their older hearers.

The pagan religions made little association of religion with ethics. Christianity took over from Judaism the insistence that religion presupposes and prescribes ethical requirements; indeed, it adopted the very standards of Jewish ethics. Whether stemming from "faith" or from the Law, the ethics of Christianity and of Judaism were strikingly similar. Pauline Christianity, accordingly, could insist that man's necessity to live by the spirit was an unabating necessity, and not simply the need to abide by the caprice of secular law. Man's actions were always under the scrutiny of God; and thereby God was a constant factor in man's life.

And, finally, the pagan religions markedly lacked anything comparable to the Jewish Old Testament. This divine literature, widely disseminated, upheld of necessity as authentic by the Jews as well even as they opposed Christianity, gave to the new movement an ever-present vehicle for validating its claims. How important to Christianity the Old Testament was is discernible not only in Paul's letters, but also in the sporadic though unsuccessful efforts from within Christianity in subsequent decades to eliminate the Old Testament as a church legacy.

It was Pauline Christianity, classifiable superficially within the description of a mystery religion, which led ultimately to the triumph of Christianity over its rivals in the Hellenistic-Roman world. The traces of Philo's Judaism, on the other hand, are so minor and scattered that for our present purposes they can be ignored. The conjectured fate of the Greek Jews and of Greek Judaism of the type represented by Philo has become a historical puzzle. The Talmud tells us virtually nothing about them — indeed, we should not even suspect from the Talmud that somebody like Philo ever existed. While occasionally some scholars believe that they detect overtones of Philo's thoughts in rabbinic literature, there is less than universal agreement in the matter. It is unquestionable, however, that Philo is abundantly quoted and reflected in the writings of the church fathers; indeed, it was the church which preserved Philo's writings. It was not until the sixteenth century, in the wake of the renaissance and of humanism, that Philo was rediscovered by Jews.

Pauline Christianity offered a way less burdensome than the regimen of the Law, yet equally efficacious. It was more attractive to pagans as the religion to which to convert than was Judaism. Pauline Christianity and Judaism each claimed to be the true Israel, each possessed the same Scripture, each offered the same type of divine grace. In eminently practical terms, a man could become a convert to Judaism only by undergoing circumcision. A detail of such deterrent character did not obstruct his entrance into Christianity; Judaism could not compete with Christianity successfully in demanding a more arduous entry-fee for the relatively similar salvation. Moreover, the Pauline principle of "faith" lent itself more readily to philosophical explanation than did the explanation of the regimen of the Law; the recourse in Philo's writings to extreme ingenuity and tortuous interpretation reveals how difficult it was to square an entire regimen of practice with a philosophical system. Pauline Christianity offered personal communion with God, through Christ, in the initiatory rite of baptism and in the recurring rite of the eucharist; Philonic Judaism offered communion with God only to rare souls, and the observance of Mosaic requirements which was the medium of its attainment could hardly have seemed more complex.

In short, Pauline Christianity was infinitely more congenial to the Greek world than Philo's complex Judaism, and not only laid the basis for the ultimate triumph of Christianity, but also it foredoomed the Jewish missionary movement to failure and to extinction. The Philonic adaptation of Judaism to the Greek climate ended in nothing. The Pauline adaptation ended in triumph.

Both the Jews and the early Christians were more aware of the difference between Judaism and Christianity than were the Roman officials, who frequently confused the two. The older movement may perhaps have been somewhat complacent and overconfident of its position; at any rate, there is always lacking in an existing institution the vigor which a new movement seems to possess. We may readily conjecture that however extensively the Greek Jews may have tried to impede Christianity or even to harass it, their recourse was primarily towards defensive measures, designed to preserve the old. The newer movement would be more aggressive and more determined. In illustration, Christianity developed even beyond Paul the Pauline formulation of God's rejection of the Jews, for the new group needed to search its soul to define its essence. In the Judaism of the comparable period we get overtones of bitterness towards a wide variety of "heretics," but so less than precisely formulated that an understandable dispute exists as to whether the heretics alluded to were Christians or other sectaries. Judaism never felt the need for delineating Christianity any more definitely than as a vague heresy, and there is in Judaism no theological formulation in assessment of Christianity like the Christian view of God's rejection of the Jews. To this day Jews, inheriting no special view of the place of Christianity in divine providence, are surprised and even shocked that they occupy a special and somewhat unsavory position in segments of Christian thought.

Pauline Christianity offered to pagans not only a more congruent Hellenizing of Judaism; it also drew on immediate and powerful impetuses towards expansion. The conviction that the End was near must have lent special fervor to the wish to save mankind; while the Jewish sense of the abiding quality of the world made the need for salvation less pressing and less promptly to be achieved.

Both Philonic Judaism and Pauline Christianity were poles apart from Palestinian Pharisaism, especially as it flowered in rabbinic Judaism. That the Old Testament was common to all provided a remote community of inspiration and of similarity in some doctrines. But just as the Greek Bible diverged only in minor details from the Hebrew and yet led to intense disputes between Jews and Christians over the question as to which version was authentic — and some church fathers accused the Jews of falsifying the Hebrew text so as to contravert Christian claims — so the developing church and synagogue, set into opposing world-views, led to specific manifestations and religious doctrines overtly different and contradictory. It requires considerable penetration to discover that Pauline Christianity and rabbinic Judaism stem from a common Scripture, because the Scripture was for each only a point of departure, and each separated in a different direction. Rabbinic Judaism retained its oriental character for several more centuries. Pauline Christianity had an ancestry remotely oriental, but it was born and nurtured in so completely Hellenized an atmosphere that it was a completely Grecian phenomenon.

# PART THREE

## THE SYNOPTIC GOSPELS AND JESUS

# XI

# The Gospel Process

PAUL STANDS OUT as such a tremendous figure in growing Christianity that it is well to remind ourselves that he was not the only Christian missionary. There were others, even in those early days, as we have learned from his writings themselves, through their mention of his involvements with opponents. Naturally, not every early Christian who differed with Paul was necessarily a direct opponent. The early disagreements probably exhibited a range from the slight to the antithetical, but all this within a framework of basic agreements. The controversies were noticeably internal, based on disagreements of viewpoint, or occasioned by the passing of time. For example, as the years and decades went by and the End, proclaimed by Paul, failed to arrive, later attitudes towards that event were to vie with the earlier ones. But the area of disagreement between Paul and some of the other missionaries which had the most marked effect on shaping the New Testament was that of method. Paul had glossed over the human career of Jesus, dwelling on the significance, and not on details; and significance had carried him into some difficult complexities of metaphysics and of Old Testament interpretation. A less abstract and hence more concrete and simpler presentation of the significance of Jesus was useful for the ordinary purposes of missionizing the pagans or of edifying the faithful. Other church leaders chose a method which was the reverse of Paul's, and instead of glossing over the human career of Jesus, they turned to it in its details.

The early church faced in regions besides Galatia the problem of its relationship to Judaism, to the Old Testament, and to the Jewish oral law. Moreover, there was the question of what was to be the relationship of the church to the Roman authorities. Or, again, what was the relative merit of a recent convert compared with one of long standing? Paul had answered some such questions by appealing to the Old Testament or to revelation, or by simply giving his own opinion; in the matter of divorce he appealed to a saying of Jesus, but this is a single and therefore exceptional instance. After Paul's time, the church more and more conceived that its own immediate problems had already arisen in the time of Jesus, and therefore its authoritative answers were to be found in his words and deeds. Details in the career of Jesus became the authoritative precedent or the decisive word for the church.

Just as Paul knew of an attitude of Jesus towards divorce, so oral tradition knew authentic details of what Jesus had said and done, and the preservative factor in oral tradition was quite strong. But some of this authentic material needed slight recasting so as to be germane for the new times. In order for the words of Jesus to apply, they often needed to be changed. Where no relevant word of Jesus existed, pious imaginations tended to create it, by envisaging Jesus in the contemporary situation and by attributing to him the solution congenial to later times.

The authentic, the altered, and the created materials existed, according to modern scholarship, in short oral units, each of which at one time was self-contained. In this stage of the growing oral tradition, there was as yet no long, connected narrative of the career of Jesus, but there were only isolated incidents; there was as yet no collected exposition of Jesus' words, but only a mass of unrelated items which Jesus, so it was believed, had said or taught.

Since many of the claims of the church rested neither on pure logic nor on ordinary historical attestation, the desire to prove them led to the searching of the Old Testament for passages which could be construed to support the church contentions. This was especially the case with the claims about Jesus. It is likely that very early in the history of the church passages from the Old Testament, usable as "proof-texts," were assembled into a collection.

Folk legends about appealing heroes became Christian by the device of inserting Jesus in the place of the traditional subject. The cure of the sick, the healing of the infirm, and, indeed, the exorcism of demons out of swine were readily usable when once the hero of such incidents became Jesus. Legends of a general character, too, were often found useful to preachers by the device of retelling them about Jesus.

The "words" or "deeds" of Jesus, and legends about him, existed in oral form, but in separate, small units. Scholars call these units "pericopes"; they are too short to be called "episodes." Each pericope at one time had some precise use or precise meaning, or precise application to some current situation. Let us now imagine a church in a small Greek city in early times. The members were partly of pagan extraction, partly of Jewish. In the same city there were "opponents," some of whom were Jews and some pagans, indeed, Roman officials. Let us imagine that certain Jews criticized church laxity in observing the Jewish oral law. The church replied with a pericope, which told that Jesus had set an example in discarding the oral law. Again, Jews complained of the non-observance of the Sabbath; the church replied that in some situations Jesus, too, had not observed it; indeed, they said, Jesus was greater than the Sabbath. Jews observed that the church was not properly obeying other Old Testament laws; the church countered with the statement that something greater than Moses had come, and that Jesus had himself departed from some Old Testament laws. Roman officials, spurred by enemies of the church, investigated its loyalty to the Roman Empire; the church declared that Jesus had said, "Render unto Caesar what is Caesar's." Pagan Christians within the church engaged in acts which by Jewish standards were immoral; when taken to task, they averred that, like Paul, they needed no law; the church replied that Jesus had announced that he had come not to annul the law, but to fulfill it.

The stamp of the church was put on virtually every pericope about Jesus. As the church grew and spread, its problems changed. The figure of Jesus was constantly the exemplar or the model, but altered circumstances made him the exemplar of altered attitudes or of altered interests. For example, the attitude of the church towards Jews and Judaism was not the same at every single moment throughout early Christendom; in Palestine the early church seems to have been but one more "sect" in Jewry, but outside of Palestine it seems to have been more keenly aware of its difference. The passing of time contributed changes in attitudes towards Judaism, and we can distinguish three periods. Initially, Christianity was content to be a special phase within Judaism; in Paul's time it became aware of its individuality, and its attitude was one of regret that the Jews abstained from entering the church. After Paul's time, regret was supplanted by unrelieved hostility. In the oral stage of separate pericopes, Jesus was the exemplar of fidelity to Judaism, of regret at Jewish blindness, and of bitter hatred of the Jews.

Other motifs unfolded with growing nuances or intensities. Doctrinal differences within the church became progressively more divisive, and Paul's lament over factionalism became increasingly metamorphosed into an awareness of orthodoxy and heresy. Jesus was the exemplar of each faction.

The natural result was that pericopes in contradiction of other pericopes were simultaneously in circulation. For example, Jewish Christians affirmed the Messiahship of Jesus through the romance of his Davidic descent, and hence we have the pericope tracing his genealogy through Joseph back to David. Gentile Christians, however, affirmed the Messiahship through the "virgin birth"; if the Holy Spirit was the father, then Joseph and his ancestors were hardly the relevant forebears of Jesus, and such a genealogy had to be contended against. Just such a pericope is preserved; in it a passage in Psalms is so interpreted as to show that David had talked to Christ in David's time, and therefore David could not be his ancestor.

The preserved traditions reveal that the office of Jesus is described variously as the Son of David, the Christ, "the" prophet, "Lord," and the "Son of Man." Of the descriptions, the latter is the most puzzling, for it was used in Judaism in different, distinct senses, simply as "a man," but also, as in Daniel, for the divine figure from whom the revelation of the future was expected. The Gospels do not permit of a single connotation for the phrase; some passages are clearly the one, and others are clearly the other, but in still other passages it is often difficult, and a matter for subjective choice, to determine the intent. That the titles are diverse is often explained as due to the geographical dispersion of Christianity, and to the tendency of a regional church to use the term most congenial to its environment. Perhaps a progression from Palestine to the Greek world ran along lines such as these: in Galilee the term was "Son of Man"; "the" prophet and the "Son of David" were Jerusalem phrases. "Messiah," after being transformed virtually into the Judaeo-Greek word "Christ," was replaced in the Gentile world by the term "Lord." Pericopes used sometimes one term, sometimes another.

Pericopes were preserved even when they were in oblique or even in direct contradiction of each other, because once a pericope was in circulation, its use for some segment of the church prevented its suppression. The appeal once made to the career of Jesus preserved a pericope — even when it was one whose existence the developing church might conceivably have regretted; for example, that Jesus had undergone baptism at the hands of John the Baptist.

The preservative power of oral tradition is even better discerned in the case of certain materials which hand on a word of Jesus but without the setting in which the word was spoken. For example, Jesus is reported to have compared something with putting a new patch on an old garment, or new wine in old skins, but the comparison was lost to the church, and therefore to us. We do not know in what connection Jesus spoke of hiding a light under a bushel, or of the nature of the "single" eye.

There were complete pericopes and incomplete ones; authentic ones, altered ones, and created ones; and pericopes often contradicted each other.

The pericopes, we have stressed, existed in oral form. Two circumstances combined to bring about the first written sequence of pericopes which has come down to us. By 70 A. D. the church had grown so much that inner diversity to the point of nihilism threatened it unless some standardization was to ensue; the time had come for a more stable, even more rigid, teaching about Jesus.

At this juncture, in Palestine, rebellion against Rome had brought about a new siege of Jerusalem by the Romans under Titus. The disputes between the Jews and the church had grown apace. In 70 Jerusalem was destroyed and the Temple utterly ruined. The church saw in the event its vindication and its triumph; its claim of exclusive possession of a new revelation was enhanced by the misfortune of its chief rival. Before 70 the church was on the defensive in its relations to Judaism; after 70 it became assertive. The calamity to its parent underscored its own arrival at maturity.

There were, indeed, still opponents and still skeptics, and these needed to be refuted or silenced. Two problems vexing to the church were still present on the lips of the unpersuaded. First, if the church claims about Jesus and his divinity were correct, why did Jesus undergo crucifixion? Second, if Jesus was what the church claimed, why was this not universally known, and why did the church have to have recourse to proclaiming what he was?

Primarily in order to answer these two questions, a writer skillfully joined together a good many oral pericopes about Jesus in a connected narrative which asserted that the crucifixion was not a defeat or even a surprise. Jesus knew about it in advance; it was the predestined divine act by which man could be cleansed of sin. And, second, the need for proclamation was the result of the fact that Jesus had deliberately kept his divinity and Messiahship a secret from all but the inner circle, and even the inner circle had had less than clear sight. The writer who assembled the materials into a connected narrative, and who invested them with the answers to these questions, is known to us as Mark; his work is the earliest of the written Gospels.

A Gospel, it must be understood, is not a full-length biography, nor is it the product of the kind of painstaking research which modern historians practise in what they call the science of history. A Gospel is an interpretation of Jesus.

Each of the surviving Gospels is a separate interpretation. All of them use the same, or virtually the same, materials; I shall be more specific about this matter presently. The similarity, or occasional identity, of materials should not obscure the distinctive character in each interpretation. Some twenty or thirty years ago a professor of creative writing submitted an outline of a short story to fourteen prominent authors, asking each to use his plot and characters, but to write the story in his own way. Each of the resultant fourteen stories was stamped by the personality of the individual author.

A Gospel is about Jesus; its chief characteristic is that it is some author's interpretation of Jesus, an impressionistic painting, and not a mere photograph.

# XII

# The Gospel According to Mark

THE READER will find it useful at this juncture to read the Gospel According to Mark, for which this chapter purports to act as a companion-piece and guide. The content of the Gospel, here outlined, is a long series of connected episodes about Jesus, which, it will be seen, fall into three natural divisions. The first records the activity of Jesus in his native Galilee, the second traces his journey to Jerusalem, and the third relates the events in the Holy City which culminated in the crucifixion and the resurrection. Throughout Mark, Jesus is portrayed primarily through what he is shown as doing rather than saying. Mark gives us incident rather than discourse.

Mark introduces us to Jesus as a mature man; he relates nothing of his birth or infancy. The first incident is Jesus' baptism at the hands of a well-known man, John the Baptist (whom we shall call, a little more precisely, John the Baptizer). We are told briefly that Jesus was led by the Spirit into the wilderness, where for forty days he was tempted by the devil. Thereafter Jesus came into Galilee, preaching: "The time is fulfilled, and the kingdom of God is at hand; repent and believe in the Gospel."

In response to his call he attracted followers. He preached in synagogues, exorcised unclean spirits, and began to gain fame. His teaching impressed his hearers as having an authority which the ordinary teachers lacked.

As he wandered about, he effected impressive cures of the sick. Those whom he cured had faith in his ability to heal. Some onlookers, scribes, noted with antagonism that Jesus, in curing a paralytic, assured him that his sins were forgiven; for them this was blasphemy, since God alone could forgive sins. Moreover, they observed that Jesus associated with sinners and with the ritually unclean tax-collectors. Accordingly, there begins in this first division of the Gospel a conflict with fellow Jews which grows sharper and more extensive. When Jesus on the Sabbath healed a man with a withered hand, the Pharisees held counsel with the Herodians as to how to destroy him.

Jesus meanwhile gathered more disciples until they numbered twelve. He attracted great crowds. Opposition continued; some of it came from scribes who had wandered down from Jerusalem; some came from friends who thought he was insane. To his twelve disciples Jesus taught some parables, the inner meanings of which he revealed to them. He set out with them in a boat; he slept while a storm arose to frighten them. Jesus rebuked the sea and wind, and they were still. The disciples asked, "Who is this that even the wind and sea obey him?"

Other exorcisms and healings ensued, until Jesus returned to his own town, where because of unbelief he was unable to do mighty work — he only healed a few people. It was at this point that Jesus sent out his disciples for them to use their power to cast out demons and to heal the sick.

The fame of Jesus had reached King Herod. The monarch wondered who Jesus could be; his interest was not a friendly one.

When the disciples returned to Jesus and many people gathered, Jesus fed a multitude of five thousand with five loaves of bread and two fishes which the disciples had. Next, they saw him walking on the water; they did not understand who he was.

He had further conflicts, and effected further healings. Again he was confronted by a great crowd, this time four thousand, who were hungry. He fed these from seven loaves and a few small fishes; there were left over seven baskets of pieces of bread. His disciples still did not understand him.

At a place named Caesarea Philippi, Jesus asked his followers who men thought he was. Peter averred that Jesus was the Christ. Jesus commanded them to tell no one. He taught them that he had to suffer many things, to be rejected by the priests, elders, and scribes, to be killed, and after three days to rise again.

On a mountain, accompanied by the disciples Peter, James, and John, Jesus was transfigured. The disciples saw that his garments became intensely white, and Elijah and Moses appeared, talking with Jesus. A cloud overshadowed them, and a voice came out of it, saying: "This is My beloved son; listen to him." The disciples looked around, and now saw only Jesus with them. Jesus said that he would be killed and would arise. The disciples questioned among themselves what rising from the dead could mean.

When the four returned to the other disciples, these were futilely attempting to cure a dumb boy who had been convulsive from birth. Jesus cured him. The disciples asked why they had failed. Jesus told them that that kind of demon could be driven out only by prayer.

As they passed through Galilee, Jesus for a second time predicted his being delivered into the hands of men, his death, and his resurrection after three days. A discussion with them about discipleship to him and its cost closes the first part of Mark.

The journey to Jerusalem now follows. Jesus crossed to the eastern shore of the Jordan and headed southward. Crowds again gathered to him, and again he found himself in conflict. The Pharisees permitted divorce, for it seems sanctioned in the Bible. Jesus contended that Moses had only made a reluctant concession, and that divorce was wrong, and that what God had joined together man should not put asunder.

A man who wanted to follow Jesus was advised to sell all his possessions and give the proceeds to the poor. Thereupon the man went away. Jesus told his disciples that it would be easier for a camel to go through a needle's eye than for a rich man to enter the kingdom of heaven. He promised his disciples that they would receive rewards a hundredfold in this age and eternal life in the age to come.

A third time Jesus predicted his death and resurrection.

Two disciples, James and John, requested of Jesus the privilege of sitting one at his right hand and one at his left when Jesus should be in his glory. Jesus replied that whoever would be great among them must be their servant, not their ruler.

At Jericho he cured the blind beggar, Bartimaeus, whose faith, Jesus told him, had made him well.

When they approached Jerusalem, Jesus directed two of the disciples to enter a village, where they would find a colt on which no one had ever ridden; they were to untie it and bring it to him. They brought the colt to Jesus, spread their clothes on it, and he mounted it. Many spread clothes on the road, while others strewed leafy branches. They called out, "Hosanna! Blessed be he who comes in the name of the Lord. Blessed be the kingdom of our father David that is coming. Hosanna in the highest." (Here the second part of Mark ends.)

Now Jesus entered Jerusalem. He went into the Temple, looked around, and then withdrew to Bethany with the twelve disciples. The next day he returned to the Temple. He drove out those who bought and sold there, and he overturned the tables of the money changers. He said: "Is it not written, 'My house shall be called a house of prayer for all the nations'? But you have made it a den of robbers."

The chief priests and scribes now sought a way to destroy him, for they feared him and they saw how great was his following. When they asked Jesus what authority he had for what he was doing, he parried their questions cleverly and did not answer them. He told them a parable: The owner of a vineyard had let it out to tenants and had gone off to another country. He sent a servant to get some of the fruit. The tenants beat him and sent him home empty-handed. He sent another servant; they wounded him in the head. He sent another, whom they killed. And so with many others. He had a beloved son whom he sent to them, thinking, "They will respect my son." The tenants, however, said to one another, "Let us kill the heir, and the inheritance will be ours." And they did so. What will the owner of the vineyard do? He will come and destroy the tenants and give the vineyard to others.

Jesus' auditors understood that he was telling the parable against them. They left him and went away, and sent Pharisees and Herodians to trap him with the catch question, "Is it lawful to pay taxes to Caesar, or not?" Jesus said: "Render to Caesar the things that are Caesar's, and to God the things that are God's."

Sadducees tried to trap him on the question of the resurrection, which they denied. A woman was married, they said to Jesus, to a succession of seven brothers; after marrying each, she became a widow. At the resurrection, of which of the seven would she be the wife? Jesus said: "When they rise from the dead they neither marry nor give in marriage." He went on to cite a Biblical passage which could refute the denials of resurrection.

On the other hand, a scribe approved of Jesus' declaring that the first two commandments are, first, "Hear, O Israel, the Lord our God, the Lord is One"; and the second, "You shall love your neighbor as yourself." Jesus told him that he, the scribe, was not far from the kingdom of heaven. He also praised a poor widow who gave a mite to the Temple treasury.

Jesus revealed to his disciples that the Temple would be destroyed. He warned them against falsifiers who would claim to come in his name and announce the End prematurely. He told them that they would undergo suffering and punishment before that time. Just when the End would come was uncertain, but the signs of upheavals and of wars and the darkening of heavenly bodies were sure portents of its nearness. "Truly I say to you, this generation will not pass away before all these things take place . . . . But of that day or that hour, no one knows . . . ."

Two days before the Feast of Unleavened Bread the chief priests and scribes sought a way to arrest Jesus by stealth, so as not to evoke the displeasure of the crowd.

At Bethany, a woman anointed the head of Jesus with some costly, pure cosmetic called nard. She was, Jesus said, anointing his body beforehand for burial.

Judas, one of the disciples, went to the chief priests to betray Jesus. They were glad, and they promised to give him money.

Jesus sent two disciples to prepare a place for him to eat the Passover. It was a large, furnished upper room. When evening came and they were at the table eating, Jesus predicted that one of them would betray him. Then he took bread, blessed, and broke it and gave it to each of them, saying, "This is my body." He passed around a cup from which they drank, and he said to them, "This is the blood of the covenant which is poured out for many."

Then Jesus predicted that they would all fall away from him and scatter; after resurrection he would go before them to Galilee. Peter protested that he would remain faithful; Jesus predicted that Peter would deny him three times before the cock crowed.

At Gethsemane, while Jesus prayed, Peter, James, and John fell asleep; a second time while he prayed they fell asleep. He awakened them, for it was time for him to be betrayed into the hands of sinners. Immediately Judas arrived with a crowd bearing swords and clubs. He identified Jesus by kissing him. Jesus expressed his indignation that they were treating him like a robber, "but let the Scripture be fulfilled."

Jesus was led to the high priest. Peter followed at a distance, even into the courtyard, where he sat by the fire. The high priest and the council (Sanhedrin) sought testimony against Jesus, but found none. False testimony was adduced: "We heard him say, I will destroy this temple made with hands, and in three days I will build another not made with hands."

To the direct question, was he the Christ?, Jesus replied, "I am, and you will see the Son of Man sitting at the right hand of Power, and coming with the clouds of heaven."

Peter meanwhile denied three times that he knew Jesus, and the cock crowed. Now it was morning, so the leaders and the council bore Jesus away to the Roman official, the procurator Pilate. He asked Jesus questions, but Jesus was mostly silent, so that Pilate wondered.

It was usual at the feast to free whatever prisoner people wanted released. They asked that a certain rebel, Barabbas, be freed. Pilate asked them if he should release the King of the Jews. The crowd insisted on Barabbas; to Pilate's question, what should he do with Jesus?, they shouted, "Crucify him!"

The soldiers led Jesus away. They clothed him in a purple cloak and put a crown of thorns on his head. They saluted him as the "King of the Jews," and struck him and spat on him, and mocked him. They stripped off the cloak and put his own clothes on him and led him out to crucify him.

A passer-by, Simon of Cyrene, was compelled to carry Jesus' cross. At the chosen place, Golgotha, they offered Jesus wine mingled with myrrh; but he refused it. They crucified him and cast lots for his garments. It was the third hour. (We would say 9 A. M.) The charge against him was inscribed: "The King of the Jews." The chief priests and scribes mocked him: "He saved others; he cannot save himself."

When the sixth hour (noon) came, darkness spread over the land and lasted until the ninth hour (3 P. M.). Then Jesus called with a loud voice, "My God, my God, why hast Thou forsaken me?" He uttered a loud cry and breathed his last. The curtain of the Temple was torn in two, from top to bottom. A Roman centurion facing him said, "This man was truly the son of God."

Some women among his followers looked on from afar. One Joseph of Arimathea asked Pilate for the body, that he might bury it. Pilate first inquired to make certain that Jesus was really dead. Joseph bought a shroud, wrapped Jesus in it, laid him in a tomb, and rolled a stone against the door.

After the Sabbath (that is, on Sunday), the women came to the tomb, bringing spices to anoint Jesus' body. They found the stone rolled away. Inside the tomb was a young man dressed in a white robe, who said, "Do not be amazed; you seek Jesus of Nazareth, who was crucified. He has risen; he is not here . . . . Go, tell his disciples and Peter that he is going before you to Galilee." They went out and fled from the tomb, for they were afraid. Thus the Gospel of Mark ends.

This résumé may adequately summarize the contents, but one can grasp the tone and tenor of the Gospel only from reading it, and preferably at one sitting. One finds a more faithful reproduction of its true character in some such modern translation as the Revised Standard Version; the majesty of the King James translation can conceal the plain, unadorned, inerudite character of the original Greek. Mark is not a polished writer, nor is he subtle, nor is he elegant. He writes for plain, common people.

It has been noted, correctly, that in several places Mark uses Aramaic words or phrases, and in these cases he translates their meaning. Where he seems sure that his readers will not understand, he tries to supply what they need, but he is so sure of their understanding most of what he is saying that he does not feel the need to explain this or that term or conception. He is writing for an audience which shares with him common understandings and with which he can communicate. He does not stop to define kingdom of God, or sin, or Christ. His readers did not need the dictionaries, encyclopedias, and commentaries which the modern age requires.

In the light of the presence of assumptions about the Christ, sin, forgiveness, and the like, it is evident that Mark writes from the standpoint of a theological position. It is not a well-worked out, systematic position; and it is much more often implicit than stated, but it is present in latent or surface form in every paragraph. What he has heard or read about Jesus is blended with those things in which he believes or which greatly concern him. His vehicle is the narrative about Jesus; but Mark is writing more than a mere narrative.

When Mark tells us that at the death of Jesus the veil of the Temple was rent, he is saying the same thing which elsewhere in the New Testament is expressed this way: in the Jewish scheme of things, only on Yom Kippur did the High Priest venture beyond the veil into the holy of holies; through the death of the Christ, however, Christians had a means of atonement which was always available. The story of the rejection at Nazareth, ending in the verdict, "A prophet is not without honor except in his own country," reflects the Christian rejoinder to the argument that Jesus' own people had not accepted him.

The story of a Syro-Phoenician woman touches on what was a delicate matter in the developing church, the question of whether Gentiles could enter as full equals. Mark relates the story infelicitously. As he tells it, the Gentile woman approached Jesus to ask him to cure her daughter. He declined to do so at first, because she was not Jewish: "Let the children first be fed, for it is not right to take the children's bread and throw it to the dogs." To the woman, and not to Jesus, is assigned the rebuke to this exclusivism: "Even the dogs under the table eat the children's crumb." The point of the episode is that the benefit of the Christ's activity is not limited to Jews.

Again, the parable of the vineyard keeper and his tenants spoken to the Jewish leaders (which is not strictly a parable, but an allegory*) begins to make sense only when we understand that the vineyard owner is God; the tenants are the Jews; the servants are the succession of prophets (Christianity developed the polemic that the Jews had always killed their prophets); the vineyard owner's son is the Christ; the punishment promised is to come at the End of things.

This allegory discloses a well-developed set of attitudes which had become common currency among Christians. It blames the

---

*A parable is a self-contained, short anecdote which provides some moral or some lesson applicable to some larger matter. An allegory is a series of symbolic persons or incidents, and is not self-contained, but becomes meaningful only through the symbols. Here is a parable: Two men owned a boat in common. Neither could swim. They went fishing. One man pulled a drill from his pocket and began to bore a hole in the boat. The other protested. The driller replied, "This is my part of the boat." Here we have a parable illustrating that our lives and fates are intertwined with those of other people. One can make it into an allegory by suggesting, for example, that the boat is Christendom, the men Protestantism and Catholicism, and the drill suspicion or rivalry.

Jews for Jesus' death, and it promises them punishment. Mark ingenuously tells it in such a way as to suggest that even before the death and resurrection of Jesus, the Jewish leaders are able to understand the allegory immediately on hearing it.

It would be beyond the present scope to show how each of the episodes finds its particular place within Mark's total thought, for to do so would encompass too many pages, and is a pursuit primarily for the diligent student. The common reader can profit from a summary view of Mark's theological attitudes, and can dispense with the details.

To begin with, Mark writes from a Gentile and not a Jewish-Christian viewpoint. He is far enough from Palestine that he needs to translate the Aramaic words and to identify place names. He is near enough to the time of Jesus to continue with Paul in the expectation that the End of the world will come soon; yet he is far enough away to have experienced the disappointment attendant upon its premature announcement by some who have declared that it was right at hand. Mark is still sure that it is some day coming, but just when no man knows.

Mark knows that Christians have already undergone persecution and martyrdom — they have drunk from the cup which was Jesus', to adopt his form of utterance. His discussion of what discipleship involves and costs is hardly a prediction by Jesus; it is a reflection of the experience of the Church.

So, too, Mark reads back into the career of Jesus the contentions of Mark's own situation. For example, he holds that there is a body of private information which Jesus gave to his immediate followers. He gets at this through the device (which may to us seem clumsy) of having Jesus relate a long parable which is crystal-clear to us, but not to his disciples, and therefore must be explained to them. "A sower went out to sow. Some seed fell along the path, and the birds came and devoured it. Other seed fell on rocky ground, where it had not much soil, and it sprang up, and when the sun arose it was scorched and quickly withered away. Other seed fell among thorns, and the thorns grew and choked it, and it yielded no grain. Other seed fell into good soil and brought forth grain, growing up and increasing a hundredfold." After Jesus has explained that the seed is the word of God, Mark assures us that Jesus explained the meanings of his parables privately to his disciples. Before the explanation, however, he tells us, astoundingly, that Jesus had had recourse to parables not in order to enlighten — which we should judge to be the true function of parables — but to render his teaching incomprehensible to outsiders. What is this all about? The undoubted answer requires the background information, that as early as Paul's time the church was plagued by "false teachers" from within, and by skeptics from without. Mark is contending that there is a body of authoritative oral information which had been confided to the proper group within the church, but which was unknown to the improper within and undisclosed to the obdurate who remained outside.

Just as timely is the narrative of Jesus in conflict with the Jews over the washing of the hands, a narrative which would be welcomed by the church which had ceased to observe the Law of Moses. The controversy depicted in this narrative moves on to the question of whether a man is defiled by what goes into him or by what comes out of him, and Mark concludes that Jesus had made all foods clean.

A series of diverse materials have it in common that through them Jesus is depicted as greater than Judaism or some single person or item central in Judaism. John the Baptizer is known from other literature; he is an authentic, historical character. The exact relationship between him and Jesus is not known, nor is it certain that there was any at all, for we read elsewhere in the New Testament that John's movement persisted long after Christianity was a separate organism. Mark tells us that John and Jesus were related as messianic forerunner and messiah. He stresses John's complete subordination to Jesus, having John tell us that he will be followed in time by someone whose sandal thongs he is not worthy to stoop and tie. Similarly, Jesus is greater than the Sabbath; he is greater than the Temple; he is greater than Moses (symbolic of the Law) and than Elijah (symbolic of the prophets).

In Mark, the Jews uniformly fail to understand or to appreciate Jesus. It is the Roman centurion from whom the telling conclusion emerges: "This man was truly the son of God." To mention something to which we shall later return, the disciples and the opponents of Jesus share in an opaqueness which has in it only this difference, that the disciples did not fully understand Jesus or remain loyal to him, whereas the other Jews were downright antagonistic to him.

Inasmuch as Mark came from a Gentile Christian environment and was thus motivated towards personifying the rivalry between Jewish and Gentile partisans in the church, it is not unexpected that there is in his Gospel a strong beginning of a motif which grows greater in later writings (and which is virtually absent from Paul), namely, that the Romans were innocent vehicles in the crucifixion, and that the truly guilty ones were the Jews. Paul has no such suggestion in any passage which remains undisputed among modern scholars, for to his mind the death of Jesus was a benefit to mankind; why, then, blame someone for conferring a benefit? Mark, on the subject, is close to a contradiction. In one breath he assures us that Jesus three times predicted his death, so that we must not mistakenly conclude that it was either a mistake or a defeat. On the other hand, there are found in Mark the beginnings of what later on flowers in the epithet which Christians addressed to Jews: Christ-killer.

This bitterness of the Gentile church towards the Jews, which Mark reflects, is more discernible in the narrative of the crucifixion than elsewhere. The episode bristles also with other problems, to which answers are only conjectural. It seems likely that whereas the preceding material reached Mark in oral form, when he comes to what Christians call the passion narrative, he uses a written source. As Mark begins, he seems to set the stage for the crucifixion to be dated prior to Passover (as the Gospel According to John dates it); then he seems to forget that, or else he gives us a notoriously false clue. (That Mark can be careless is provable from his opening verses, where he attributes to Isaiah a passage partially from Malachi.) By allocating the events to Passover, Mark would have us suppose that there took place on a holiday an all-night session of the council, followed by a hearing before Pilate, and by the crucifixion. When it is recalled that Jewish holidays begin and end at sundown, we see that all these events are compressed within the holiday. Our knowledge of Jewish practices is in total conflict with the juridical processes; it would be as reasonable to suppose that an American lower court held an all-night session on New Year's Eve and transferred the proceedings to a higher court on New Year's morning, and that the sentence was carried out on the same day. Some Jewish scholars have attempted a step-by-step refutation of the procedures described.

The entire trial business is legendary and tendentious. The date of Passover, or its eve, was selected in order to equate Jesus with the sacrificial Passover lamb of the Bible. The church, by Mark's time, did not know when Jesus was crucified, but naturally chose a date which would make it seem clear that his death was predicted in the Old Testament. Bitter controversy prevailed in some quarters of the church because the date selected was, for the Gospel of Mark, the fifteenth of Nisan, and for the Gospel of John, the fourteenth. Had it been known when the crucifixion occurred, it would not have been possible for conflicting dates to arise.

We read that at the trial true testimony was not available, so that false testimony was introduced. What we struggle in vain to see is some genuine basis on which a wish to have Jesus crucified could rest. We read of Jewish animosity and of Roman disinterest; Pilate, indeed, is willing to release Jesus. Mark supposes that the council's condemnation comes when Jesus replied that he is "the Christ, the son of the Blessed." This reply totally lacks anything which would suit it to a Palestinian Jewish setting; Christ, son of the blessed, is a term from Greek Christian circles such as that from which Mark came.

Moreover, in the light of Mark's supposition that it is blasphemy, not political revolt, which occasions the wish on the part of the Jews to have Jesus crucified, we become puzzled by the titulus inscribed over the cross, "The King of the Jews." Nothing in the first fourteen chapters of Mark has prepared us for Jesus to be addressed or spoken of as a king. Nothing which he had been portrayed as doing squares with the phrase.

Earlier in the Gospel the word Christ is very rare. It occurs in the first verse, but that may be part of an added subtitle to the Gospel. The term which Mark usually has Jesus use in self-description is the enigmatic "Son of Man." The term is found in Ezekiel and in Daniel; also, an extra-Biblical book uses the term as a kind of synonym for Messiah. It chances that in Aramaic the term can have both that very pregnant meaning, or else it can have the simplest of meanings, "I."

Why, then, does Mark use the locution Son of Man in place

of Messiah? Why does he abruptly introduce the phrase, The King of the Jews?

The term Messiah, we saw in looking at Paul, was meaningless among Greek Gentiles. To Jews, however, it had a connotation which was as much political as religious. Son of Man, on the other hand, was an innocuous and non-political phrase. It is to be suggested that Mark, writing in a time when it was expedient for a rising sect to assure the Romans of its political harmlessness, prefers Son of Man, which has no revolutionary connotations, as the title for Jesus. The titulus, however, suggests the probable historical basis for the crucifixion, namely, that it was a Roman punishment meted out to a supposed insurrectionist, as any Messianic claimant would have appeared to the Romans to be. We must conjecture that common knowledge of the titulus was so strong in the tradition which Mark inherited that even despite his inclination to represent Jesus as non-political, he was impelled to reproduce the words, "The King of the Jews." We can only conjecture that this is so, for our sole evidence of the political aspect of Jesus is the titulus itself, as interpreted for its logical meaning. It needs to be added that whatever there may have been initially in the movement which Jesus led that was politically revolutionary, it is not to be found in any of the sources. Since the Gentile Christians saw a cosmic rather than a national significance in Jesus, they may have winnowed out of the tradition material relating to a Jewish revolutionary movement, in which they were not interested. The fact remains that such material has not survived in the tradition, if it was ever present.

Mark begins with the formula, the Beginning of the Gospel of Jesus Christ, to which many ancient versions add, the Son of God. It must be borne in mind that Mark is not describing the career of a man, but the human career of a divine being. Since it is a human career, Mark will occasionally veer to the excessively human. In the Passion narrative the desire to elicit pathos from his reader leads him to portray Jesus as praying in one breath that the cup be taken away from him, and in the next breath, "Not what I wish but what You wish." It is in part pathos which leads Mark to portray Jesus on the cross as saying, "My God, My God, why have You forsaken me?" This is a quotation from Psalm 22, which is used throughout the Passion narrative and which is the probable source, rather than history, for such other details as the scornful mockery and the casting of lots for the clothes.

The vivid depicting of such responses occasions passages which later evangelists find troublesome in Mark. Baptism in Christian thought effects remission of sins, and to depict Jesus, as Mark does, as undergoing baptism can amount to imputing sin to him. Mark's imputation gives other writers a problem with which to struggle. These human descriptions can obscure from a reader the reality that the Christ in Mark is not less metaphysical than in Paul. He is the Son of God, greater, as we have seen, than Moses or Elijah, and in his own being as focal in the rising church as the Temple was in Judaism. Though Mark, at Jesus' entry into Jerusalem, tells us of proclamations of the coming of David's kingdom, he includes a paragraph which, as if in contradiction, denied that Jesus was descended from David. It is a strange passage to our eyes, for it involves a mode of reading the Old Testament which is unfamiliar to us; moreover, in the passage we should notice that it is Christ, not Jesus, about whom the issue is raised: Jesus . . . said, "How can the scribes say that the Christ is the son of David? David himself . . . declared, "The Lord said to my Lord, Sit at my right hand . . . . David himself calls him Lord; so how is he his son?" We need not look pedantically at the details, for the conclusion

alone is significant. The Church at one and the same time har-
bored those who transmitted the Jewish conviction that the
Messiah was of Davidic stock, and also the view, as in this
passage, that Jesus was an eternal being. If it seems surprising
that the passage implies that Christ was in existence in David's
time, that is nevertheless exactly what the passage intends to say.
Similarly, in the Fourth Gospel we read: "Before Abraham was,
I am." The strongest affirmations of Jesus' descent from David
come from Matthew and Luke, who supply genealogies to
illustrate Jesus' descent.

We are dealing, then, with the human career of an eternal
being. His first coming was preparatory. His return is awaited.
Mark portrays Jesus as saying: "You will see the Son of Man
(that is, me) sitting at the right hand of Power (that is, God) and
coming with the clouds of heaven."

The feeding of the multitude with fishes and bread seems
intended to relate an agreeable miracle, and at the same time
to suggest more subtly that it is "spiritual" food which the
Christ provides. One account of the feeding tells of five thousand
persons and the other of four thousand. The culmination of each
incident brings Mark's comment that the disciples did not understand about the loaves. It is primarily in the Fourth Gospel that
we read of the Christ's being spiritual bread, or a vine, the staff
of life. That is the intent here. The fish appears to have been an
ancient symbol of immortality; it was a widely used Christian
symbol, too.

The twin ceremonies of communing with the Christ, baptism
and the eucharist, are handled in different ways. Baptism is
taught merely through portraying Jesus' undergoing it. He is
represented as instituting and enjoining the eucharist, at the last
supper. There is little likelihood that this is historical; it is rather
a wish to attribute the important ceremonial to Jesus himself.

The basis of the doubt is double; the ceremonial with such a meaning fits in ill with Palestinian Judaism, and, secondly, it is so thoroughly Christian in its tone as to suggest the likelihood of its being still one more church item for which the authority of Jesus himself was sought.

The Gospel through several incidents commends faith in the Christ. Faith produces freedom from sin, which in the ancient world was usually thought of as the cause of disease. Mark's way of commending faith is to illustrate it through those who are cured through it, or who can move mountains or walk on water.

In addition to the more significant aspects of the contents of Mark discussed here, there remains to be considered what the occasion for its writing might have been and what the more special interests, revealed through the recurring motifs, were. As to the time and place, modern scholarship gives answers quite different from what is contained in the traditions of the Church fathers. There one reads that Mark was Peter's interpreter or secretary in Rome, and that Mark wrote down what he heard from Peter, but not in order.

It is, in my judgment, useless to try to be definite about where Mark was written. Rome would do as well as any other place. As to when, it is reasonable to follow those who interpret Mark 13 as referring to the destruction of the Temple at Jerusalem in the year 70. We thereby get both a date, and probably an occasion. The anti-Jewish feeling between the Church and its Mother Judaism prompted the writing of this Gospel shortly after the Mother had experienced its great discomfiture. The loss of the Temple would, to an opponent, seem a vindication of its own way. A reasonable date for Mark is the year 75.

Three major motifs, some already alluded to, give Mark its essential character. The first of these is known as the Messianic secret. It is frequent in Mark that only the demons recognize who Jesus is; and when Jesus effects a cure, he cautions the cured to keep silent. The usual explanation of this motif is that through it Mark is replying for the Church to the question, Why is it necessary to proclaim Jesus? Why is his worth not universally known?

The second motif is the recurrence of Jesus' advance knowledge of his death and crucifixion. We know from Paul that the crucifixion made difficulties for Christian missionaries, for it repelled as well as attracted. Mark is setting forth that the crucifixion was not a surprise or a defeat, but rather part of the predetermined scheme of necessary events.

The above two motifs are handled competently in the usual scholarship. I would add a third. I believe that when one looks at Mark without being influenced by centuries of tradition and by the other Gospels, one will be struck by the ignoble role which the disciples play. They do not understand who Jesus is, they lack the faith which he expects of them, and they abandon him when he is arrested; and the Gospel ends without portraying the Risen Christ as appearing to them. It is my opinion that Mark is here suggesting that it was not the immediate followers of Jesus, such as Peter or James, who truly comprehended him, but remote and later persons. Not disciples, but apostles, understood Jesus; even his immediate Palestinian adherents did not understand or grasp him.

The danger in an exposition of details or summary is that it can fail to transmit the flavor of what is under description. A reader sympathetic to Mark, not boggling at this or that detail, would find the Gospel quick-paced and dramatic. So, undoubtedly, did the usual Christian in the last quarter of the first century find it. Mark is short enough to read at one sitting. The reader, in identifying himself with Jesus, goes through exciting and triumphant incidents. When he has read through the Gospel, he has experienced a great emotional release.

The Gospel According to Mark was designed for such reading. It is almost impossible for the modern man to read it in that way. Unclarities are there; doubts intervene; recollections from other Gospels, now available but then unwritten, intrude. Yet for the man of nineteen hundred years ago who was attuned to it, the Gospel of Mark was an exciting, a moving literary and religious experience. It edified him, and by answering questions and dissipating some doubts and uncertainties, it strengthened his faith.

# XIII

# Beyond The Gospel According to Mark

As TIME WENT ON Mark's Gospel, for all its dramatic force and power, answered some pressing contemporary questions, only to raise even more. Indeed, there were passages in Mark to which thoughtful and analytical persons might take exception, such as the last words on the cross, or the notion that Jesus underwent baptism, as though he was like any other man. Accordingly, additional Gospels came to be written. Two of these, Matthew and Luke, we have said, used Mark as a source both in content and in order of arrangement. The knowledge of the way in which they used Mark is the key to the understanding of why these later Gospels were written. Our next step is to get some glimpse of the essential differences in style, structure, and content of the later Gospels.

Only about a half of Matthew and of Luke is taken from Mark. The rest is "teaching materials," that is, "words" spoken by Jesus which are not found in Mark. Where did Matthew and Luke get this source material? A reasonable conjecture — but only a conjecture — is that they had before them, in addition to Mark, a collected body of "words" as their "second source." This second source could well have existed only in an oral form, as part of the as yet unwritten tradition, and a minority of scholars hold to this view. But the words of Jesus appear in substantially the same form in Luke as they do in Matthew. Jesus spoke in Aramaic; Matthew and Luke, in the Greek, give almost identical wordings. Since independent translations of the same Aramaic texts would hardly yield Greek sentences so largely identical, it is natural to suppose that Matthew and Luke utilized collections of Jesus' words in written Greek and not in oral form. The usual view among scholars is that Matthew and Luke each used this second source independently of each other. A convenient symbol for the second source is "Q," standing for the German word *Quelle*, "source."

It needs to be noted, however, that a somewhat different but not unreasonable alternative explanation is at hand, that is, either that Luke used Matthew, or that Matthew used Luke; in either case, no written form of Q needs to be assumed. Those who would deny that Q existed in an independent, written form argue that had it been available, the author of Mark would hardly have ignored it so completely. The assumption, however, that Matthew used Luke, or Luke Matthew, raises hypothetical questions of comparable cogency. Certainty is absent, and one needs to be content with probabilities. Most scholars hold to the existence of Q. I do not share this view.

The words of Jesus, as indicated earlier, were preserved in some authenticity. But the church shaped these words, altered them, and created words, reflecting its own later attitudes, which it put into the mouth of Jesus. Accordingly, whether there was a written source Q, or whether the source was amorphous and oral until either Matthew or Luke recorded it, it should be noted that in the form in which the words appear in the Gospels they are not primarily what Jesus himself actually said, but rather what the later church earnestly wished that he had said or piously and sincerely believed that he had.

The Gospels of Matthew and Luke are implied criticisms of Mark. Using his Gospel, they feel constrained to edit as they adapt. A demonstration in miniature that this is so may be useful before we characterize Matthew and, later, Luke, so that the reader may have some sense of the bases on which the conclusions rest, and see part of the process through which some judgments are reached. The use of a synopsis makes the differences easier to note. For example, here is how the incident of the baptism of Jesus appears in the synopsis, except for my added underlining:

| Matthew 3:13–17 | Mark 1:9–11 | Luke 3:21–22 |
|---|---|---|
| (13) Then Jesus came from Galilee to the Jordan to John, to be baptized by him. (14) John would have prevented him, saying, "I need to be baptized by you, and do you come to me?" (15) But Jesus answered him, "Let it be so now; for thus it is fitting for us to fulfill all righteousness." Then he consented. (16) And when Jesus was baptized, he went up immediately from the water, and behold, the heavens were opened and he saw the Spirit of God descending like a dove and alighting on him; (17) and lo, a voice from heaven, saying, "This is my beloved Son, with whom I am well pleased." | (9) In those days Jesus came from Nazareth of Galilee and was baptized by John in the Jordan. (10) And when he came up out of the water, immediately he saw the heavens opened and the Spirit descending upon him like a dove; (11) and a voice came from heaven, "Thou art my beloved Son; with thee I am well pleased." | (21) Now when all the people were baptized and when Jesus also had been baptized and was praying, the heaven was opened, (22) and the Holy Spirit descended upon him in bodily form, as a dove, and a voice came from heaven. "Thou art my beloved Son; with thee I am well pleased." |

138

The words with the single underlining are the changes made in Matthew and Luke, while the double line shows Marcan material omitted by Matthew and Luke. Some of the changes are stylistic; Mark uses simple declarative sentences; but Matthew and Luke prefer more complex ones with subordinate clauses of various kinds. Mark tells with great simplicity that Jesus was baptized by John; the two other Gospels find this troublesome, since baptism was a rite to wash away sins, and they saw the suggestion of sinfulness attributed to Jesus. Hence, Matthew portrays John as unwilling to perform the rite, and Jesus as apparently agreeing to its not being required of him, but nevertheless consenting to it as an example to emulate. Luke passes over the baptism so that it draws little attention, and serves only as the prelude to what follows. The spirit in Mark is altered to the Spirit of God in Matthew and to the Holy Spirit in Luke. Matthew and Mark describe the descent as dove-like, but Luke tells us that the spirit was embodied in a physical dove.

Or, again:

| Matthew 19:16–18 | Mark 10:17–19 | Luke 18:18–20 |
|---|---|---|
| (16) And behold, one came up to him, saying, "Teacher, what good deed must I do, to have eternal life?" (17) And he said to him, "Why do you ask me about what is good? One there is who is good. If you would enter life, keep the commandments." (18) He | (17) And as he was setting out on his journey, a man ran up and knelt before him, and asked him, "Good Teacher, what must I do to inherit eternal life?" (18) And Jesus said to him, "Why do you call me good? No | (18) And a ruler asked him, "Good Teacher, what shall I do to inherit eternal life?" (19) And Jesus said to him, "Why do you call me good? No one is good but God alone. (20) You know the commandments: 'Do not commit adultery, Do not kill. Do not steal, Do |

| Matthew 19:16–18 | Mark 10:17–19 | Luke 18:18–20 |
|---|---|---|
| said to him, "Which?" And Jesus said, "You shall not kill, You shall not commit adultery, You shall not steal, You shall not bear false witness." | one is good but God alone. (19) You know the commandments: 'Do not kill, Do not commit adultery, Do not steal, Do not bear false witness, Do not defraud, Honor your father and mother.' " | not bear false witness, Honor your father and mother.' " |

The introductions vary: Matthew abridges Mark's description of the asking of the question, while Luke changes "a man" into "a ruler." In the question, Luke alters the "must" into "shall"; Luke omits "do not defraud." Matthew, however, changes the question; it is addressed to "Teacher," rather than "Good Teacher"; and Matthew focuses on the good deed that needs to be done. Mark and Luke portray Jesus as rejecting the adjective "good"; Matthew, however, by removing the "good" before "Teacher," has no point of departure for Jesus to reject the adjective; instead, Matthew makes Jesus' answer focus on what is the good; thereby Matthew avoids the implication that Jesus denied his goodness. Mark and Luke simply quote from the Ten Commandments, but Matthew portrays Jesus as commanding or, better, as affirming them.

Or, a Q passage:

| Matthew 22:1–10 | Luke 14:15–24 |
|---|---|
| (1) And again Jesus spoke to them in parables, saying, (2) "The kingdom of heaven may be compared to a king who gave a mar- | (15) When one of those who sat at table with him heard this, he said to him, "Blessed is he who shall eat bread in the kingdom of God!" (16) But he said to |

| Matthew 22:1-10 | Luke 14:15-24 |
|---|---|
| riage feast for his son, (3) and sent his servants to call those who were invited to the marriage feast; but they would not come. (4) Again he sent other servants, saying, 'Tell those who are invited. Behold, I have made ready my dinner, my oxen and my fat calves are killed, and everything is ready; come to the marriage feast.' (5) But they made light of it and went off, one to his farm, another to his business, (6) while the rest seized his servants, treated them shamefully, and killed them. (7) The king was angry, and he sent his troops and destroyed those murderers and burned their city. (8) Then he said to his servants. 'The wedding is ready, but those invited were not worthy. (9) Go therefore to the thoroughfares, and invite to the marriage feast as many as you find.' (10) And those servants went out into the streets and gathered all whom they found, both bad and good;. so the wedding hall was filled with guests. | him, "A man once gave a great banquet, and invited many; (17) and at the time for the banquet he sent his servant to say to those who had been invited, 'Come; for all is now ready.' (18) But they all alike began to make excuses. The first said to him, 'I have bought a field, and I must go out and see it; I pray you, have me excused.' (19) And another said, 'I have bought five yoke of oxen, and I go to examine them; I pray you, have me excused.' (20) And another said, 'I have married a wife, and therefore I cannot come.' (21) So the servant came and reported this to his master. Then the householder in anger said to his servant, 'Go out quickly to the streets and lanes of the city, and bring in the poor and maimed and blind and lame.' (22) And the servant said, 'Sir, what you commanded has been done, and still there is room.' (23) And the master said to the servant. 'Go out to the highways and hedges, and compel people to come in, that my house may be filled. (24) For I tell you, none of those men who were invited shall taste my banquet.' " |

The introductions vary; in Matthew, Jesus simply tells a parable, but in Luke, the parable is the rejoinder to one who sits at the table. Matthew tells of a marriage feast for a king's son, while Luke tells of a man's giving a banquet. Matthew has servants sent out, Luke only one servant; and Matthew has the servants go out on several occasions. Luke portrays the invited guests as reluctant to come, for reasons of preoccupation, but Matthew interprets the reluctance as hostility to the point of the abuse and killing of the servants. Luke's householder in anger withdraws the invitation and extends it to the poor and the maimed, but Matthew has the king send out to destroy the murderers and burn their city.

What we are dealing with here is fundamentally a parable on the virtue of preparedness; the parable may well go back to Jesus in the form simply of an account of a host who found his invited guests unprepared, and therefore supplanted them. But Matthew and Luke here have expanded the parable by applying its details to situations and events of their own times. In Luke, it is no longer the crystal-clear parable of preparedness, but an explanation, more clearly, of how God has rejected the Jews and turned to the church; there is still room in the church, and missionaries should go out and compel people to come in.

Matthew, too, turns the parable into a series of symbols. An anti-Jewish contention, frequent in the church from the end of the first century on, that Jews were responsible for the death not only of Jesus but also of earlier prophets, has been super-imposed upon the parable with the result that we get such incongruous matters as guests injuring and killing the host's servants, and the marriage feast remains always ready while a military expedition destroys a city and its inhabitants; this latter, of course, is a reference to the destruction of Jerusalem and the Temple in 70.

If one studies the entire Synoptic Gospels, as we have quickly glanced at these sections, one will discern for oneself what the differences are among them. The results of such study, as scholars have pursued it, is the notice that the changes fit into a rather consistent pattern for each Gospel; and one who notes, for example, how Luke rewrites the early chapters of Mark can predict with astonishing accuracy what the rewriting of subsequent chapters will be.

The study of such changes is the key to the motives and purposes which underlie the Gospels of Matthew and Luke. A notice of motives and purposes in turn leads to a recognition of church situations and interests out of which these emerge. The differences between Mark, on the one hand, and Matthew and Luke, on the other, show us with unmistakable clarity how the problems, doctrines, and needs of the church developed and reached a crystallized expression.

# XIV

# The Gospel According to Matthew

THE GENERATION which needed Mark's assurance that Jesus was indeed the Messiah though not so recognized in his own lifetime was followed by one in which continued growth and development of the church tended to make earlier issues less pressing; the novelty of a "messianic secret," when accepted as a part of tradition, assumed a usualness, and indeed a casualness, which withdrew from Mark's Gospel its timeliness and vivid relevance. New issues had arisen, and these were to claim more attention than matters by now considered settled.

The church had grown so much that variety in local manifestations or practices could result only in arguments about proper doctrine and correct forms of practice. Divisiveness could be reduced as uniformity could increase, and uniformity could be attained primarily through adequate regulation by the appropriate church leaders.

The urgent need for some regulation was due not only to a prevalent diversity, but also to the logical circumstance that the abolition of the Law of Moses, as urged by Paul, could seem to imply the complete absence of any regulation. Though the Pauline doctrine of liberty implied that proper attitude would yield proper conduct, some even in Paul's own day interpreted liberty to mean that there was in conduct no issue of good or bad. Both in Paul's time and in later days such libertines were a vexing problem to the church.

The dilemma before the church was that libertinism was increasingly more intolerable, yet a revalidation of the Law of

Moses was no longer possible — indeed, not at all desirable. One way out of this dilemma was taken by the Epistle of James; it accepted the Pauline premise of the primacy of faith, but insisted that overt conduct ("works") was important, too, for salvation. Although the Epistle thereby pointed to conduct as a somewhat relevant norm, it fell short of what to Christians would have been the pitfall of re-establishing the Law of Moses.

A similar but more far-reaching way out of the dilemma is the substance of the Gospel According to Matthew. Beyond the position taken by James, Matthew was not content that works should be only a random Christian criterion. He introduced something quite new and for its time a significant landmark: church law. This he accomplished by portraying Jesus as a lawgiver who provided a new manual of regulations for believers. The new Law of Christ was not the same as the old Law of Moses; Jesus was a newer and greater lawgiver who laid down a better and more valid law which displaced and supplanted the Law of Moses.

Subsidiary interest, too, entered into Matthew's recasting of Mark's Gospel. Mark's implication that Jesus became the Christ only at his baptism (a view which was known as "adoptionism" and which, in the eighth century, blossomed into a full-grown heresy) had its attractiveness in missionary activities, for it seemed to say to prospective converts that as the nature of Jesus was changed by baptism, so the nature of a convert could change. But to urge such an imitation of Jesus was perilously close to suggesting that the original nature of Jesus was little different from that of the convert, and the disadvantage in adoptionism lay in the implied reduction of the character of Jesus.

The assertion of the transcendent character of Jesus required that his Messiahship should rest on something more than adoptionism and on something anterior to his baptism. Accordingly,

Jesus was portrayed as the offspring of a virgin birth, with the Holy Spirit as the "father." Such a portrayal was not without precedent in the Greek world with its ancient mythologies and with its popular religions, and it did not elicit from the ancient mind the skeptical attitudes of present-day rationalists.

Except for noting the tone of the characteristic deviations from Mark's narrative, we need not linger over Matthew's narration of the same material. In summary, almost everywhere that Mark ingenuously displays either Jesus or his disciples in unflattering act or speech, Matthew rewrites the passage or omits it. Two such examples will suffice. First, in his version of the rich man, Matthew winnows out Mark's implication that Jesus denied his goodness. Secondly, where Mark had attributed to disciples, the sons of Zebedee, the desire for priority among the disciples, Matthew makes it a request from their mother, thus shielding the disciples from the unseemly ambition.

There are other kinds of recasting, one example of which, of greater import, is worthy of note. Whereas Mark has Jesus forbid divorce entirely, Matthew allows it on the single ground of unchastity.

But Matthew does more than recast. He also presents material not found at all in Mark. He arranges his material, both the old and the new, whether of incident or of teaching, in systematic groups. He never has a single utterance or statement, but either three or seven. The assembled blocks of teaching material total five. The Gospel According to Matthew is not a haphazard work, or one written in the glow of warm impulse. It is coolly and deliberately planned. But within the coldness of the framework, the evangelist wrote with both skill and emotional appeal.

Matthew begins with a genealogy which starts with Abraham and leads up to Joseph (1:1-17). The latter part of the genealogy is found in varying forms in the ancient manuscripts, as a result of conscious changes found necessary in the divergent views of the church. Joseph is described in some of the texts as the husband of Mary, of whom Jesus was born; in at least one he is described as the father of Jesus. The relevance of the genealogy would disappear if it did not in some way include Jesus; but the inclusion of Jesus would tend to contradict the virgin birth which immediately ensues. Hence the texts vary in the end of the genealogy. The unsolvable problem for the modern reader is whether or not Matthew himself was aware of the inconsistency of beginning with a genealogy of men, and then of proceeding to the virgin birth. Whatever may be the truly proper end of the genealogy, Matthew exhibits no awareness of the inconsistency between his genealogy and his account of the virgin birth.

Matthew's account of the virgin birth is totally different from Luke's and beyond reconciliation with it. The Matthean version is the well-known account of the three Magi from the East and the star which led them to Bethlehem. Significantly, Matthew's account is replete with texts from the Old Testament which Matthew avers are being fulfilled. The citation of the Greek version of Isaiah 7:14 demonstrates that the prediction, "a virgin shall conceive and bear a son," is being accomplished.

Animosity on the part of Herod leads the parents to flee with Jesus to Egypt so as to permit the fulfillment of Hosea 11:1, "Out of Egypt I have called my son." Herod tries to kill all the male children under two years of age; Matthew does not quote the similar action by Pharaoh in Exodus 1:16. The subsequent lamenting is to be found "predicted" in Jeremiah 31:15. Throughout the Gospel Matthew cites verses from the Old Testament; where passages in Mark seem only reminiscent of them, Matthew goes on to quote them.

The first of the blocks of teaching material comes early in the

Gospel. This section, known traditionally as the sermon, was given on a mount; Moses, too, had given his teaching on a mount.

"Blessed are the poor in spirit, for theirs is the kingdom of heaven.

"Blessed are those who mourn, for they shall be comforted.

"Blessed are the meek, for they shall inherit the earth.

"Blessed are those who hunger and thirst for righteousness, for they shall be satisfied.

"Blessed are the merciful, for they shall obtain mercy.

"Blessed are the pure in heart, for they shall see God.

"Blessed are the peacemakers, for they shall be called Sons of God.

"Blessed are those who are persecuted for righteousness' sake, for theirs is the kingdom of heaven."

However many of the particulars of this section of the Sermon on the Mount, known as the Beatitudes, go back to Jesus, the Sermon in its present assembled form is the work of Matthew. Its impact as a cohesive unit is a strong one, and the section is justly esteemed as a magnificent expression of religious emotion. Each individual beatitude is paralleled in Biblical or rabbinic writings, and the Beatitudes can be considered as rather characteristic expressions of the piety of Palestinian Judaism.

Matthew follows the Beatitudes with injunctions for disciples (5:13–20); some scholars have called the section the "handbook for a Christian missionary." He attributes to Jesus an affirmation of the perpetual validity of the Law and the prophets ("not a jot or tittle will pass away"), intending thereby not only to deny the claims of extreme followers of Paul, but also to perpetuate the ensuing requirement which he conceives of Jesus as formulating. The new law demands a righteousness exceeding that

148

of the scribes and Pharisees. Matthew is affirming the law of Jesus, not the law of Moses.

The new law is next specified (5:21 to 6:2) in a series of seven contrasts between the law of Jesus and the law of Moses. Not alone murder, but also inward anger against a fellow man, is sin. An adulterous desire is a transgression the equivalent of actual adultery. As to divorce, it is prohibited. (But here Matthew portrays Jesus as permitting divorce for a single cause, adultery, against Mark and Paul, who forbid it for any reason whatever.) The old law enjoined complete honesty in oaths, but the new law forbids an oath under any circumstance, since recognized honesty can satisfy with a simple yes or no. In place of retaliation one should not resist evil. But if anyone should strike you on the right cheek, turn to him the other also; if anyone forces you to go one mile, go with him two miles. In place of hating an enemy, the pious should love him. The pious should love their enemies as well as their neighbors; they should be perfect "even as your Father in heaven is perfect." And prayer should not be recited ostentatiously, but in a private room, and briefly.

In these contrasts, the evangelist portrays Jesus' new law as a sharp criticism of antecedent Jewish practice. It needs to be noted that most liberal commentators deny that these antitheses go directly back to Jesus, but hold that they were put into the mouth of Jesus by Matthew. What purports here to be the Jewish Law or the Jewish way is unrecognizable to Jews, as it would have been to Jesus himself, and for a reason which is not remote. We have here not an accurate or fair appraisal of Judaism, but, indeed, only a travesty. It is the result of the arbitrary device of listing seven items of Old Testament law or of supposed Jewish practice as typifying Judaism. "Hate thy enemies" is quoted here as though it were a part of the Old Testament; it is found neither there nor in any of the vast contents of early and later Jewish literature, and it is the clue to Matthew's procedure. He constructs a list of seven items which he describes as the Jewish law, and follows them by extensions or modifications which are for him the new and improved law of Jesus.

This new law embodies a rigorism which is as little viable, as in the case of the prohibition of an adulterous desire, as it is extreme. It can be estimated applaudingly as ideal legislation; and it has inspired Christians (such as Quakers) to noble accomplishment. But it is hardly practical legislation. An abundance of literature of self-criticism by modern Christians reveals how remote from implementation is the new legalism which Matthew presents as being so vastly better than the Jewish Law.

Matthew portrays Jesus as instructing his disciples in prayer (6:5–13). The Lord's Prayer get its Christian character from its association with Christianity. The words themselves are quite congruent phrases of prayer in habitual use in the Talmud:

> "Our Father who art in heaven,
> Hallowed be thy name.
> Thy kingdom come,
> Thy will be done,
>    On earth as it is in heaven.
> Give us this day our daily bread;
> And forgive us our debts,
>    As we also have forgiven our debtors;
> And lead us not into temptation,
>    But deliver us from evil."

An additional phrase is found in only some of the manuscripts, "For thine is the kingdom and the power and the glory, forever, Amen."

As the sermon proceeds, Jesus is portrayed as giving regulations on fasting, on material treasures, and on the anxiety that abides with little faith (6:16–34). Jesus urged considerateness in judging others: "Why do you see the speck in your brother's eye" — but not to the point of disregarding the character of those whom one encounters: "Do not throw your pearls before swine." He assured them that God answers prayer ("Ask, and it will be given unto you"); and in typical rabbinic fashion he summed up Scripture in the Golden Rule, "Whatever you wish that men would do to you, do so to them" (7:1–12).

Few motifs are more widely universal in folk wisdom than the Golden Rule. Christian pietists who attribute its authorship to Jesus do so from narrow horizons, while Jews, in citing the similar formulation from Hillel or from Leviticus 19:18 as the truer origin, also fail to note that the motif is well attested in virtually every literature. Indeed, the Golden Rule recurs in Matthew 22:39, explicitly as a quotation from Leviticus 19:18, and without any effort to suggest that it originated with Jesus. The only relevant issue which might be rescued from the discussion of origins is whether Hillel or Jesus was the first so to summarize Scripture as equaling the Golden Rule. While Hillel was indeed earlier than Jesus, it is not unlikely that the equation was older than both, and that each drew on the same common source.

Matthew's formulation of the Golden Rule, like that in Leviticus, is in the affirmative. Hillel's formulation was in the negative: "What is hateful to you, do not do to your neighbor." A curious, and quite gratuitous, literature exists which tries to demonstrate the superiority of one of these formulations over the other, as Christian and Jewish partisanship has felt the need for exalting its form of the tradition over the other's. That greater profundity lies either in the positive formulation or in the negative is, in my judgment, not to be discerned; the formulations mean precisely the same thing. The common assessment in both traditions of the essence of Scripture is surely more worth noting than is any polemic over originality or supposedly greater insights.

The difficult experience of the church is reflected in Jesus' word that his followers would not have an easy way. That only few could enter by the narrow gate which leads to life (7:14) reflects the resistance from pagans which the growing church found in the Greek world. Matthew portrays Jesus as warning against internal difficulties in the form of false prophets (7:15–23); the passage reflects a concern with heretical doctrines, dealt with abundantly in other New Testament writings. Immediately after this warning ensues the statement that simply to hear the words and not to do them was futile and insufficient (7:24–27); heresies of that time, made known to us through the writings of the Church fathers, seem to have carried the Pauline doctrine to an oblique absurdity in asserting that the faithful need conform to no standard of conduct. The passage, like the Epistle of James, argues that faith without works is empty. An injunction to obey the commandments is a fitting conclusion to this first block of teaching material, and a "colophon" (a closing formula) rounds off the section (7:28–29).

After some narratives of healings and of conflicts, a second block of teachings ensues. These all focus on discipleship. Disciples are few, and prayer is needed to increase their number (9:35–38). Jesus now had twelve disciples. These he sent out with injunctions to restrict their activities to Jews: "Go nowhere among the Gentiles, and enter no town of the Samaritans, but go rather to the lost sheep of the house of Israel" (10:1–6).

Some Jewish interpreters have been led astray by the passage. Failing to note that it occurs in the context of a long Gospel, they seize upon it as though it were an isolated detail. They contend that this, indeed, is the true reflection of the historic Jesus, whose fidelity and even "nationalistic" devotion to Judaism were never broken. That the passage can readily yield this interpretation in isolation from the rest of Matthew is to be conceded. But what this interpretation misses is no less than the direct intent of the Gospel as a whole, namely, that the Jews were given the chance, and the first chance at that, to accept Jesus, but they refused to; and only thereafter was the Gospel offered to the Gentiles. The abstract notion, as in Paul, that the blindness of the Jews led God to turn to the Gentiles, is made concrete in Matthew in a narrative form. The passage is not a self-contained story, but an initial incident whose conclusion is found at the very end of Matthew, where the risen Jesus sends a mission out to the entire world. The present passage does not reflect the historic Jesus; it does no more than relate in the first of two incidents the Christian conviction of the process by which Gentile Christianity came to supplant Jewry as God's people.

The injunctions here put into the mouth of Jesus are the rules for the missionaries of the growing church. These were to preach that the kingdom of God was at hand; they were to heal the sick, raise the dead, cleanse lepers, and cast out demons. For these tasks they were to receive no pay. They were to travel light, and to expect to be sustained by those whom they served. In coming to a new city they were to seek out worthy people. Punishment was assured for those who rejected the disciples. Shrewdness ("be as wise as serpents and as innocent as doves") was incumbent on them (10:7-16).

They could expect to be brought up before synagogue authorities and flogged (as was Paul's experience), and dragged before imperial governors and kings. Flight from one town to another would be necessary. They would have to bear hatred, but those

153

who remained constant would be saved (10:17–23). But, continues the text, in reassurance, even before they should have gone through all the towns of Israel, the Son of Man would have come (10:23).

Few verses in the New Testament are more troubling than this last one. On the one hand, for Fundamentalists, the prediction is so obviously clear and unmistakable that the failure of the prediction to materialize has necessitated stupendous feats of exegesis; on the other, many liberals have felt the reluctant necessity of saying that in expecting the End so soon, Jesus was wrong.

That this is an authentic word of Jesus, I am inclined to doubt. It seems to me that the context in Matthew requires that the evangelist could not have been so acutely unaware that he was recording an unfulfilled prediction. In my judgment, the evangelist is not dealing at all with the mission throughout Palestine in Jesus' own day; he is expressing the pessimistic thought that the End would come, in his own day, before all Palestine was preached to and converted. From his standpoint the prediction was partly fulfilled in that the destruction of the Temple in 70 intervened before any anticipated conversion of all of Palestine. Writing from the vantage point of accumulated time, he is stressing here the obduracy of Jewish Palestine, and not the nearness of the End. He is speaking with reference to the missionaries of his own day, rather than the disciples of Jesus' time.

Those to whom such an explanation is unconvincing and who prefer to regard the passage as an authentic utterance of Jesus must in some way explain not only how Jesus could have been wrong, but also why the evangelist, who was so alert to recast items in Mark, or to omit them, left this item unchanged.

One more word may be added. Matthew has a view of the

End which is quite different from Paul's expectation of an event very soon to come. To this I shall presently revert.

In their task, which will be overtaken by the End, the disciples could expect no better fate than that of Jesus, yet they were not to vie with each other for supremacy (10:24). They need not experience anxiety and fear, for the same God who watched over sparrows would watch over them. Discipleship would involve great difficulties, even to the point of splitting families — undoubtedly an allusion to actual experience — yet devotion to one's family was not comparable to devotion to Jesus. Even martyrdom was not to be avoided ("He who loses his life for my sake shall find it") — again a reference to church experience. For men to receive a disciple was like receiving Jesus himself and would bring them an ultimate reward (10:24–42). Here Matthew ends the second block of the words of Jesus (11:1).

The third block is a series of parables on the kingdom of heaven. Matthew portrays the imprisoned John the Baptizer as sending a question to Jesus: "Are you he whom we have been awaiting, or shall we look for another?" Jesus replied: "Tell John what you hear and see: the blind receive their sight and the lame walk; lepers are cleansed and the deaf hear, and the poor have good news preached to them" (11:2–5). The answer is significant even beyond its words, for it is the clue to a solution by the church of the problem that the End had failed to arrive. When Paul dealt with the problem in the Thessalonian Epistles, he resorted to the explanation that delay was intervening, but the End was nevertheless still to be expected. Matthew's solution is to suggest, here and elsewhere, that the End was not in reality a matter for the future, but that it had indeed begun, in the miracles which were taking place, though it was as yet not completely accomplished. The new scheme of things, accordingly, was not a matter of the future and of the Second Coming;

the new scheme, rather, had already begun with the first coming of Jesus.

Matthew does not eliminate the words of Jesus which point to the future, because the full consummation of the End is still to be realized. But he neutralizes the vividness of futurity by this section and similar ones. Beyond Matthew, the Fourth Gospel interprets the "future" End as completely in the past, having come with Jesus. Between the probably authentic preachment by Jesus of an early future End, and the subsequent implicit denial of futurity, we stand here at the midpoint.

Matthew portrays Jesus as continuing to evaluate John the Baptizer. Although John was a great man, his importance was less than that of any member of the "kingdom of God"; for John belonged to the old age, not to the new one (11:11–15). Here again Matthew weakens the futurity of the End by identifying the "kingdom of God" simply as the Christian church. So much, for our purposes, for the third block of discourse.

In the fourth block Matthew depicts Jesus as giving instruction on how to deal with the erring and the wayward. God's interest in the erring and His joy at their return are comparable to the situation of a man who had a hundred sheep, one of which had gone astray. The joy of the man on finding the one lost sheep was greater than his joy over the ninety-nine. As for men, an offended person should seek out the offender and talk to him privately. This failing, he should visit the offender, accompanied by witnesses. This, too, failing, the matter should be brought to the church. If the offender is still obdurate, he should be ousted from the church (18:10–17). While the parable of the shepherd may possibly go back to Jesus, the entire passage in its present form gives regulations for church conduct which it reads back into the time of Jesus.

Jesus conferred on the church full powers sanctioned by

heaven; the passage uses figurative language, like the rabbinic *halaka*, of loosing and binding, permitting and prohibiting. When in the church agreement exists, the matter agreed to is confirmed by heaven: "For when two or three are gathered in my name, there am I in the midst of them." The rabbis, somewhat similarly, give assurance that God's Shekina rests on two or three persons who are gathered for study of the Torah. This section in Matthew has gone a long way in the growing identification of the Christ with God.

In the fifth block, Matthew appends to the Marcan version of Jesus' revelation of the future a series of parables dealing with the End. It would come suddenly, as the flood had come in the days of Noah. As Noah was saved in the general destruction, so some would be saved at the End. As a householder, alert for burglars and apprised when and to what part of the house they will come, is fully prepared, so, too, the faithful should be alert and prepared. A faithful and wise servant is he whom the returning master — allegorically, Christ returning — finds doing the right thing; a wicked servant is one who uses the delay in the master's coming for misdeeds. Preparedness is illustrated, too, by the difference between five wise virgins who prepared to meet the bridegroom by having oil for their lamps, and five foolish ones who made no such preparations, and who were accordingly rejected when he came (24:37 to 25:3).

In waiting for the End, the faithful can learn from the servants of a man who, going on a journey, entrusted each of them with varying sums of money. Some invested their entrustment wisely and earned reward and the phrase "Well done, my good and faithful servant." But one of them, rather than invest it, simply buried his sum in the ground. For this failure to use opportunity the worthless servant was cast into the outer darkness when the master came home (25:14–30).

At the End, Jesus would come accompanied by angels, and sit on his glorious throne for judgment. Those who had been kind to his followers would go into eternal life; for "as you did it to one of the least of these, you did it unto me." Those who had been evil would go into eternal punishment (25:31–46). In these terms Matthew ends the fifth block of the words of Jesus. It is to be recalled that the Law of Moses is in five books; perhaps the five blocks are a conscious imitation of the five books.

We have noted in the third discourse that the kingdom of God in Matthew is often interchangeable with the Christian church. We have by now moved completely outside of Judaism, and the Church is both acutely conscious of its own individuality and, like any dissident religious movement, also greatly antagonistic to the rock out of which it was hewn.

We are still many decades before the time when Christian writings were gathered into a New Testament which conceivably could have served as the authority in church matters. In this still formative period, with Jesus' lifetime a thing of the past but with the collected New Testament as yet a thing of the future, authority lies in individuals believed to be authoritative. Such an individual, emerging in the Gospel of Matthew, is Peter.

At Caesarea Philippi, as in Mark, Peter recognized Jesus as "the Christ"; to this designation Matthew adds, "the Son of the Living God." Matthew says, further, that the recognition could have come to Peter only as a revelation from God. As Peter means "rock," Peter is the rock on whom the church is founded (16:13–20).

This high recognition of Peter intrudes in Matthew, and is absent from the parallel sections in both Mark and Luke. Peter, in Mark, is last portrayed in his three denials of Jesus; he is last mentioned in Mark in 16:7, in which verse the angel bids the two Marys to tell Peter and the other disciples to go to

Galilee, where Jesus will appear to them. Only by this passing mention has Mark indicated in any way that Peter's defection was a temporary one and that it was forgiven. In Mark, as we have seen, Peter plays a role which is quite ignoble. In Matthew, he plays a similar role, but the present passage seems to point to him, nevertheless, as the chief figure among the disciples, and to suggest that if he had ever fallen from an eminent position, he was restored to it. Luke becomes specific about Peter's restoration (Luke 22:32): "But I have prayed for you that your faith may not fail; and when you have turned again, strengthen your brethren." The turning and the strengthening are depicted in Acts 1:15. An appendix to the Fourth Gospel, its Chapter 21, portrays the risen Jesus as designating the erstwhile swerving Peter as the new shepherd of the sheep.

In the basic account in Mark there is at Caesarea Philippi no mention of future eminence for Peter; from Mark alone only verse 7 of Chapter 16, with its laconic mention, would suggest that the role of Peter was any but a consistently dark one. Perhaps some historical basis underlies the account of Peter's earlier defection from Jesus, although I doubt it. But if, as I have suggested, the Gospel of Mark represents a branch of the church which was Pauline, perhaps Matthew represents another branch which, in turning away from Paul's "liberty," looked to Paul's rival mentioned in Galatians, Cephas, as the proper apostolic guide.

Peter, it must be conceded, is quite an elusive figure to the historian. Was the Cephas of Galatians the same person as the Peter of the Gospels? Peter means "Rock" in Greek; Cephas means "Rock" in Aramaic. Christian tradition has assumed that the two were the same person; the two names are brought together in John 1:42, along with the name Simon. The problem is knotty, and its solution uncertain. It seems to me likely that

Simon Peter and Cephas were two different persons. As merged into one in the growing tradition, Simon-Peter-Cephas became the symbol for that branch of the church in the East which was more Jewish both in make-up and in orientation than the Western church, which was predominantly Gentile, and whose symbol became Paul.

Matthew rewrites Mark so as to rehabilitate Peter. Once rehabilitated, as here and in the later Gospels, Peter could be pointed to in the second-century church, by those who espoused a more conservative, settled form of church practice, as the true successor of Jesus, and as the person from whom true succession could be traced — all this in opposition to libertine churches of the second century which would have traced their charter back to Paul. The Roman Catholic Church, which follows a harmonizing trend to be discerned in Acts, traces itself back both to Peter and to Paul, but it bases its claim to sole legitimacy among the contemporary, multifarious versions of Christianity on the "keys of the kingdom" passage.

Another area in which Matthew goes considerably beyond what is stated by Mark is that of antagonism towards Jews and Judaism. We may note initially that Matthew occasionally adds a narrative to his Marcan base. Jesus, he tells us, was approached by a Roman centurion on behalf of a paralyzed slave. Jesus heals the slave, and the episode closes with the point of the anecdote: Jesus declared that he had not found anywhere in Israel an equal to the faith of the Roman, and that, accordingly, the Gentiles would supplant the Jews as the heirs of Abraham, Isaac, and Jacob.

Since Matthew is setting forth a legalistic Christianity, he cannot directly repudiate the legal process of the Pharisees, but only the Pharisees themselves in the series of bitter denunciations appearing in Matthew 23. These reflect the Christian side of mutual animosities which had grown up between synagogue and church. No comparable denunciations of Christians are preserved in Judaism, either in intensity or in bitterness, though they may well have been expressed. Unhappily for the subsequent history of the Jews, the words here are enshrined in the Christian Scriptures. Although Pharisees is the term used, Jews are meant; the later church's attitude is attributed to Jesus. According to the passage, Pharisees like external show and honors; they preach but do not practice; they do all their deeds to be seen by men. The title which they use, rabbi, is not to be used by the church (23:1–8).

"Woe to you scribes and Pharisees, hypocrites," is the repeated imprecation by which Jesus is depicted as introducing the seven grievances against the Pharisees. The allusion in the first woe, that the Pharisees themselves do not enter the kingdom of God, and yet prohibit others, is not fully specific, but it probably alludes to their preventing Jewish would-be converts from consummating any intention of joining the church. The second woe tells that the Pharisaic missionary movement succeeds only in making a convert twice as much the son of hell that a Pharisee is. Third, the Pharisees respect the gold of the Temple more than the Temple itself. Fourth, they observe minute details of the law, but forget justice, mercy, and faith. Fifth, they observe outward ceremonial purity, but neglect inner purity. Sixth, they appear outwardly to be righteous, like whitewashed sepulchres, but inwardly they are filled with uncleanliness. And seventh, they adorn the sepulchres of the righteous, but these very righteous men are the prophets whom their ancestors slew. Though the descendants aver that they would not have joined in the slaying of the martyrs, they confess thereby that they are the descendants of murderers. On them rests blood from the first murdered man, Abel, through the most recent, Zechariah the son of Berachiah. (The identification of Zechariah is uncertain; but he is probably a figure known from Josephus, *Wars*, IV, 5, 4, killed in 67 or 68 A. D.) All the responsibility for this bloodshed will come on the "present generation." Jesus laments for Jerusalem, whose children (23:32–35) might have been gathered to him, but were obstinate.

The conservative Christian who is determined to preserve the passage as the authentic words of Jesus needs to ponder whether he can then with intellectual honesty hold fast to a usual Christian view of Jesus as a benign and kindly soul. The passage is not from Jesus; it is a partisan utterance from a period of extreme antagonism; least of all is it to be taken as a fair or accurate description either of Pharisaism or of Judaism.

Matthew follows Mark rather closely in the accounts of the arrest, the crucifixion, and the resurrection. He supplies the name of the high priest, Caiaphas, which Mark had lacked (26:3). In Mark, the priests had given Judas thirty pieces of silver without being asked; Matthew tells us that Judas asked for the silver before betraying Jesus (26:14–16). To the man who cut off the ear of the high priest's slave Jesus issued a rebuke; twelve legions of angels could be summoned if Jesus wanted them, but how, then, would the fulfillment of Scripture take place (26:51–54)?

Mark had said that the high priests and the council had sought testimony to put Jesus to death; Matthew puts it that they sought *false* testimony (26:59). Where Mark had written, "Some stood up and bore false witness against him, saying, 'We heard him say, "I *will* destroy this Temple that is made with hands and *in three days* I will build another, not made of hand," ' " Matthew writes, "At last two came forward and said, 'This fellow said, "I *am able* to destroy the Temple of God and to build it in three days." ' " (In even later tradition, as in John 2:18 ff., Jesus is portrayed as actually saying that which Mark reports as false testimony). Matthew, though declaring the testimony to be false, reduces Mark's phrase from intention to one of ability, that is, from "I will" to "I am able." Mark had said that the testimony had failed to agree; Matthew omits this statement, for he does not wish the inference to be drawn that it was the disagreement of the testimony rather than its falseness which was the issue. The Marcan statement, "some stood up and bore false witness," implies that there were many who spoke out against Jesus; Matthew's "at last two came forward" suggests that in desperation a charge was concocted out of the whole cloth by only two people. Mark's version, with the mention of the Temple not made with hands, especially when read in the light of John 2:18 ff., could seem to sound too entirely credible to be dismissed as false testimony; by omitting it, Matthew strengthens his suggestion that it was not disagreement in the testimony, but the complete falsehood of it, which constituted the injustice done to Jesus (26:59–61).

After Jesus is delivered to Pilate, Matthew inserts a paragraph (27:3–10) to the effect that in remorse for the betrayal, Judas hanged himself; thereby Matthew emphasizes the innocence of Jesus. The thirty pieces of silver were used to buy a potter's field, for the burial of paupers, in fulfillment of a passage in Zechariah which Matthew wrongly attributes to Jeremiah. This is but one of two tales of the sad end of Judas; in Acts 1:18 it is told that Judas bought a field with the money, but he fell and "burst open in the middle and all his bowels gushed out."

In the scene before Pilate, Matthew adds a note to intensify Jewish guilt. Pilate's wife sent word to Pilate to have nothing to do with the righteous Jesus, because she had suffered about him that day in a dream (27:19). Matthew crowns the Jewish guilt by portraying Pilate as washing his hands, symbolic of his innocence; while all the Jews gathered there answered, "His blood be on us and on our children" (27:24–25). A Jewish commentator has said of this passage: "This is one of those passages which have been responsible for oceans of human blood, and a ceaseless stream of misery and desolation."

The drink offered to Jesus, which Mark described as "wine mingled with myrrh," becomes in Matthew "wine mingled with gall." The wine with myrrh was an analgesic, offered humanely; in Mark, Jesus refused it in order to die with full consciousness. In Matthew, the drink is a bitter one which Jesus first tasted and then rejected (27:34). "Wine mingled with gall" is an Old Testament phrase (LXX Psalms 69:22).

To Mark's statement that after Jesus' death the Temple curtain was torn, Matthew adds an earthquake which opened tombs. Bodies of saints were resurrected, and the resurrected went about the city, appearing to many (27:51–53). This is in conformity with the purpose of Matthew, to show that the End began in the past. It was the earthquake and the resurrections which prompted the Roman centurion to say, "This man was truly the son of God."

After the burial, Matthew adds a paragraph which tells that the priests and Pharisees obtained a guard from Pilate to watch over the tomb in order to prevent Jesus' disciples from stealing the body and falsely proclaiming that a resurrection had taken place (27:62–66). The passage reflects Christian and Jewish dispute over the credibility of the resurrection.

When the women came to the tomb on Sunday, there was no need, as in Mark, to wonder about rolling the stone away, for Matthew provides an earthquake, and an angel who both rolled the stone away and also made the guards become like dead men (28:2–4). But the Jews, Matthew tells us, bribed the soldiers to lie and to say that the disciples came by night and stole him away. Indeed, "This story has been spread among the Jews to this day" (28:11–15).

The eleven disciples (Judas was the twelfth) went to Galilee, to a mountain. There, when they saw Jesus, they worshipped him. Some, however, still doubted (28:16–17).

Jesus then said to his followers, "All authority in heaven and on earth has been given to me. Go therefore and make all nations into disciples, baptizing them in the name of the Father, and of the Son, and of the Holy Spirit" (28:18–19). This is the only mention of the Trinity in the usual text of the New Testament; the appearance of the formula indicates the distance traveled between the time of Jesus and the church with its set procedures.

Matthew, true to his bent, closes his Gospel with the injunction to the disciples to teach their successors to observe all that Jesus had commanded. The final word was the assurance that Jesus was with them always, to the end of the age.

According to church tradition, Matthew was originally written in Aramaic and thereafter translated into Greek. Modern scholarship, however, does not hold that the present book is a translation. If there was indeed a Gospel in Aramaic, it was not the present Matthew.

Scholarship seems almost unanimous in declaring that "Matthew" was a Jew who became a Christian, and that his Gospel represents "Jewish-Christianity." The view rests on several assumptions. One of these, paradoxically, is the rejected church tradition, just mentioned, that the Gospel was written in Aramaic, the Jewish vernacular of the time.

A second basis, which seems to me equally insecure, rests on the fact that Matthew is replete with quotations from the Old

Testament. It is assumed that such a knowledge of the Old Testament would have been the possession only of a Jew, especially at a period as relatively early as the year 100. But, on the other hand, how could the Christian movement, which as early as Paul used the Jewish Scriptures, have continued to grow without some dexterity in Scripture? It does not seem to me reasonable or likely that when the Christian movement was over a half century old, facility in the Greek Scriptures should have been outside the grasp of a Gentile Christian.

A third assumption notes, correctly, that Matthew promulgates a Christian "law." In the view of Christians, especially of modern Protestants, Paul's greatness was that he shattered legalism. "Legalism" for such minds is a regrettable, second-rate tendency, and it tends to be identified in some Christian minds as a quality only of Jews. The line of argument seems to run: there is legalism in Matthew and legalism in Judaism, therefore Matthew must be Jewish. Jewish, that is, until he became a Christian — then he was able to rise above "racialism" and "nationalism" and end up with his injunction to a world mission, found at the close of the Gospel. Indeed, it is contended, the crowning proof that Matthew was a Jew is the unrelieved bitterness of his attacks on Jews, since only one who has left a communion is apt to exhibit such bitterness towards it. (The miserable work of Jewish converts to medieval Christianity could bear out the insight in this contention.)

But if a moment's thought is given to the circumstance that a break with legalism, as in Amos and in Paul and others, is as equally a characteristic of Judaism as legalism itself, then the naïve or partisan identification of Judaism and legalism can be abandoned. Thereafter one can move to the more tenable observation that legalism, and its opposite, "Prophetism," are qualities or manifestations universal among peoples, and in any religious communion. It is somewhat strange to Jewish ears to hear Catholics, with their elaborate canon law, or Anglicans with theirs, or Methodists with their Discipline, ascribe to Jews exclusively a tendency equally persistent in themselves.

Protestants have been acutely aware of the legalism in Catholicism, but apparently not nearly so vividly alert to it in peculiarly Protestant forms. Denomination after denomination in Protestantism has extolled Paul for breaking the shackles of narrow legalism; and denomination after denomination has felt compelled to devise its own, equally necessary, legalism. Paul himself felt called upon to give specific advice and injunctions, abstaining thereby from a total reliance on "fruits of the spirit."

Both facets of the double notion that legalism is exclusively Jewish and that legalism is necessarily bad are products of what cannot escape delineation as a conceit. The Code of Theodotius, the Siete Partidas, the Common Law of England, and the Napoleonic Code were not produced by Jews. These monuments of legalism have been assessed with somewhat less derogation than has been accorded the Talmud.

The Gospel According to Matthew, in my judgment, was composed not by a Jewish Christian, but by a Gentile, out of the awareness that law and regulation are inescapably necessary for religious discipline in a growing and developing entity.

Matthew has little regard or respect for the Jewish law; it is a new Christian law which he is introducing. Matthew reflects the church experience that no denomination can flourish with all its members prophets. Followers as well as leaders are needed, and orderliness and stability require set and stated procedures. Matthew's new law is the initial bill of particulars, as it were, for a phrase found in Paul, the "law of Christ."

Matthew's phrase, "to fulfill Scripture," has a connotation of its own. The rabbis use a similar phrase, in this sense, that some present-day action conforms to or falls in with the ancient Scripture. In Matthew the intent of the phrase goes further. It is not that some contemporary circumstance has managed to coincide with what is written in Scripture — but that something entirely new has arisen which brings Scripture to a fullness previously unrealized. To fulfill Scripture in the rabbinic sense is to measure up to the standard; in the Matthean sense it is fulfillment in the sense of the creation of a new standard for which Scripture is only a prologue.

With new regulations for the new entity, the church, the break between Judaism and Christianity has become virtually complete. Church and synagogue have become so thoroughly distinct that the overt differences are greater than are the similarities. For the church, the Law of Moses is not only reckoned as superseded, but indeed obsolete.

We do not know what considerations dictated the order of the books in the New Testament. It seems hardly an accident that the first place is held by Matthew, a book of church law. This position of emphasis inevitably is an endorsement of the tacit assumptions of the Gospel of Matthew, that out of disorder, order must arise; out of uncurbed factionalism, regulatory discipline; out of diversity, uniformity and harmony. Just as the Old Testament, with its prophetic, historical, and poetical writings, precedes these by the Law of Moses, so, too, the various books in the assembled New Testament are preceded by the laws of Christ.

# XV

# The Gospel According to Luke

THE THIRD GOSPEL opens with a formal preface, of a kind frequent in the literature of the time, in which the author dedicates his book to a man named Theophilus. We do not know who Theophilus was. The preface goes on to say that many others have already written about Jesus and the church, and that now the author is providing another account, this time accurate and orderly.

What does this reference to other writings mean? Some have interpreted the phrase as simply a literary cliché and do not think that anything is referred to, while others believe that Luke is alluding to actual books, such as the Gospels of Mark and of Matthew. This latter opinion seems to me to be the more likely, as the contents of Luke show clearly a use of earlier writings, specifically Mark and the collection of sayings of Jesus usually described as Q.

But if one were to assume either that Matthew used Luke, or that Luke used Matthew, then the sayings of Jesus found in the one Gospel would have come from the other — and we should not need to suppose that Q ever existed as an independent collection. Accordingly, a minority of scholars consider it unlikely that two different evangelists each independently followed the same procedure of combining Mark and Q, and such scholars suggest instead the use of Matthew by Luke, or vice versa. The majority of scholars, however, continue to hold that both Matthew and Luke combined Mark and Q, to which each added some special source or superimposed some extensive editorial additions.

Among those who are in that minority, the usual view is not that Matthew used Luke, but that Luke used Matthew. It is believed that the view of the Christ in Luke is advanced beyond Matthew, and therefore it is Luke which is the later writing. Accordingly, the reference in the prologue would be to Mark and Matthew, and possibly to other Gospels which have wholly or partly disappeared.

The evidence by means of which to solve the problem is less than conclusive; one is dealing with probabilities, not with certainties. I hold with the minority view; I believe that Luke was composed out of Mark and Matthew, and that Luke is not trying to write just another Gospel, but rather *the* Gospel. This effort leads him into editorial changes of quantity and significance; indeed, the important aspect of Luke's Gospel lies rather in how he presents his material than in what he presents. Luke's effort to be "orderly and accurate" implies his dissatisfaction with Mark and with Matthew. It seems to me that in the case of Matthew, Luke's dissatisfaction extends to the point of rejecting Matthew's basic contention that Jesus was the giver of a new law. He scatters Matthew's assembled discourse. Luke will insist that Jesus is not the creator of something which is new, but that he represents the continuation, at its highest point, of that which is old.

But it is not only the dissatisfaction with earlier Gospels which motivates Luke. He has positive convictions which he wishes to offer, and a sturdy insistence, in his revision of older views, which he is impelled to offer. These matters will unfold as we proceed. But a preview of them will be helpful along the way.

In place of Matthew's emphasis on Jesus as the new lawgiver and on his church as the heir of the new order, Luke insists that the church is not a new order but the continuation of Judaism. For him the period of Jesus is only one part of a larger account, which he extends into the career of Paul. The Acts of the Apostles, which scholarship has established as also written by Luke, can be considered as the second volume of Luke's Gospel, and the evangelist's theme is the same in both volumes. Luke writes from the standpoint of Gentile Christianity, and he defends the proposition that Gentile Christianity is the true Judaism. Jewish Judaism, that is, the Judaism which did not become Christian, is an error-laden movement, and the Jews have been rejected by God. So false, indeed, was Jewish Judaism that it failed to recognize the Christ, and it failed to discern the complete fidelity of the true Judaism to the historic past. Neither Jesus nor the subsequent Christians ever broke with Judaism; rather, they were the natural and proper heirs of the true Judaism. It is true, Luke seems to concede, that the Christian movement and Judaism are hardly friendly to each other. But the fault lies with the Jews. Jesus, Peter, and Paul had not broken with Judaism; the Jews had, despite this fidelity, broken with them.

In addition, any unfriendliness on the part of the Romans towards Christianity rested on the false assumption that there was some basic tension between the Romans and the Christians. Luke avers that this was not true; indeed, it was never true. The Christian movement had had in itself no real difficulties with the Romans, or at a minimum the minor difficulties encountered were the result of the mischief perpetrated by the Jews. Accordingly, the Roman authorities might well look with favor on the Christian movement.

In setting forth Christianity as the true Israel, Luke diverges from Mark and Matthew, who had allocated the appearance of the resurrected Jesus to the remote Galilee, rendering it possible to suppose that the Christian movement came only from the fringes of Judaism. Luke, instead, depicts Jerusalem as the place where Jesus appeared after his resurrection: Christianity came from the very heart of Judaism.

Against this background, the structure and the peculiarities both of the Gospel According to Luke and of the Acts of the Apostles provide within themselves a consistent pattern. Luke's attitudes move him to a quite free use of his sources, and we shall see later that he is as little bound to authentic history in Acts as he is in his Gospel to Mark and to the sayings of Jesus.

Although Luke reflects Paul's point of view that the Law of Moses is obsolete as a means of salvation, Luke does not stress the rejection of the Jews. To do so would hardly comport with the view that the Christian movement had been undeviatingly faithful to Judaism. Nor can Luke go to the other extreme of Matthew's supplanting of the old Law with a new Law, since he wants to argue for Christianity as the continuity of Judaism and not as a rupturous displacement. This, which is central in Matthew, is by implication directly repudiated in Luke.

Our survey above of Mark and Matthew has recounted most of the contents of Luke. It is not necessary here, then, to recapitulate the contents, but only to show the character of the Lucan additions or editorializing which reveal his purposes and preferences. While Luke follows the basic divisions of a period in Galilee, a journey to Jerusalem, and the events in that city, the structure of his Gospel has some significant variations.

Like Matthew, he begins with the birth and background of Jesus, though in a manner utterly divergent from Matthew's. In place of Matthew's rather mechanical use of proof-texts, Luke gives a highly polished and literary account of the foreshadowing of the virgin birth of Jesus. Luke begins not with the birth of Jesus, but with the birth of John the Baptizer. To John's father, Zechariah, appeared an angel, not anonymously, but specifically named Gabriel, announcing the birth of a son destined to be a forerunner like Elijah, and to prepare the people not, as we might have expected, for the Messiah, but rather, as Luke puts it, for the "Lord"; customarily, Luke so alludes to Jesus. The appearance of Gabriel to Zechariah took place in the Temple; as a result, Zechariah was stricken dumb. He went home to his wife Elizabeth, who became pregnant (1:5–25). In the fifth month of that pregnancy Gabriel appeared in Galilee to Mary, here described as Elizabeth's kinswoman. Just as the barren Elizabeth, an old woman, was miraculously pregnant, so Mary, barren through being unmarried, would conceive through the Holy Spirit (1:25–38).

Mary then went to visit Elizabeth. The baby in Elizabeth's body leaped with joy at Mary's greeting, and Elizabeth was moved to exclaim to Mary, "Blessed are you among women, and blessed is the fruit of your womb." Even before birth John the Baptizer knew that Jesus was to come (1:26–45).

Luke next reproduces a poetic prayer (the Magnificat), which most manuscripts attribute to Mary, although some manuscripts credit it to Elizabeth (1:46–55).

Mary remained for three months, apparently until just before Elizabeth's baby was born, and then returned home. At the birth of the baby some wanted to name him after the father, Zechariah. The father, unable to talk, and apparently deaf, too, wrote on a tablet, "His name is John." Promptly the disabilities left him, and he was able to talk and to bless God. The story of this miracle spread throughout the region, and people wondered what the child would become. Zechariah prophesied that the child would go before the Lord to prepare the way. John went out into the wilderness and remained there until the day of his manifestation to Israel (1:56–80).

Mary, now with child, was taken by her betrothed, Joseph,

from Nazareth to Bethlehem to be listed in the Roman census which was then being taken. The time for the birth arrived and, because there was no room for the parents in the inn, the child, wrapped in swaddling clothes, was put in a manger. To shepherds in the vicinity an angel appeared, telling them that on that day a Savior, Christ the Lord, had been born (2:1–11). The birth of the Savior, it seems to be suggested, coincided with the census, a great step in the establishment of orderly government and administration in the growing Roman world. We deal here with developed legend, as the complex phrase, "Savior, Christ the Lord," indicates. The shepherds were instructed to look for a child in a manger. Suddenly an angel, accompanied by a heavenly host, praised God (the passage is known as the Gloria) in these words: "Glory be to God in the highest, and on earth peace among men with whom He is pleased." The shepherds, finding Joseph, Mary, and the child, praised God for all that they had heard and seen (2:12–20).

Eight days later the child was circumcised and named Jesus. In further fidelity to Jewish practice, he was later brought to the Temple at Jerusalem for the redemption of the first-born son (*pidyon ha-ben*) — Luke here seems less than sure of the nature and procedures of the two Jewish practices. At the Temple, a pious old man named Simeon, who had been promised that he would not die before he should see the Christ, picked up the child and said, "Lord, now let me depart in peace." That is, he regarded the promise as now fulfilled. Another person at the Temple, a prophetess named Anna, likewise recognized in Jesus the one to whom all were looking forward (2:21–38).

When Jesus was twelve, he was taken to the Temple at Jerusalem at Passover time. Through an oversight, his parents set out for home without him. They returned to Jerusalem to find him sitting with teachers in the Temple and discussing profound questions. Told by his mother that they had been looking for him, Jesus replied that he had to be in his Father's house. His parents did not understand this cryptic answer (2:41–52). Such tales increase in number and in legendary character in Gospels which were not admitted into the New Testament; and such cryptic words, which appeared even in Mark, become more usual in the Gospel According to John. Some commentators equate the incident with bar-mitzvah, a ceremony for a Jewish boy at the end of his twelfth year. It is not a happy or correct equation. Bar-mitzvah probably did as yet not exist, but is a later institution. Moreover, it was (and is) a ceremony for the synagogue, not for the Temple. Finally, a youngster at bar-mitzvah exhibits his supposedly beginning maturity; the narrative in Luke, however, is a legend of how a divine being was, as a wonder-child intellectual, more mature than the finest teachers.

Luke has almost finished his prologue at this point. Fidelity to Jewish ways is his theme; there is no echo of the Gentile maze of Matthew.

After supplying some historical framework about kings and governors (3:1–3), in the usual ancient style, Luke introduces the now mature John the Baptizer. While he mentions Jesus' baptism by John, he glosses over it, appending it as an afterthought to his summary of John's career and imprisonment (3:4–22).

A genealogy, somewhat like the one with which Matthew had begun, appears in Luke immediately after the baptism. Matthew began with Abraham and progressed to later times; Luke begins with Jesus and works back not to Abraham, but to Adam (3:23–38). The genealogies are not completely in accord with each other. Also, Luke exhibits much interest in women in the line of descent. A genealogy beginning with Abraham is a genealogy of Jews; the genealogy from Adam is the genealogy of all men.

When Luke relates the temptation by the devil, he adds, artistically, that the devil departed from Jesus for a more opportune moment (4:1–12) — thereby foreshadowing the betrayal by Judas, occasioned by the devil.

As Luke relates Jesus' preaching in Galilee, he allocates virtually to the start of the mature career of Jesus the "rejection at Nazareth" (4:14–30), which the other two Gospels assign to a later time in Jesus' career. Luke is telling us that Jesus was rejected by the Jews right at the beginning. In his account Luke supplies what Mark and Matthew lack, that is, the particular teaching at Nazareth which they had described as eliciting astonishment. Luke tells us that Jesus, as was his custom, was in the synagogue. He stood up to read, and the book of Isaiah was handed to him. He turned to Isaiah 61:1–2 and read: "The spirit of the Lord is upon me, because he has anointed me to preach good news to the poor. He has sent me to proclaim release to the captives and recovery of sight to the blind, to set at liberty those who are oppressed, to proclaim the acceptable year of the Lord." Jesus gave the book back to the attendant and sat down. The eyes of all were fixed upon him. He said to them: "Today this Scripture has been fulfilled in your hearing."

There is not in Luke any suggestion, which scholars have affected to find in Mark, that there was in Jesus a "growing awareness" of his special role. I doubt that Mark intends any such idea; if he did, it is a motif uncongenial to Luke, for whom at all times Jesus is fully aware of a special mission.

The first response of the Jews to Jesus reads in the Greek that "all bore witness to him." The Revised Standard Version paraphrases the passage: "they all spoke well of him." While this paraphrase seems to go beyond the meaning of the Greek, it is quite faithful to the intent, namely, that Jesus' first words evoked approval. But in their subsequent wondering about him and in their asking each other, "Is not this Joseph's son?", Luke finds suspicion and doubt, to the point of interpreting their astonishment not as neutral bewilderment, but as antagonism. He portrays Jesus as replying to their question that no prophet is acceptable in his own country; moreover, Luke adds that Jesus spoke of the older prophets, Elijah and Elisha, saying that they, too, had done works of healing, but only to Gentiles. At this point Jesus was driven from the synagogue.

The section is quite difficult, especially if the initial response of the Jews to Jesus is intended to be a favorable one. It would seem to be Luke's purpose to see in Elijah and Elisha the prefiguring of his own conviction that the Jewish message was for Gentiles, and that the objection of the Jews to Jesus did not lie in any claims made by him or for him about a unique role, but only in Jesus' assertion that his appearance was specifically on behalf of Gentiles. Luke is saying, in short, that the Jews were ready to believe that Jesus was the awaited divine agent; they resented, however, his proclamation that his coming was not on their behalf. We shall notice presently how differently from Matthew Luke portrays the sending out of the twelve disciples.

Luke adds to the synoptic parable enjoining against putting new patches on old garments and new wine in old skins the comment, "No one after drinking old wine desires new, for he says the old is the good" (5:37–39). Some texts read, "the old is better." Whichever reading is correct, it is unmistakable that Luke does not want the parable to be interpreted in its natural way as a comparison between Christianity and Judaism as the new and the old. For him, Christianity is the continuation of the old, and must not be described as new.

In Luke, the Beatitudes are delivered from a plain (6:17), whereas in Matthew they are part of a sermon delivered from a mount. There are some minor differences in the two versions, but a general correspondence. There is in Luke's preface to the Beatitudes no suggestion of a "new law" enjoined from some mountain.

The anointing of Jesus by a woman, which in Matthew takes place in Passion Week, is found in Luke in the Galilee period (7:36–50). This occurs at a dinner where the host, a Pharisee, is rebuked — in context quite needlessly — for seeming inhospitality contrasted with the devotion of the woman. The point of the discussion between the Pharisee and Jesus is whether Jesus was to be recognized as a prophet. The Pharisee argued that Jesus could not possibly be, for otherwise Jesus would have known the woman's sinful past. In reply, Jesus forgave the woman's sins and rested his prophetic role on his loving forgiveness. The story is followed shortly by the mention of other women who were followers of Jesus (8:2–3). Luke is very much interested in women; it is likely that the exceedingly subordinate status of women in traditional Judaism was in marked contrast to their broader role in Gentile Christianity. The later books of the New Testament try to limit women in the holding of church offices — a reflection of their prominence.

Luke, in his account of Jesus' sending out the twelve disciples, has no mention of a limitation on them to preach only to Jews. "They departed and went through the villages, preaching the gospel and healing everywhere." Matthew does not expressly tell of the return to Jesus of the twelve. Luke, like Mark, does mention it, but most briefly, as though not too greatly interested in it (9:1–6, 10). It is to be recalled that there were twelve tribes of Israel; the twelve disciples are to be interpreted as a mission to Jews, though one of little success. As we shall presently see, Luke has still another account of the sending out of apostles.

Luke recasts Jesus' journey to Jerusalem (9:51 ff.). Significantly, the route followed runs from Samaria towards Jericho, always west of the River Jordan; it is more consistent with Luke's purposes than with the natural geography; neither Mark nor Matthew brings Jesus into Samaria, but they have him cross the Jordan in the North at Galilee and recross at Jericho. The motive for Luke's change is to show that Jesus' ministry was not limited to Jews, but extended to their enemies, the Samaritans.* The Samaritans did not welcome Jesus. By means of the section, however, Luke has prefigured the universal scope of the Christian message.

Shortly thereafter, Luke narrates that Jesus commissioned seventy other apostles (10:1–20). Seventy is the symbol, following Genesis 10, for the supposed number of nations of the world, a device frequent in rabbinic literature. The place from which the seventy are sent out is presumably Samaria. Earlier, the return

---

*The Jews and the Samaritans regarded each other as false pretenders to the ancient heritage of divine choice and revelation. The Samaritans were, from the viewpoint of the Jews, the descendants of alien tribes transported into the northern kingdom of Israel after the Assyrians had exiled the ten northern Israelite tribes from the region in the eighth pre-Christian century. These exiled ten tribes were probably swallowed up among the peoples where they were moved, but popular fancy conceived of them as lost in some ancient Shangri-La; subsequent fancy has found them in the Esquimaux, the American Indians, and even in the British people. The Samaritans and the Jews had their greatest difficulties at the time of Ezra (450 B.C.), and subsequent relations were exceedingly bitter. A temple, located on Mount Gerizim, served the Samaritans as the counterpart of the Temple at Jerusalem. Rival claims by each group asserted the validity of its temple and the invalidity of the other's. At the time of Jesus the Samaritans were numerous, and spread throughout the Mediterranean world; some literary fragments in Greek by Samaritan authors have survived. Today the Samaritans are still to be found, at Nablus, in Palestine, but in a community of less than two hundred souls.

of the twelve is passed over with little comment: "On their return the apostles told him what they had done." Here, however, Luke says: "The seventy returned with joy, saying, 'Lord, even the demons are subject to us in your name.'" It is as though Luke is suggesting that the mission of the twelve to Jews was fruitless, but that of the seventy to Gentiles was successful.

Luke uses material which in Matthew is the question about the greatest commandment and which culminates in the Golden Rule. The question addressed, according to Luke, is, however, not: "What is the greatest commandment?"; it is: "What shall I do to inherit eternal life?" It is the questioner, not Jesus, as in Matthew, who speaks the Golden Rule. Here the questioner, at Jesus' prompting, quotes from Scripture, while in Matthew Jesus quotes the Scripture himself; there Jesus is portrayed as describing the love of God as the first and greatest commandment, and the love of one's neighbor as the second commandment. Luke consistently avoids the suggestion that Jesus uttered anything like commandments, and his portraying of the questioner as the one citing Scripture is not accidental. In the context in Luke the section serves, moreover, as the prologue to a parable. The questioner goes on to ask, "Who is my neighbor?" Jesus' reply — which does not really answer the question — tells of a man journeying from Jerusalem to Jericho who was beset by robbers and beaten. A priest and then a Levite passed by the man without helping him. A Samaritan, in contrast, did succor the man (10:25-37). The parable answers, What is neighborliness?, not, Who is my neighbor? It is a touching tale of the callousness of religious officials contrasted with the kindliness of the humble. The cast of characters is hardly accidental, however, for the parable has the secondary purpose of aspersing Jews by means of an unfavorable contrast.

Several parables in Luke are so shaped that they are not simply pithy anecdotes, but sets of symbolic details. Jesus, when a guest at a meal, urged his host to invite as guests the poor and maimed rather than the wealthy who might repay his hospitality; the parable, which we have seen above, is that of the ruler who supplanted at the banquet those (the Jews) who did not respond with others (Gentiles) who were to be brought in (14:12–24). Another parable, about the prodigal son, tells of the younger of two sons who received his part of the family means, traveled to a distant country, and there squandered his property in loose living. Sad experience made him penitent, and he turned to his father, humbled and uncertain of his reception. The father welcomed him gladly, to the point of killing the "fatted calf" for a feast. So far the parable is an effective illustration of God's love of the repentant sinner. The account goes on, however, to depict the older son, who stayed at home (that is, the Jews), as refusing to go to the party (15:11–32).

Still another parable illustrates prudence; it tells of a dishonest steward who, to save himself from embezzlement charges, cleverly falsified the accounts. The parable has occasioned two difficulties to the traditional interpreters. One could obliquely infer that dishonesty is being commended, for the text reads: "The master commended the dishonest steward." The interpreters have wondered if "master" meant Jesus (the Greek word is the same as the Greek for Lord), or the steward's employer. Such difficulties fade when the parable is regarded as no more than the urging of prudence. Its mention of money, however, is followed by other comments on money and its proper use, and promptly the Pharisees are mentioned as lovers of money (16:1–14).

The mention of Pharisees leads to a comment on the Law, and here Luke's position is clearly set forth. "The law and the prophets were until John; since then the good news of the kingdom of God is preached. . . . But it is easier for heaven and earth to pass away than for one dot of the law to become void." Luke is telling us that the climax in the history of revelation has come through Christ, but that the old is by no means annulled. These passages, which are joined together in Luke, demonstrating the continuity of the Gospel with what has gone before, do appear in Matthew, but they are widely separated from each other, and appear in contexts that give different meanings. Matthew tells us that not a dot of the Law will pass away, but in the context of the new law, set forth in the Sermon on the Mount (5:17–18); his statement that "all the prophets and the law prophesied until John" comes in a later passage (11:13), in a discussion of John the Baptizer. That the two parts are brought together in Luke conforms with his consistent view that Christianity was not a new movement or a disruptive one, but the natural continuity.

Moreover, Luke uses the teaching about divorce to buttress this contention. Luke abstains from reproducing the view in both Mark and Matthew that the Mosaic sanction of divorce was a mistake; he makes the statement against divorce follow the assertion of the continuity of the Gospel with the Law and the Prophets. He intends thereby to illustrate what he has just said, that no dot of the Law can disappear, as witnessed by the circumstance that the Gospel not only does not abolish the requirements of the Law, but even prohibits the divorce which the Law has permitted (16:15–18). Christianity, again, is not a break with Judaism, but rather its natural extension.

Luke uses a story illustrating the doctrine of reward and punishment in the after-world in his usual symbolic way, again as a parable of Jesus. A rich man — he is unnamed, but often spoken of in New Testament studies as Dives, the Latin word for rich — and a poor man, Lazarus, have both died. The rich man went to "hell," where he thirsted. Lazarus, however, was received into the bosom of the patriarch Abraham. The suffering rich man could look over and see the happy Lazarus. It chanced that when both were alive the rich man had withheld help from Lazarus; now, however, he begged Lazarus for some water. Abraham replied that punishment or reward in the after-life was destined to counterbalance the experience of this life (16:19–25). So far the parable might have been told by any rabbi, but the narration continues. A great chasm has been fixed between the rich man and Abraham — an attitude in conformity with Luke's usual exaltation of the poor and animosity towards the rich. In replying, the rich man said to Abraham: "Then I beg you, father, to send Lazarus to my father's house, for I have five brothers, so that he may warn them, lest they also come into this place of torment." A rejoinder issues from Abraham: the brothers (that is, the Jews) have Moses and the prophets; let the brothers listen to them. The rich man responded: "No, father Abraham, but if some one goes to them from the dead (that is, the Christ), they will repent." Abraham said to him: "If they do not listen to Moses and the prophets, neither will they be convinced if some one should rise from the dead" (16:26–31).

There is nothing in the narrative to indicate that Lazarus has been resurrected from the dead, though this is to be obliquely inferred from his continued existence. In the Fourth Gospel a lengthy story relates Jesus' raising the dead man Lazarus. The parable here in Luke reflects the annoyance of the church at Jewish obduracy. Luke includes with his charge that Jews did not accept the Gospel the accusation that they were not even faithful to the Law or to the prophets.

An anecdote, described as taking place when Jesus was passing between Samaria and Galilee, relates that ten lepers appealed to Jesus for help, and he responded. Of these only one, and he a Samaritan, praised God for the healing (17:11–19). Again Luke is contrasting Jews unfavorably with non-Jews.

A question about the kingdom of God elicits from Jesus the reply: "The kingdom of God is in the midst of you" (17:20–21). The meaning of these words has led to acute difference of opinion. Do they mean that the kingdom of God is in your hearts? If so, then the delay in the coming of the End seems to have led to a reinterpretation of the kingdom as an inner security and serenity. Or, as others insist, do they mean that the kingdom of God is not in the future, but has already begun? Or do the words mean that it has not yet begun, but is very near? I incline to the second view.

In speaking of true piety, a parable draws the contrast between a self-righteous Pharisee, who thanked God for not being like other people, sinners, and a humble tax-collector who penitently beat his breast and, acknowledging his sins, prayed for mercy (18:9–14). The parable is a most effective one; as usual, however, the villain of the anecdote is a Jew.

As Luke relates the events of Passion Week, his changes, though minor, are significant. He omits the verse in Mark which seemed to set the time as shortly before the Passover; he adds minor touches specifically identifying the time as Passover itself and the meal as a Seder (such as Luke 22:7–8). The devil, who had departed at the Temptation, now returns to enter Judas. Luke rewrites the interview between Judas and the Jewish officials; these, according to Luke, were glad and engaged to give him money, although Luke does not specify thirty pieces of silver. As we noted above, Luke defers until Acts his account of the death of Judas.

Luke makes no mention of Gethsemane by name, as did Mark

and Matthew; but he reproduces the substance of the earlier Gospels. For Mark and Matthew, Gethsemane represents the passive acquiescence of Jesus in the painful incidents about to ensue; for Luke, the section becomes an example, intended to inspire emulation, of how Jesus withstood temptation. Luke intensifies the motif of temptation by portraying vividly the extreme agony through which Jesus passed. An angel came from heaven to strengthen him. He prayed earnestly "and his sweat became like great drops of blood falling down upon the ground." This vivid passage seems to be pointing to the example for those undergoing torture. It is absent, however, from many ancient manuscripts. The verses were either omitted by those copyists who objected to the vividness as unseemly human emotion in Jesus; or else they were added to those manuscripts which have them by some later hand in order to encourage the church under Roman persecution. It is impossible to decide which is the case; in my judgment, however, these words are basic to the text, and not a later interpolation.

The kiss bestowed by Judas is, in Luke's account, recognized by Jesus as the kiss of betrayal (22:47–48). The ear of the slave, which in Mark was cut off, is in Luke miraculously healed by Jesus' touch (22:50–51). Such an increase in vividness and the miraculous is for scholars a token of the growth of traditions as time passes on.

After the arrest, Luke specifies but one "trial" before the Sanhedrin, at dawn, in contrast to Mark's two meetings, the first at midnight and the second at dawn (Mark 14:55 and 15:1). Mark's time scheme seems to have given Luke some difficulty, since Mark has put into the available hours more incidents than the time would normally allow.

Luke omits completely the mention of an accusation that Jesus had threatened to destroy the Temple; he does not tell, as Mark did, of "false witnesses" who brought such an allegation. Jesus is tried, according to Luke, simply and only on the charge of being the Christ or the Son of God (22:67–71). The omission of the Temple matter is deliberate. This is consistent with Luke's rejecting, throughout the Gospel, of any suggestion that Jesus was ever disloyal to any Jewish institution. Earlier in the Gospel, Luke had glossed over Mark's account of the cleansing of the Temple, and he had abstained from reproducing Mark's assertion that the action evoked priestly hostility. As Luke tells it, the cleansing incident goes almost unnoticed, both by the priests and then by the reader of the narrative. Moreover, even after the cleansing, Luke tells us, Jesus was teaching daily in the Temple; the priestly hostility, therefore, which is present in Mark-Matthew, and which Luke apparently felt was too well-known to omit, is shown as being directed against the teachings of Jesus, not against the deed of cleansing. From Luke's standpoint, nothing in the teachings of Jesus is unfaithful to Judaism, and the hostility of the Temple officials is a result of their own perversity (19:45–48).

With this as background, the complete absence of any mention of the accusation about the Temple is to be discerned as the result of careful pruning. As we shall see again in Acts, the viewpoint which Luke is offering is that Christianity had only theological differences with Judaism; Luke upholds the Christian side of these "differences" as proper Judaism, even as he insists that Jesus never deviated in his fidelity to Judaism. Christian personalities, whether Jesus or Paul or others, were unfailingly loyal to Jewish requirements and practice. Luke has found uncongenial the implication in Mark and in Matthew that the Sanhedrin dealt with charges relating to specific deeds, or words, of Jesus.

Similarly, Luke omits the statement in Mark 14:64 that the

Sanhedrin condemned Jesus to death. Some scholars explain that Luke knew "historic facts," that the council lacked the authority to pronounce capital punishment; but other scholars retort that the council did have such authority. The question of the council's authority may be interesting, but it is hardly relevant here. Luke will not concede that an authoritative Jewish body found any reason to condemn Jesus. By eliminating a judicial sentence of death, Luke is better able to suggest that Jesus was the victim of illegality (22:66–71). The mocking and beating of Jesus, which in Mark followed the trial and were done by Roman soldiers, take place in Luke before the trial, at the hands of the Jewish guards (22:63–65).

In the scene before Pilate, Luke lists specific charges, numbering three, made by the Sanhedrin to the procurator; Mark has no specific charge. The items which Luke specifies are that Jesus perverted the nation, that he forbade tribute to Caesar, and that he claimed to be Christ the King. The absence of a charge in Mark might have invited incredulity in those who know Roman procedure, since the scene would hardly conform to Roman practice without some bill of particulars. The threefold charge, when read in context, would immediately remind the reader of the earlier section (20:2–26), in which Jesus had authorized the payment of tribute to Caesar, and the falsity of the second charge would impugn the honesty of the other two. The threefold charge, accordingly, can hardly fail to strike the reader as mere malice — this in conformity with the encompassing view that the troubles of the Christians with Rome were always traceable to the Jews. The first and third items maintain the form of theological differences, rather than infractions of legal requirements.

Three times in Luke's narrative (23:5, 14, and 22) Pilate is made to declare that Jesus was innocent; the Jews, and not the

Romans, it would seem, were the guilty ones. Indeed, Luke adds that Pilate took advantage of the presence in Jerusalem of King Herod of Galilee to send Jesus to him for examination. At Herod's hand, Luke admits, Jesus was ill-treated, but Herod, the proper Jewish authority, found no crime in him. Pilate thereafter wished only to chastise Jesus and then to release him. The mob protested; Pilate for a time persisted in his wish, but then he bowed to its desire (23:1–25).

The royal apparel, which, in the earlier Gospels, had been put on Jesus by Roman soldiers, is in Luke put on by the Jewish soldiers of Herod (23:11).

At the crucifixion some manuscripts, as we have mentioned, put into the mouth of Jesus the words: "Father, forgive them, for they know not what they do." The passage (23:34) is absent from some of the best manuscripts, and seems to be an interpolation.

Only after leading Jews had scoffed at Jesus on the cross did the Roman soldiers mock him. Luke makes the crucifixion of two "robbers," in an account more detailed than Mark's or Matthew's, coincide with that of Jesus. One of the robbers recognized that injustice was being done, and Jesus gave him the assurance of future bliss (23:35–43). Luke omits Mark's statement that the crucifixion took place at the third hour, about 9 A. M., possibly because such an hour left too little time for trials before the Sanhedrin, Pilate, Herod, and again Pilate. At the sixth hour, as in Mark, darkness came over the earth; many·early texts of Luke explain that an eclipse of the sun took place (23:44). Astronomically, this is impossible at the full moon of Passover; other texts omit this incongruous statement.

Luke replaces Mark's "My God, my God, why hast thou forsaken me?" with "Father, into thy hands I commend my spirit." Luke changes the words, which Mark said that a Roman centurion spoke, into the judgment, "Certainly this man was innocent."

The burial of Jesus is described as taking place on Friday night; he is put into a new tomb. Luke adds about Joseph of Arimathea that though Joseph was a member of the Sanhedrin, he had not consented to the accusations against Jesus. Although the women are mentioned as resting on the Sabbath, Luke inconsistently assigns to that day the preparation of spices and ointments. No mention is made of the stone put before the tomb; but, oblivious of the omission, Luke tells us that "the stone" was rolled away (23:50 to 24:4).

The one young man of Mark becomes two angels in Luke, as the miraculous steadily grows. The words which in Mark prefigure a resurrection appearance in Galilee are completely altered, resulting in the omission of a proposed appearance in Galilee. For Luke, the risen Christ appeared in Jerusalem in proximity to the Temple. In his portrayal of Christianity as the true continuation of Judaism, Luke cannot relegate the resurrection appearance to Galilee, the fringe of Palestine. Luke relates that the women promptly told the disciples and other followers of the visit to the tomb, but they were not believed (24:5–11).

For the remainder of his Gospel (24:13–53) Luke lacks a Marcan basis. He tells us that two disciples were on their way to Emmaus, a village near Jerusalem. Jesus drew near and went with them, but they did not recognize him. They told him the story of Jesus, of the crucifixion and the empty tomb. Thereupon Jesus rebuked them for their slowness of belief, and he interpreted for them in all the Scriptures the matters concerning him. But only when they reached the village, and when, at the supper table, he broke bread for them, did they recognize him. He promptly vanished from them. The two returned to Jerusalem, where the disciples were gathered. Immediately they were informed that Jesus had already appeared to Simon (Peter).

At this point Jesus appeared again. The people were afraid, thinking that they were seeing some disembodied spirit. Jesus asked them to look at his hands and feet, apparently for the marks of the nails used in the crucifixion. He asked them to touch him, to see that he was substance and not a mere spirit. Moreover, he asked for food, and he was given some fish, which he ate.

Jesus then reminded them of words which he had spoken to them earlier, that the Christ would suffer, that he would rise on the third day, and that repentance and forgiveness of sins should be preached in his name to all the nations, beginning from Jerusalem. He directed them to remain in Jerusalem until divine power should come upon them — this touch foreshadows an event, "Pentecost," to be related in Acts.

Jesus lifted his hands and blessed them. Then he parted from them — some texts add that he was borne up to heaven. Acts tells us that the period between the resurrection and the ascension was forty days; here, however, no indication of elapsed time is given. The disciples, Luke concludes, were continually in the Temple, blessing God.

By his additions, omissions, and rearrangements, Luke has carried through his motifs with striking consistency: Christianity was the true Judaism, undeviatingly loyal and emerging from the center. Its difficulties were never with Romans but only with "Jews," whom God has rejected and supplanted as the true Israel by bringing Gentiles in instead.

The Gospel of Luke comes from the Greek dispersion at some time between 100 and 140. An occasional scholar would carry the date even as far as 150. I would date it nearer 150 than 100. The usual view assigns the Gospel to Rome.

For Christianity to have rested only on Matthew's view that Christianity was a new church with a new law was to forfeit what in the ancient world (as in the modern) was a precious possession: the claim to antiquity. The Jewish historian Josephus, in writing about the year 90, in order to commend the Jews to the Romans, deliberately called his book "The Antiquities of the Jews." Josephus spends several chapters in demonstrating by quotations from Greek writers how truly ancient Judaism was. So, too, Philo and other Graeco-Jewish authors stress the high antiquity of the heritage.

Luke wishes to avoid the charge that Christianity was new or marginal; he insists that it is central and truly ancient. Though he does not go so far as some of the later church fathers, who made veritable Christians out of the Biblical forebears, Luke points the way to the next step.

Regarding Matthew's view of a new law, Luke is too deeply Pauline to be favorable to a "legalism." The disinclination of most scholars towards the view that Luke used Matthew is based on their assumption that Luke would never have broken up such blocks of Matthean material as the Sermon on the Mount. In holding with the minority who affirm that Luke used Matthew, rather than Mark and Q, I believe that Luke consciously and deliberately excised the Matthean legalism. Luke retains the Beatitudes, but not as a prescribed code; he holds on to what Matthew tells us Jesus taught, but never in the form of a commandment from Jesus.

Over and over again, especially in Acts, Luke speaks of the "Holy Spirit." So abundantly does it appear that some scholars have aptly suggested that Luke's two volumes are less a history of the visible church than an account of the historical working of the Holy Spirit. Direct divine inspiration, rather than conformity to some antecedent code, is Luke's principle of attaining unity in the church. He does, it is to be conceded, portray and counsel obedience to the proper church officials; but these, it is to be remembered, function through possessing the Holy Spirit.

No words are too extravagant to praise Luke's literary art. Not only is his skill revealed in the technical aspects of fine writing, but his warmth, his capacity for eliciting the responsive sympathy of the reader, and his gift for characterization and for human touches are unmatched in the New Testament and, indeed, are equalled in very few works of literature.

# XVI

# The Historical Jesus

ABOUT THE TIME of the American Revolution, a leading intellectual doctrine called Rationalism emerged in Western thinking. The movement, which exalted man's reason and common sense and looked askance at the supernatural and the miraculous, has persisted as a dominant trend into recent times. It was under the impact of Rationalism that the beginning was made in the historical study of the Gospels.

It was inevitable within this framework of thought that the view became crystallized that much of the New Testament had lost its authority. The Epistles of Paul bore the brunt of an attack on mysticism, and ultimately a Christian scholar was to declare that Paul had substituted a religion about Jesus for the religion of Jesus. The Gospels, it was then averred, were irrational accounts, with incredible details; but there were some fine ethical teachings by Jesus, which were valid, even if the framework in which they were preserved was not. If only the Gospels could be stripped of the legendary and the supernatural, so the argument ran, then the ethics of Jesus would emerge more clearly, and the historical Jesus would be discernible as a man whom rational men could imitate. The need, accordingly, was to "recover" this "historical Jesus."

What manner of man was Jesus? Was he a Jewish Messiah? A great teacher? A prophet? The end of virtually all scholarly Gospel study was directed to the goal of answering this most insistent question. The Gospels had to be studied for themselves and for their relationship to each other; their broad background needed minute investigation. It is no exaggeration to say that virtually every phrase, or even every word in the Gospels, was scrutinized with exacting care. No stone was left unturned in the great quest.

Along the way, a number of efforts were made to answer the question, "What manner of man?" The answer almost invariably was influenced by some special interest of the answerer. The man who learned rabbinic literature quickly noted Jesus' resemblance to the rabbis, and the answer was given simply, Jesus was a rabbi. Or, another who drew together some clews from here and there answered that the historical Jesus, like a more typical Jewish messianic claimant, had been a political rebel against Rome. Christian Old Testament scholars saw him as the last and greatest of the prophets. For several decades men interested in social problems were sure that Jesus was a social reformer. Then, later, a school of mythologists used the term Christ-myth to express the conviction that there had never been a historical Jesus at all. More recently, some popular authors have indirectly depicted Jesus as a liberal rabbi, a Quaker, a Unitarian, or, in one atrocity, an advertising expert.

It is quite easy to be glib about the historical Jesus. Some popular novelists who have written about the life and times of Jesus are able to speak with a facility that an earnest student lacks. Their works give us not history, but imaginative portraits. The insistent question remains, What manner of man was the historical Jesus?

Jesus is mentioned in the rabbinic literature, but the passages are rather late retorts to post-New Testament Christian claims. They are of no value for the history of Jesus. A mention of Jesus in Josephus is regarded by most scholars as an interpolation; and the handful of conservatives who do not declare in favor of the interpolation concede that the passage is so reworked as to be of no historical value. Jesus is not mentioned in

Greek or Latin histories of the period. Only one bit of writing that purports to be in his hand is extant, contained in a legend, of no historical relevance, of his having written in Greek to a certain king, Abgar.

The Gospels, then, are our only real source. But, we have said, they came at least two or three generations after Jesus; not from Palestine, but from the Diaspora; and they were written in Greek, not in Aramaic. Some pericopes, we have said, were shaped by the church, while others were created by it. Within almost every pericope the hand of the growing church can be discerned. It is only within the narrowest limits that one can discern readily separable layers of traditions. The Gospels do not in reality tell us about Jesus; they tell us about the faith, the problems, and the interests of the church which created them.

If the hand of the church is so clearly discernible, is it not possible to remove later accretions and get back to a historical kernel? Scholars have found it partly possible. Even the most skeptical scholars of our day do not deny that some materials in the Gospels go back to Jesus. For example, it is unlikely that the church, forming the Gospels generations after Jesus, would have deliberately ascribed to him a prediction of the early End which by their time was so clearly wrong, unless it was part of an authentic tradition. Thus many scholars consider the Gospel materials to have a large measure of historical reliability about Jesus, though they would not insist on the historicity of every detail, and they would concede that the historical materials are shaped considerably by the developing church. Other scholars, perhaps fewer in number, find that the accretions in the pericopes are so thoroughly blended with what may have been authentic materials that to remove the accretions leaves a formless remainder; and to retain them yields a totality so obviously comporting with the later church of the dispersion that it supplies no great illumination for the historical Jesus. Perhaps we might call the first group of scholars the moderates and the second group the extremists.

There appears to be among moderates no thorough agreement as to what sections of the Gospels can yield historical data about Jesus, and two moderates can often be quite far apart from each other. What the moderates have in common is not an agreement on what is historical, but rather the conviction that there is much historical material about Jesus in the Gospels. The moderates, accordingly, go in the direction of the extremists, but not nearly so far. Indeed, among the moderates there are perceptible differences in the distances which now one and now another travels.

Most moderates would probably conclude that no secure biography of Jesus can be written. But not even the extremists would permit this circumstance to lead to a denial that Jesus is a historical character. In the 1910's a few scholars did argue that Jesus never existed and was simply the figment of speculative imagination. This denial of the historicity of Jesus does not commend itself to scholars, moderates or extremists, any more. On the basis of simple human experience, it seems to most scholars more likely that a historical personality was elevated into divine rank, than that a speculative abstraction was turned into some fictitious person. To believe the latter would raise the problem of why a Jew, of Galilean origin, would have been hit upon as the fictitious embodiment of a divine being. Why not a Roman, of noble birth, of great education and wealth? The obscurity and humbleness of the background of Jesus, preserved by the church even in the face of its deification of him, form a compelling argument that he was a historical character.

While the liberal scholar will concede that some, or much, or even most, of the data which the New Testament reports about Jesus is unhistorical, he concludes that to deny his historicity entirely is neither necessary nor reasonable. It seems perfectly natural that behind the accrued beliefs there was a historical person; and the burden of proving a case would today seem to fall upon those who would deny that Jesus ever existed, not upon those who affirm it. Indeed, when resort is made to tolerably reasonable proofs, the weight seems in the direction of affirming that Jesus lived, even though Jewish and Roman sources of his day fail to mention him. The mention of a mother and of brothers and sisters of Jesus in the Gospels, and the mention of James in Paul's First Epistle to the Corinthians, are understandable only as genuine historical reminiscences, but not as possible by-products of speculation, since their very nature would tend to be refuted by the speculative deification. In short, the New Testament has so many overtones about Jesus which point to a historical person that it is excessive skepticism to doubt the direct statement that he was a historical person who was born, lived, and died. The "Christ-myth" theories are not accepted or even discussed by scholars today.

The quest for the historical Jesus, that is, for the precise biography of the man, began with optimistic certainty that it would be successful in all details, and more than one premature cry of "eureka" has echoed through the scholarly world. But modern scholarship appears to be skeptical of the long expected success. Indeed, some of the extremist scholarship even concludes that we cannot be certain that any single incident about Jesus, or any word attributed to him, is genuine. More moderately, others would hold that a general portrait of Jesus is discernible; a portrait perhaps like one painted in oil which must be viewed from some distance.

The political rebel, or the social reformer, or the teacher par excellence, or the rabbi, or the prophet was never the center of the New Testament faith. Sentimentality may invest parables attributed to Jesus with a value far beyond what the words carry, or obscure statements may be considered to be pertinent to a given cause. Yet it must be insisted that the church did not worship the Christ as a master of parable, nor as a climax in the line of Amos or Hosea, nor as a precursor of Thomas Jefferson or of Abraham Lincoln. The church worshiped him as the Christ in whom God was revealed. Whatever it preserved or created in the Gospels was retained because it had some direct or indirect relationship to God's revelation and to the need of the church. The church insisted that the revelation of God in Christ was in the historical Jesus, but the New Testament faith is centered in the divinity of the Christ, not in the historical man Jesus.

The quest for the precise, human Jesus has not been successful. Indeed, we can see now that it was foredoomed to failure since it essayed something impossible, on an attractive but deceptive premise, that literary materials created out of supernatural beliefs would submit to scholarly sifting and yield a naturalistic residuum.

A single, unified catalogue of the teachings of Jesus proves to be as impossible to extract from the Gospels as is the historical impression of Jesus himself. To a question such as, What was Jesus' view of sin?, three varying answers, according to Matthew, Mark, and Luke, present themselves. Did Jesus prohibit divorce? The precise answers to such questions cannot be direct, but must be conditioned by the fact that Mark and Luke may say one thing, but Matthew another. Or, each evangelist may give a different answer. Or one or two may be silent on the matter.

Only if one wants a semi-historical answer, or an unconsciously or deliberately mendacious one, or a careless summary, can one stop at the statement, Jesus said this, or Jesus taught that. It is possible to report on Jesus only as the evangelists report on him.

Many of the statements attributed to Jesus are paralleled in the ancient Jewish literature. Some Jewish scholars have used this circumstance to deny originality to Jesus, while others have used it to show the "essential Jewishness" of Jesus.

One needs to note that the parallels have usually been scrutinized for facets of similarity, and not nearly so often for facets of difference. Moreover, the rabbinic literature has been used with considerable carelessness, not only by Jewish scholars, but also by Christians. Not alone has the motive existed either to glorify Jesus at the expense of the rabbis or the rabbis at the expense of Jesus, but ordinary cautions of primary concern in the historians' method have been tossed aside. Excerpts from the difficult rabbinic literature, available in convenient translation, especially in a highly commendable five-volume German commentary (known as *Strack and Billerbeck*), have encouraged both the imprudent and, one must say, the impudent.

Even when bias and partisanship are absent from the hearts and minds of scholars, the comparisons are seldom capable of realization. This is true not only because the Jesus of the Gospels, as we have seen, is not completely the "original" Jesus but has been enriched with additions by the church, but also because of significant factors in the rabbinic literature.

Rabbinic traditions, parables, and statements are older than the time of Jesus. Some of these appear in non-canonical works, such as the Book of Jubilees; some appear in Josephus. But the earliest rabbinic collections, which contain the oldest material, were written down two centuries after Jesus. The material in the collections includes some which undoubtedly antedates Jesus — but to separate the layers in the rabbinic literature is a task of great delicacy, and one which has yielded, for the few who have tried it, no abundant agreement. Much of the parallel material comes from rabbinic collections, which were made in Babylonia, and not in Palestine, in even later centuries; these later collections admittedly also contain very old material, but again the uncertainty exists about the age of relevant passages. Some Jewish scholars seem to believe that since some of this material is demonstrably older than Jesus, potentially all of it is; and some Christian scholars, overlooking the fact that late collections contain quite ancient materials, declare that the true priority and hence the inherent virtue of originality belong to Jesus. But since controlling criteria are absent, these quarrels about priority are as useful, and truly as relevant, as that about the chicken and the egg.

Even when the rabbinic literature is used in a non-partisan manner, it does not furnish a full and exact understanding of the time of Jesus. Just as the Gospels reflect, in their presentation of older material, the newer times in which they were recorded, so, in their own peculiar way, the rabbinic collections reflect the interests of the editors. Pharisaic in its outlook, rabbinic literature has little that is charitable to say about the Sadducees. So selective is it in what it offers that it mentions neither Philo nor Josephus; we should not know from the rabbinic literature about the mere existence of most of the other preserved Jewish writings called Apocrypha and Pseudepigrapha. Traditions older than the year 70 are to be found in the rabbinic literature, but only in the form of stray bits.

It is to be remembered that between the time of Jesus and the time of the recording of rabbinic literature, the tremendous upheavals of 70 swept the Pharisees into the ascendancy. The destruction of the Temple in 70 ended the Temple cult and the Sadducean movement which presided over it. The Pharisees, who had been until then an active but possibly small minority among many minorities, rose with their institution, the synagogue, to become practically synonymous with Judaism.

Is the historical Jesus to be reckoned as close to the Pharisees, despite the anti-Pharisaic tone of the Gospels? Or is he, a Galilean, more aptly to be joined with some now obscure sectarian group, possibly the Essenes or the Fourth Philosophy? Was he an *am ha-aretz*,* as some scholars have suggested (though they have not agreed on the meaning of the term) on the basis of the contempt expressed in the Pharisaic literature?

Since the period before 70 in Palestine is not readily to be recovered from rabbinic literature because of its Pharisaic one-sidedness, these variables tantalize the historian. (The Dead Sea Scrolls serve most conspicuously in underlining the limitations on, and the uncertainties in, our knowledge; they do not materially increase our specific knowledge, but only offer some corroboration of what was already known.)

The end result is that the more closely we look for exactness in details, the more elusive it is. The reluctant conclusion seems to me this, that to attempt to fit the historical Jesus into his Jewish setting is to put a somewhat uncertain figure into an uncertain background. We are on the safest ground when we are the most general; when we proceed to specific matters, definiteness eludes us.

Moreover, respecting the comparison of Jesus and the rabbis, there would seem to be little gained from contrasting a single individual with a host of individuals. It needs to be said, again if necessary, that the motives in such comparisons, even when they are unconscious, are not without some impetus to exalt the one party at the expense of the other. Some writers, especially

---

*It seems to me that this variously explained term means simply a rural person.

Jews, taking their cue from the Fourth Gospel, speak of Jesus as a "rabbi," even though that title was not used by Jews until after the time of Jesus. This title would, from one aspect, "raise" Jesus from the supposedly low level of a political rebel, or, from another, it would lower him from a supposedly loftier one of uniqueness. For many Protestants the role of rabbi seems understandably insufficient; their tradition, having broken with priestly Catholicism, puts great store on the laymen. Some Protestants, accordingly, insist that Jesus was not a rabbi but a "lay" prophet who broke with the priesthood of his day — and some such Protestants seem mistakenly to equate the rabbinate — a thoroughly lay institution — with the priesthood! The motive in terming Jesus a prophet is to counter the priestly claims of Catholicism; in Catholicism, Jesus is the prototype of the priest, a view derived from its explicit formulation in the Epistle to the Hebrews.

Since motive, of aggrandizement or of reduction, enters into the comparisons, objectivity fades and even disappears. This is as true of comparisons made by partisans of Protestantism and Catholicism as it is true of Christian and Jewish partisans.

The viewpoint advanced here is not that the comparisons should not be made between the rabbis and Jesus, and not that the effort to set Jesus in his Jewish background is unworthy. On the contrary. But scholarship has tried, even desperately, to do exactly that and on substantial basis; but when more than generalities have been considered, the effort has failed. Because the tools for an objective comparison are lacking, whatever comparisons emerge are the result of predisposition and partisanship.

Since in the past, and even in the present, the epithet of "Christ-killer" has been directed by some Christians at Jews, and the epithet has often been accompanied by physical on-slaught — and this may well continue in the future, too — the search for the historical facts relating to the crucifixion has long been a Jewish concern. Jews have written abundantly, and feelingly, to show that the epithet does not rest on sound histor-ical bases. Crucifixion was a Roman form of punishment; hence, it is argued, the Romans, and not the Jews, crucified Jesus; secondly, the judicial procedures described in the Gospels do not accord with Jewish practices, and therefore the Gospel accounts are not historical. To the first point, the reply has been made that while the Romans, indeed, did the actual crucifying, it was at the behest of the Jews; on the second point, there exists a huge literature elaborately defending the supposed authenticity of the Gospel record by demonstrating that the trial was in conformity with such irrelevant judicial processes as those, for example, of British Common Law. The Jewish retort may be just, but it has hardly been widely effective.

For those Christians for whom there is meaning or satisfaction in blaming Jews of two thousand years ago for something which transpired, and who enjoy exacting from Jews of our day, or from their children, some penalty for the transmitted guilt, the recourse to historical scholarship is totally useless. So, too, is the appeal to conscience or to Jesus' summary of the Golden Rule, or to any standard of ethics or justice. There have been, are, and probably will be forever some Christians to whom this single item of New Testament tradition is more vivid than anything else, and Jews must face the reality of the fact. Especially in the week before Easter, Jews need not be surprised to read in their daily newspaper abstracts from sermons derived from the crucifixion account which may upset them.

There are many Christians for whom a distinction between the Jews of two thousand years ago and those of our day still seems possible, yet whose fidelity to their training conditions them to affirm and transmit the blame of the ancient Jews for the crucifixion. Such Christians can wholeheartedly oppose discriminations against the Jews of our day — which are often abetted unconsciously by the words and phrases which these people use.

There are, however, Christians in abundance who recognize the circumstance that the anti-Jewish tone of the New Testament is the product of an age and of a set of conditions. They point out that the progressive shift of blame from the Romans to the Jews in the developing Christian literature, both within the New Testament and beyond it, is a result of the need to appease the Romans, and, further, that the church conviction that it had taken the place of the Jews in God's favor made concrete the blindness attributed to the Jews by extending it to the point of malicious, premeditated responsibility for the death of Jesus. These Christians deny that anti-Jewish sentiment is a necessity for the Christian faith. There is quite an extensive literature, written by Christians for Christians, deploring the intrusion of anti-Jewish feeling into the New Testament. Such Christians have recognized that the New Testament can be, for those who wish it, the source and the justification for hatred of Jews; they have made sincere efforts to forfend against a use of this kind in the preparation of the textbooks which they use in their religious schools.

Among such Christians, the crucifixion narrative is handled in such a way that the virulent hatred of certain of its passages is neutralized. The opponents of Jesus cease to be simply "Jews," but are interpreted as the wayward universally found in every land or religious communion; the Pharisees cease to be typical of all Jews, and become a type of communicant recognizable within any Christian denomination. And the telling questions are asked, If the crucifixion brought a benefit, atonement, to mankind, then why should hatred be expressed against those who were involved in the incident? And if the crucifixion was divinely ordained, then was not the role of the crucifiers fixed by God, rather than capriciously chosen by man?

Just as there are both Jews with prejudice and without it towards Christians, so, too, despite the anti-Jewish bias of the New Testament, there are many such Christians without prejudice against Jews. Their approach to the crucifixion narrative is constructively gratifying. Yet it, too, cannot be called historical, for it is commendable interpretation, but still interpretation.

The historical circumstances which led to the crucifixion of Jesus, in my judgment, are beyond recovery.

The scholarly conclusion that the "historical" Jesus is not to be "recovered" emerged shortly after World War I. Since that time, as we know, mankind has been in the most serious straits in the recorded history of humanity.

Rationalism, and optimism about man's potentialities, had led in the nineteenth century to a view of man directly the opposite, we may say, of Paul's view. Paul believed that man needed God's redemption; nineteenth-century liberalism believed that man could redeem himself.

Since World War I Paul has been, as it were, rediscovered, as many theologians have seen in contemporary history the confirmation of Paul's view of man. The older premise that Paul might well be discarded has been supplanted by a growing conviction in exactly the opposite direction, with the result that Pauline doctrine has been extolled with refreshed approbation. The unavailability of the historical Jesus has promoted an ascendancy of the Pauline Epistles; and if Paul has not quite supplanted Jesus in contemporary thought, it is little exaggeration to report that the Epistles have been more emphasized than the Gospels in much of current Protestant theological concern.

For some such theologians the authority of Paul is, understandably, insufficient, and, naturally, they turn to Jesus. But here such theologians run headlong into the conclusions of the scholarship which this volume tries to mirror, that the historical Jesus is not readily to be recovered. It is not surprising that these theologians have been considerably dismayed at failing to elicit from specialists in the Bible the desired confirming word. Some have been understandably incensed, and they have not hesitated to express their displeasure at the tone of Biblical scholarship. From such circles there has emanated a repeated disparagement of Biblical scholarship, on the grounds that the career of Jesus was "suprahistorical," and therefore historical scholarship is a wrong and useless tool. An outsider suspects that the efforts to discredit the historical approach would be less arduous if the historical approach were not so inconvenient to the discreditors. There are a perceptible number of theologians who, bypassing the scholarship of the New Testament, go on to affirm conclusions more congenial to their own dispositions. Such theologians appear to be in the minority, and do not seem to include the leading theological figures of the day.

The leading theologians seem to feel, on the contrary, that to disparage Biblical scholarship is to be guilty of intellectual blindness or dishonesty. These would not only not discourage such scholarship, but even encourage it, however extreme its conclusions. But they are also critical of "liberal scholarship," yet in a completely different way; the Bible specialist among these would reject the label "liberal" in favor of the term "radical." The inadequacy which these theologians note in the liberal scholarship is an alleged failure to proceed beyond historical study into an assessment of the meaning of the history studies. The "radical" will confirm the "liberal" conclusion that no satisfactory life of Jesus can be written. But for the "radical" the "truth" of the Gospel is not the accurate records of events,

but the way in which the events illustrate or elucidate the fulfillment of divine purposes in history. For such theologians the
traditional terms of the Christian faith, even when abundantly
reinterpreted, are still: "creation," "the redemption of man,"
and the "events of the End"; accordingly, they contend, the
results of modern Biblical scholarship must be shown in some
positive relationship to the traditional terms.

The distinction to be drawn between the two groups is that
the former disparages the liberal scholarship and dismisses it as
wrong; the latter is, indeed, critical of the uses of the scholarship,
but endorses it as right as far as it goes, insisting that it must go
farther.

But since out of the theological discussions there emanate from
time to time random phrases and sentiments in criticism of the
liberal scholarship, it has seemed to me desirable to digress for
the brief mention of these movements for the purpose of making
the conclusion unmistakable.

Though a voice here and there questions the validity of the
liberal scholarship, the prevailing view is this: the evangelists
disclose Jesus to us only after the church has meditated on his
significance as the Christ. The form of the Gospel writings is
such that it is not always possible to penetrate effectively beyond
the Gospel portraits of Jesus to Jesus himself. We can know what
the evangelists saw in Jesus the Christ. We can know what the
evangelists report of his teaching; we can be sure that however
the Gospels have shaped his words, some echo of them is discernible. But we cannot describe with exactness and precision
the details of the life and career of Jesus.

It certainly does not follow, since the "historical" Jesus is not
"recoverable," that the place of Jesus in the liberal Protestant
mind has therefore given way to a vacuum. On the contrary.
It means only that glibness and careless pigeonholing are re-

placed by some sturdy efforts to conceive of Jesus in more tenable ways. Perhaps this is more often implicit than articulate among liberals. But, to begin with negatives, the liberal scholar would avoid "modernizing" Jesus; that is to say, he would not describe Jesus in some category in which the modern age is interested and which would ill suit the Jewish world of almost two thousand years ago. The liberal might use a term—how can he speak without using terms? — such as prophet, or teacher, but always with the sense that the term is only an approximation. For him the figure of Jesus is beyond whatever description he can accord it; therefore he necessarily has both reservations and also implied overtones in his mind as inevitably his wish to communicate leads him to use specific terms in his description.

Such a person is likely, also, to see in the words of the Gospels not a literal truth, but symbolic or ineffable truth. He would not insist necessarily that Jesus did or said some particular thing recorded in the Gospels, but he would proclaim himself attuned to what the intent of the Gospel is in attributing that detail to Jesus. In illustration, such a person might, as many do, deny the virgin birth; or else he might deny the physical aspect involved; and he might aver that he sees in Jesus an exalted person whose essence the First and Third evangelists try to portray through the medium of the virgin birth. He would focus not on the virgin birth, but on the implicit exaltation.

Obviously, variety exists among such New Testament scholars, and no single description can fit all. But however negative the results from pure historical study, they have not been accompanied in liberal Christianity by negative approaches to the significance of Jesus. The usual liberal Christian has a positive conception of Jesus, difficult as it may be to contain it within definitions. It may be said, in general, that Jesus, as a man, serves the liberal as the model for those things which he considers the most cherished human ideals. Uncertain as he may be about details of the career of Jesus, even to the point of rejecting this or that item of the traditional faith as unreasonable, or as untenable, he sees in that career the supreme idealism which he considers worthy of imitation. In this, at least, he concurs in the faith of the evangelists, who saw in Jesus the pinnacle of human achievement, love, and solicitude. To an outsider, it may appear that an idealized man, not a real man, has been accepted as the model to emulate; to the liberal Christian, Jesus seems to be not an idealized man, but the ideal man of history.

From this conception, the liberal can derive inspiration, and also an imperative which influences or guides his conduct. His actions and his attitudes can therefore be self-effacing, noble, and exalted. There are Christians whom I know to be such persons. They would attribute their attainments not to their own merit, but, in humility, to him whom they call their Master.

In the Jewish tradition there have been many men who have inspired in modern Jews ideals such as self-effacement, nobility, and exaltation, yet neither the Old Testament nor rabbinic literature depicts the ancient worthies — Abraham, Moses, David — as perfect. Not perfection, but goodness, has been the Jewish demand from the individual, a goodness which we Jews have urged upon ourselves as a personal responsibility to be as nearly perfect as possible. But we Jews have not equated strict perfection and goodness as interchangeable. If this standard seems deceptively to be lower than Christian perfectionism, we Jews would reply that the standard is not less exacting, but only more humanly tolerable. In the Jewish view, there have been many great men, but not any perfect man to be exalted above all others.

# PART FOUR

## OTHER WRITINGS

# XVII

# Catholic, Johannine, and Pastoral Epistles

SEVERAL LETTERS AND TRACTS in the New Testament, coming from the end of the first century or even as late as the middle of the second, carry headings which ascribe their authorship to Peter, or Paul, or other worthies of the generation following that of Jesus. This practice of giving authority to a new writing by attributing it to some earlier person of eminence was a literary custom of the New Testament age, and was commonly used both among the Jews and among the Greeks. The mores of the day sanctioned this whim, and no modern sense of wrongdoing attached to it. A long Greek word, pseudepigraphical ("falsely titled"), is a convenient term by which to allude to such a late writing which has an appearance of being early. The term, however, has an overtone of moral judgment and of deploring which reflects our modern revulsion against "plagiarism," and which does injustice to the ancient intent.

As distinct from the authentic letters of Paul, which usually dealt with the specific and the local, these later New Testament writings deal with rather general subjects. They often lack the vividness and crispness of a person writing in controversy in a concrete situation. The precise moments or situations which called forth each writing are not readily to be recovered. Indeed, general situations of quite long duration rather than burning crises motivate the writings.

We have moved in these writings beyond Judaism and beyond the infancy of the church into its late adolescence or even early maturity. In the time which they reflect, the recollection of the crises of childhood has grown dim, or the problems, in having been resolved, have become unimportant. The missionary activity, though still proceeding, is sufficiently normal so that the problems are no longer those of regulating newly founded congregations, but of stabilizing the relatively old ones; internal development rather than external growth occupies the center of attention. Externally there was added to the resistance of individual pagans the growing opposition of Roman authority which sporadically flowered into active persecution. There is sounded repeatedly in the writings the need for courageous fidelity in the face of outer animosity and repression.

There is also the need to distinguish the local ill will of some single official from the settled imperial policy. The persecution in the first instance would represent the outcome of caprice, while in the second it would be the result of a deliberate attitude on the part of responsible high authorities. In the New Testament period, as we know from outside sources, Christianity underwent both types of persecution, but we cannot always be certain to which type of persecution some particular writing has reference.

Beyond the need for the encouragement of the faithful to remain passively firm against opposition, there arose naturally the wish active to end the oppression and to forfend against its reappearance. A fundamental objective was to induce the imperial authorities to alter unfriendly policy, and thereafter in local situations to counter the ill will of a local official by means of those steps which would insure his conformity to imperial wishes. The procedure was obviously to marshal arguments which would commend Christianity to official Rome as worthy of toleration and protection.

As the child of its parent, Christianity naturally would hope for the favorable status which Judaism had earlier obtained. Initially it could be argued that the child was entitled to the legacy of its parent. But when Christianity had matured, it went a step further; it ceased to regard Judaism as its parent, but rather as a kind of misbegotten stepbrother. The Judaism of the day was regarded as of illegitimate birth; it was the Judaism of the past as whose legitimate heir Christianity had come.

The conviction that Christianity was the true heir led to various formulations which would prove the claims. It was at first external pressure which led to the consideration of the relationship to Judaism; later an inner tension, combined with this external consideration, made the precise explanations urgent.

A second note in these later writings is the insistence that the proper internal doctrine is of great importance; helter-skelter growth within was no longer to be looked upon favorably. The overarching unity of the church was threatened by local or individual accentuation of some single facet of the inherited faith. The overaccentuation led some to what others regarded as distortion, and distortion came to be equated with heresy. The writings abound with warnings against the teachers of "false doctrines." Occasionally these teachers are identifiable, as in connection with some interpretation of the Second Coming; at one extreme there were those who expected it momentarily and who gave precise information about it, especially about its nearness; at the other extreme were those whose interpretation tended towards the virtual denial of it. The charge of "false teacher" could emerge, furthermore, as mere recrimination growing out of an unseemly, personal rivalry for leadership. But more often false doctrine is to be associated with some particular assessment of the nature or significance of the Christ which to some other person seemed wrong or marginal. Abundant illumination about this comes from the early church fathers; these marginal views are usually classified as "gnosticism."

The scholarly world seems to use the word gnostic in two related though somewhat different senses. A gnostic was someone who "knew," that is, he knew the way to God. As a general term it can include personalities like Paul and Philo. But more usually by gnostics are meant those Christians whose assurance of their knowledge about the Christ led them into specific extremes. Such gnostics were not only "Dualists," they were extreme dualists, and in their minds there was no possible reconciliation between flesh and spirit. For them the Christ could not possibly have been a man of the flesh; that would have imputed evil to him. Therefore, they interpreted the tradition of the humanity of Jesus in such ways as to deny that he ever had physical form; they insisted that he only *seemed* to have. In whatever of the various forms this doctrine of seeming, "docetism," was expressed, the New Testament opposed it. Christ was, in the church view, both human and divine, and the denial, within the church, of his humanity was as uncongenial as any external, skeptical denial of his divinity.

But the gnostics did not stop simply with a doctrine about Christ. The Jewish ancestry of the church brought the Old Testament into their ken. Since Genesis attributes the creation of the world to God, and since the world as a physical creation was necessarily evil, the God of Genesis was regarded by them as evil. The repudiation of the God of the Old Testament led to the denial of the validity of the entire Jewish Bible; the gnostics went on to the point of making great heroes out of the Old Testament villains, such as the serpent of the Garden of Eden and Balaam, the Gentile prophet of Numbers. Gnosticism brought the church face to face with the problem of its relationship to the Old Testament.

We cannot accurately identify every allusion to false doctrine of a gnostic variety. But we can often glimpse its character from the positive doctrines which the writings put forward, unfortunately only in sporadic expositions rather than in systematic, thorough presentations. In general, it can be said of these positive views that while the Synoptic Gospels try to tell us in detail who Jesus was, the other writings meagerly allude to who he was in the context of a conviction of what he was. The expression of the conviction of what Jesus was varied from individual to individual, especially in abstruse details. No single view prevails in the writings with which we are now concerned. Modern scholarship is undoubtedly more alert to "inconsistencies" than were the ancients; combinations of opinions which to us may seem illogical seemed quite consistent to them.

Moreover, the views on the significance of the Christ were not static, as the writings show. There was an almost steady progression towards equating Christ not with God's Logos, but with God Himself. Meditative piety, taking its cue from Paul, read the Old Testament in such a way that it increasingly interchanged God and Christ in those pages. As a result, the Jewish Bible tended to become interpreted as the record of the activity of Christ before the climactic moment of his incarnation in Jesus. The Jewish Bible, so interpreted, combined with items from the folk mythologies of both Semites and Greeks to blend into elaborate conceptions of the functioning of Christ in the whole history of the human race.

As the conception of the Christ extended in dimension and in scope, even those who did not share the extreme opinions of the gnostic heretics seem to have found some individual matters distasteful and uncongenial. Even items now found in the Synoptic Gospels were not universally assented to; we saw Luke gloss over the baptism of Jesus. As we shall see, in the Fourth Gospel the baptism of Jesus is entirely omitted.

Omission was not the only possible way to deal with an

uncongenial item. As another possibility, symbolic or allegorical interpretation tried to make the uncongenial more palatable.

The growth of the conception of Christ led at the same time to newer attitudes towards a variety of traditional matters. This was true not only in the realm of doctrines, such as the Second Coming, but even in practical matters, such as church organization. Irregularity or lack of system in the functions of Church officials, noted in I Corinthians, gives way to the assignment of more precise tasks to the holders of specific offices, and questions of qualification, eligibility, and jurisdictional authority become more frequent and more detailed. Recourse to the names of great men of the past as the authors of some of the later books was an effort to extol the past leadership in the interest of commending obedience to the leadership of newer times.

The writings to which we now turn use the materials of the past to create a more sedate and settled church. These writings are the link between the primitive church of Paul's time and the early Roman Catholic Church.

# XVIII

## The Epistle of James

EARLY CHURCH TRADITION ascribes this essay — James is not really an "Epistle" — to the brother of Jesus; the book carries the superscription that it comes from a "servant of God and of the Lord Jesus Christ." Some scholars think that they discern a "Jewish" tone in it. The essay lacks explicit doctrines of Christ, and seems more concerned with human conduct than with faith. Indeed, since Luther's time, the book has not been in the highest repute among Protestants, because Luther did not consider it to be as lofty as other parts of the New Testament. While various theories have arisen which suppose that we have here a book originally written in Hebrew or Aramaic and then translated, modern scholarship almost unanimously regards the book as originating from the Greek world and in the Greek language. The view that the book was originally the product of a Greek Jew is not farfetched, for the specifically Christian touches number only two, the first verses of the first and of the second chapter; it is quite likely that we have here a "Jewish" book adapted for Christian use. However, while most scholars seem convinced that the author, or the original basis, was Jewish, I find nothing in the book to preclude its having been written about the year 100 by a Gentile Christian.

But we need to look beyond the origin and to see instead the use to which its inclusion in the New Testament puts the book. James is a book of sound and moral guidance. Prudence and sagacity are its chief characteristics, not vivid or startling originality. Steadfastness in belief and in the face of persecution are commended; slander and unbrotherly anger are condemned. The End should be awaited patiently; meanwhile, brotherly love should abide. One who goes astray should be brought back by the brethren. The sick should offer prayer; the sinful, confessing one to another, should pray for forgiveness.

The most significant section, as we have noted passingly above, deals with the problem raised for the church by those who carried Paul's doctrine of faith to an absurd conclusion. While Paul had taught that salvation lay in faith and not in the works of the Law, he had gone on to insist that the effect of proper faith was proper conduct. There were those in the church who unwittingly, or even deliberately, overlooked the fact that while Paul had denied works as a means of salvation, he had not discounted at all the importance of proper conduct.

The device by means of which James takes the extreme Paulinians to task is to appeal, as Paul did, to the example of Abraham. But where Paul had shown that Abraham first had had faith and only then had achieved salvation, James insists that Abraham was measured by his works as well as by his deeds; indeed, Abraham's "faith was completed by works."

Though James uses faith as a rather static profession of belief, whereas Paul had used it as an intensive moment of inner experience, James is not contending against Paul. His target, instead, is the perverter of Paul's intent and of Paul's message. James does not subtract one iota from Paul's contention that salvation comes from faith; he is only adding that works, too, are important. "He who looks into the perfect law, the law of liberty" acts properly, and thereafter is blessed.

James and Matthew have in common that they are both reactions against extreme Paulinism. At one point (5:12) the injunction against swearing echoes Matthew 5:37 so strikingly that one is tempted to conjecture some close relationship between the two writings. There are, indeed, other echoes of less striking nature between Matthew and James. But these do not carry enough weight to suggest that Matthew's new law is the bill of particulars for which James is the statement of general principles. It is more likely that the two are similar but independent criticisms of excessive Pauline "freedom."

The type of essay which James represents is akin to the type used by the Stoics and known as the "diatribe." The morals which James commends are universal rather than specifically Stoic; there is no particular sense in which they are strongly Jewish or Christian. It is the binding of these morals to the question of the relationship between conduct and faith which gives these morals their specifically Christian cast.

# XIX

# The First Epistle of Peter

FIRST PETER, as this Epistle is frequently called, purports to be a letter written to some churches in Asia Minor. It closes with a greeting from the church in "Babylon," a cryptic name for Rome, and the latter city is presumably the place from which the "Epistle" is sent.

A dominant note in the writing is the danger from persecution, which hangs over the church, both in the present and for the future. The recipients of the letter are urged to remember that in the ordeals which lie ahead they will be sharing the suffering of the Christ. They should be proud to suffer as Christians, trusting in God's purpose in permitting the suffering.

In the meantime, their leaders — they are termed "elders" — are to tend their flocks "not by constraint but willingly, not for shameful gain but eagerly, not as domineering over those in your charge but being examples to the flock." The flock, in turn, are to be subservient towards the elders and humble towards each other.

The suffering is a test of the genuineness of their faith, and it will be followed by glory. Fear must not move them to slip back into the heathen ways, from which they had been ransomed by the blood of Christ to become "a chosen race, a royal priesthood, a holy nation." It is incumbent on them to maintain good conduct among the pagans, to fear God, and to honor the (Roman) emperor. Slaves should submit to their masters, and Christian wives to their pagan husbands, so as to win them to

Christ by their reverent behavior. Husbands should be considerate of their wives, "bestowing honor on the woman as the weaker sex." Unity of spirit, love of each other, and tenderness should prevail among them all.

As Christ has suffered abuse from the outside, so should they be willing to suffer for doing right. "For Christ also suffered for sins once for all, the righteous for the unrighteous, that he might bring us to God, being put to death in the flesh but made alive in the spirit; in which he went and preached to the spirits in prison, who formerly did not obey, when God's patience waited in the days of Noah during the building of the ark, in which a few, that is eight persons, were saved through water." The "preaching to the spirits in prison" is known in Christian tradition as the "harrowing of Hell"; some modern translations which object to the theology of the passage render it in such English as to disguise its meaning. In the Middle Ages elaborate fancy both of the written word and of the painter's art depicted the scene with considerably more detail than the New Testament here, or in an even more laconic parallel in Ephesians 4:9, provides. In context, the matter is of minor concern, but its appeal to vivid imaginations has often made this passage almost the substitute for the entire Epistle. The idea behind the "harrowing" is that the Gospel was preached to the righteous souls who lived before the time of Jesus, so as to enable them to share in the benefits offered in the age subsequent to theirs.

The careful reader of Genesis would be more apt to judge that Noah was saved not *by* the flood waters, but *from* them; such freedom of interpretation increases as time goes on; the flood of Noah's day is regarded as a foreshadowing of the Christian rite of baptism. Indeed, the text goes on to say that baptism saves the Christian as water saved Noah. Baptism is not a removal of dirt from the body (as was the Jewish rite of dipping), but it is "an appeal to God for a clear conscience through the resurrection of Jesus Christ, who has gone into heaven and is at the right hand of God."

A repetition of the motif that suffering means release from sin leads to the warning that those whom the "Epistle" addresses are not to join in the profligacy of the Gentiles as a means of escape; it is enough, urges the Epistle, that they had done so in the past, presumably before their conversion.

Church tradition tells us that Peter was martyred in Rome about 64 A. D.; conservative scholarship, holding the Epistle to be genuinely by Peter, interprets the persecutions as those known in the time of Nero. More recent scholarship tends to regard the opening and closing salutations as additions designed to give the appearance of Petrine authorship to what was a sermon delivered to pagan converts on the occasion of their baptism into Christianity. Modern scholarship is uncertain as to the place of origin of the writing; a date about 100 is neither too definite for objection nor too vague to be entirely meaningless. But perhaps a confession is in order that neither the date nor the place of origin is discernible.

The usual sequence that led to the production of some writing attributed to an ancient worthy was the wish of a later person to gain a hearing for something specific which he had to say. It does not seem to me that such was the order of events in the case of the present Epistle, since the figure of Peter was not one of universal respect. We have already seen that in Matthew 16:18 Peter was assigned a leadership which seems unearned, in view of his unadmirable role in the events of Passion Week. It seems unmistakable that Matthew is trying to give Peter an eminence which he did not universally enjoy.

Conjecture and not certainty can try to explain the events and the series of motifs in First Peter. It is reasonable, on the basis of the two Epistles to the Corinthians, to assume that in the earlier church there was rivalry to the point of bitterness both on the basis of who founded a particular church and on the questions of proper forms of worship and proper doctrine. Let us assume, further, that the Pauline form of freedom from the Jewish Law clashed even more widely than is indicated in Galatians with a Petrine form of fidelity to the Law also described in that Epistle. Can it be that in the interest of the Pauline form our earliest Gospel, that of Mark, relegates both Peter and the twelve disciples to an ignoble role, for which there may have been no basis in history, but only the partisan motive of the Pauline school? Is the repeated blindness of the twelve, so abundantly emphasized by Mark, an effort to discredit the surviving Jewish Christianity by aspersing its founders in favor of Paul? Is it accident that the traditional churches down to our day base their legitimacy on "apostolic succession," that is, succession from such leaders as Paul who came to the church after the lifetime of Jesus, rather than on succession from "disciples," the immediate followers of Jesus? Is "apostolic" authority at its root a denial of the validity of succession from the twelve? Were there at the time of Mark's composition an inherited antagonism and rivalry between the successors of the "apostles" and the successors of the "disciples"? Is Matthew a retort to Mark's aspersions of Peter and the twelve? Is Luke's picture of ancient harmony designed to idealize the past, in the effort to reconcile the remnants of disunity in his own day?

If this series of conjectural questions throws any light, then we may suppose a sequence like this: Peter's eminence was maintained in some early churches and denied in some others.

Mark's reduction of Peter was followed by Matthew's elevation of him. Luke met the difficulty by assigning a validity to both Peter and Paul; in his Gospel he abstains from derogating Peter as pointedly as Mark had done, or from exalting him as Matthew had done, and in Acts he accords Peter and Paul an equal eminence.

The circumstance that no writing had survived from Peter, the fountainhead of part of the church, as it had from Paul, the fountainhead of other parts, may be the clew to the assignment of the present Epistle to Peter. It was part of the process of rehabilitating Peter, by giving him an abiding voice among the writings reproducing the voices of the past.

# XX

## The Epistle to the Hebrews

THE CONTINUED GROWTH of Christianity and a maturing sense of its individuality made it natural that there was written a book such as Hebrews in which more direct and specific explanations of the church's relationship to Judaism should supplant the explanations of earlier times which were sporadic and general. Hebrews differs from earlier assessments not only in its greater general thoroughness, but also in two particulars.

First, it is written with some calmness and gentility, and it avoids the slur and the patently polemical. It exalts Christianity not by deprecating Judaism, but by restrained praise of it. The virtue of Christianity for the author is that it is even better than Judaism. He draws elaborate contrasts not between a bad and a good, but between a good and a better.

Second, the contrasts gain stature by being blended into a philosophical pattern, derived from Platonic and Aristotelian circles, and couched along lines of thought found also in Philo and in some Stoic philosophers. We saw above that Philo had used the Platonic pattern of distinction between the "ideal" and its "imitation"; specifically, we saw that Philo had taught that the Law of Moses was an "imitation" of the Law of Nature, but the best possible imitation and in conformity with nature. The Epistle to the Hebrews does not deal with the simultaneous existence of the ideal and its imitation. Introducing a time sequence, it presents the pattern wherein the imitation is an early foreshadowing, followed later by the ideal. For Hebrews, Judaism is the worthy imitation which has been succeeded by the coming of Christianity, the ideal.

The contrasts which Hebrews draws revolve around Old Testament institutions and Christian conceptions. So much of its detail is drawn from the Old Testament that in the following discussion of the book, in the interest of succinctness, I enclose in quotation marks some of the words and phrases out of which the contrasts grow, so that these will stand out more readily for the eye.

In Judaism, God had spoken, in olden times, through prophets; in Christianity, God spoke through a Son, and in recent times. Formerly there existed a Law, ordained through angels; now there was Salvation through the Son. Indeed, the Son had partaken of flesh and blood and had even tasted death; in order that he might be perfected. He had suffered and had been tempted, so as to be able to bring help to others who know temptation.

Moses was faithful in God's "House"; Jesus, however, was the builder of that "House," and therefore more glorious. Moses was a faithful "servant," but Jesus was a faithful Son. Moses had led Israel out of Egypt, hoping to lead them to the land spoken of (in Psalm 95:11) as God's "rest"; but rebellion and infidelity had moved God to "swear" that the disobedient would not reach the "rest." Now a new and abiding "rest" was available, successfully to be reached by the faithful.

Judaism had had its high priests, called to the priesthood by God, as Aaron was called. A priest can deal gently with the wayward because he, too, has human weaknesses; a priest, being human, needs to offer sacrifices for his own sins as well as for the sins of the people. Christianity has its high priest, Christ, appointed by God, to whom the verse, Psalm 110:4, applies,

"Thou art a priest forever, after the order of Melchizedek."*
Having made the identification of Jesus and Melchizedek, the
author of Hebrews is aware that it is a bold step, and he digresses
to tell his readers that hitherto they have been exposed to a
doctrine fit, like milk, for babies; now they need something more
solid and more mature. This will emerge out of his thorough
examination of Jesus and Melchizedek.

Abraham had given Melchizedek a tenth part of his possessions, and Melchizedek had blessed him. Since it is the superior
who blesses the inferior, Abraham was obviously inferior to
Melchizedek. Melchizedek, like Christ, was without a father
or a mother or a genealogy,** and had neither a beginning nor
an end of life. The Jewish priests, mortal men, were burdened
for their eligibility with the need for a proper descent. Moreover, one might even say that the progenitor of the Jewish priests,
Levi, was already in the loins of his forefather Abraham, so that
the Jewish priests, as it were, paid tithes to Melchizedek.

The Jewish priests had been worthy. Perfection, however,
was not attainable through this priesthood. Otherwise a new
priesthood, of the order of Melchizedek, would not have been
needed. A new and different priesthood arose, for Jesus was
of the tribe of Judah, and in his becoming a priest, the line of
Levi and Aaron was set aside.

---

*In Genesis 14:18–20 Melchizedek is the "priest of the most high God" whom
Abraham encountered after his victory over the kings and his rescue of his nephew
Lot; Melchizedek was also the "king of Salem." Genesis makes no mention of
Melchizedek's parentage or of his career. Philo, following some older tradition,
saw in "Salem" the Hebrew word for "peace," and he designated Melchizedek as
the "Prince of Peace," as does this Epistle. In our day it is frequent for one to hear
Jesus spoken of as the "Prince of Peace," though it is on Melchizedek rather than
on Jesus that the New Testament bestows the epithet.

**It may be going too far to infer that here Hebrews is protesting against the
genealogies in Matthew and Luke. But a similar sentiment is found in another late
writing, I Timothy 1:4, and the latest of the Four Gospels avoids the genealogy.
If "protest" is too strong a term, then perhaps disapproval is more apt.

Jesus had not become a priest through the mere possession of some proper lineage. His fitness was his indestructible life. Now that a new priesthood has been substituted for the old one, the entire Law which contained the rules for the old priesthood was set aside.

The Jewish priests were many in number, succeeding each other as at a death one career ended and another began. The priest of Christianity is one and eternal. The Jewish priests needed to offer sacrifices for their sins and for those of the people day after day after day. Jesus had made the sacrifice of himself only once. The Jewish priests, being mortal, were not perfect; Jesus, ordained a priest at a time later than the writing of the Law, had first been made perfect and only then was made a priest.

The Jewish priests function on earth in a replica of the heavenly tabernacle; Jesus is seated at the right hand of the throne of Majesty, in the ideal sanctuary and tabernacle. The earthly copies were made by men; the heavenly sanctuaries were the work of the Lord.

Jesus functions as the heavenly high priest under a new testament (covenant), which is better than the old covenant in the same high degree to which the priesthood of Jesus was better than the old. The new testament, indeed, abrogates the old. If the old had not been imperfect, there would have been no need for a second one. That a new covenant had come into being is evident from God's oath, "Thou art a priest forever"; moreover, Jeremiah 31:31–34 predicted that a new covenant would come which would not embody a written Law. In speaking of the new covenant, Jeremiah had already treated the old as obsolete and ready to disappear.

Under the old covenant, the regulations for worship provided for an outer tent and within it a curtained-off place known as the Holy of Holies. Common priests did their daily tasks in the outer tent. Only the high priest went into the Holy of Holies, and just once each year. He took with him the blood of animals as the medium for atonement. But when Christ appeared as the high priest of the perfect tent, he entered once and for all into the holy place, and the blood which he brought was not that of animals, but his own. The old covenant had been ratified, in the days of Moses, by the blood of calves and goats, and the book of that old covenant had been ratified by being sprinkled with blood.* Under the Law almost everything was purified by blood. But in the ideal, heavenly tabernacle Christ has completely put away sin by entering into the Holy of Holies a single time with his own blood. Having destroyed sin, Christ would appear a second time — not to deal with sin, for it has already been dealt with, but to save those waiting for him.

The Law was only a shadow of the good things to come. The same sacrifices repeated year after year, as in Judaism, cannot bring perfection, for otherwise they would not need to be repeated. Indeed, Christ has abrogated sacrifices, for it was he who spoke the words of Psalm 40:6–8, "Sacrifices and offerings hast thou not desired. . . . Then I said, 'Lo, I have come to do Thy will, O God,' as it is written in the roll of the book." Christ abolished the offerings required by Law in order to establish the doing of the will of God apart from the Law, in somewhat the Pauline sense.

Since sin was now forgiven, the daily offerings by the Jewish priesthood are no longer needed. Christians, freed from sin in baptism, have the confidence of entering the heavenly sanctuary through the blood of Jesus. Since Christ was perfect and his

---

*The passage which the Epistle paraphrases, Exodus 24:6 ff., does not mention any sprinkling of blood on the book of the covenant.

sacrifice perfect, perfection is demanded of the Christian believer. A Christian who sins is much worse off than a Jewish transgressor. The Jew receives his punishment for apostasy from human hands, by stoning (Deuteronomy 17:2–6). One who falls away from Christianity, however, falls into the hands of the living God. Indeed, a Christian who falls from grace can never be restored. *

The contrast, here so thoroughly worked out, that Christianity is the perfect realization of imperfect Judaism, has dominated and even directed the approach of Christians to Judaism, throughout the ages, and even into our own day.

The contrasts, since they are in a book of the New Testament, have for Christians the authority of Scripture, and the one-sidedness of the argument of Hebrews, as well as the artificiality of its predetermined pattern, seems often to escape the traditionally minded Christian. Indeed, until the last thirty years even liberal Christian scholarship was strongly enough influenced by the tone if not by the details of Hebrews so that it discerned an even wider array of "imperfections" in Judaism than Hebrews portrays. In the Middle Ages Judaism was not infrequently described by Christians elegantly as superstition or less elegantly as vomit. The author of Hebrews would undoubtedly have rejected such ascriptions, but they are a logical though less genteel sequel to the comparisons couched in the polished prose of the Epistle.

For whom was Hebrews written? The title would suppose that it was intended for Jews, and the vagaries of scholarship have turned up likely candidates among ancient Jewries. Conservative

---

*The fall from grace is examined also in First John; there a more tolerant view distinguishes between mortal sins and lesser sins which are not mortal. The two passages served the medieval church for its distinction between venial and mortal sins.

scholarship would date the Epistle in the period before the destruction of the Temple in 70, and it has been thought that it was written either to Palestine Jews influenced by Greek culture or else to a circle like Philo's in Alexandria. But it is unlikely that Jews were intended as the addressees. The Judaism described in Hebrews is the Temple cult of the Old Testament, and not the synagogue Judaism of Palestine or of the Greek dispersion. Its knowledge of Judaism comes from the reading of the Bible, and not from firsthand knowledge of a local Jewish synagogue.

The title, Epistle to the Hebrews, like most New Testament titles, is a late addition to the writing. Modern scholarship considers the writing to have been designed for cultured Christians, for whom it provides a quasi-philosophical substantiation of Christian claims. The author takes no notice of the synagogue, but instead constructs his contrast on the more ancient institution, the Tabernacle of Israel's wilderness period. He focuses, accordingly, not on some secondary manifestations of Judaism, but on its basic foundations. The Epistle presupposes that its readers have had some possibly formal philosophical training and that they are persons who have become reasonably well versed in the Greek version of the Old Testament. While tradition associates the Epistle with Rome, and a good many modern scholars point to Alexandria, Hebrews could have been written in almost any large center in the early part of the second century.

The Epistle sounds repeatedly the note of the need for fidelity in the face of false doctrines, and it urges faithful patience during the continued delay of the Second Coming. It appeals to the example of Old Testament personalities as models of such fidelity: Abel, Enoch, Noah, Abraham, Isaac, Jacob, Moses, the

Israelites who crossed the Red Sea — and all these are regarded as the distinguished forebears of the author and of his Christian contemporaries. Abraham, for example, had "faith," in that he went to a place to which he was bidden without knowing exactly where he was going; he did not truly settle down in Palestine, but continued the temporary existence of tent life. He, and indeed Isaac and Jacob, were seeking the true homeland in which to dwell, heaven; they were strangers and exiles on earth — the motif is frequent among the Stoic writers and is found in Philo that the true "sage" is a stranger on earth. The significant thing about these laudable ancestors is that they had true faith, even though they did not actually receive that which had been "promised," for the fulfillment of the promise had been deferred until the time of the Christians.

The bond between Christianity and the Old Testament was strengthened through the presence of such a résumé of Israel's history. This résumé, similar to those in the Psalms, the Apocrypha, and rabbinic literature, led the church to read into the Old Testament characters the personality and qualities of its own profession. The church came to regard the Old Testament, now, as it were, incorporated within its own Scripture, as its special possession. Indeed, some Christian books which were not included in the New Testament collection go further and suggest that the Hebrew version of the Old Testament, in the proud possession of the Jews, was an invalid forgery of the Christian Greek Scripture. The occasional Christian desire to do away entirely with the Old Testament was met by the overwhelming and prevailing response which is well articulated in Hebrews: The Old Testament was good, but had some limitations. One need only subtract from the Old Testament the outlived validity of the Law of Moses, and the rest is completely valid for Christians, and is indeed their Testament.

The Epistle to the Hebrews, through identifying Christ as a priest, served in its influence on subsequent Christianity as the justification for the establishment of the priesthood, as in the Catholic Church. In the sixteenth century, after the break with the Catholic Church, the Protestants proclaimed the theory of the "priesthood of all believers," and bitter debates ensued on the necessity for any special priesthood. Defenders of the priesthood pointed to this Epistle for support, while deniers rejected the suggestion that the priesthood envisaged in Hebrews was fulfilled in the Catholic Church — and they referred to the other twenty-six books of the New Testament where no mention of priesthood is made. The Epistle seems to be more significant to Catholics than to Protestants.

The Epistle does not begin with a salutation; it ends with one which, however, is probably from a later time, designed to give the writing the appearance of being by Paul. Without the epistolary ending the writing would be clearly recognized for what it is, an essay and not a letter. A cliché in the liberal scholarship puts it that the Epistle of Paul to the Hebrews is not by Paul, not to the Hebrews, and not an Epistle.

# XXI

# The Johannine Epistles

Five books of the New Testament are often grouped together, as having been written by a certain John. One of these is Revelation, another is the Fourth Gospel, and the other three are Epistles.

Who was this John? Tradition knows of two men by that name, the one a John the son of Zebedee, a disciple of Jesus, and the other a church official known as the Elder who flourished in Ephesus, in Asia Minor, around the year 100. One form of tradition merges these two Johns into a single character, concluding that the John who in his youth had been a disciple became in his old age the leading figure of Ephesus. This tradition emphasizes the extreme youth of John when he was a disciple, so as to account for his being alive and active some seventy years after the crucifixion. The effect of merging the two Johns into one is to strengthen the claim of the Fourth Gospel that it was written by an eyewitness of the events about Jesus which it describes; thereby the manifestly late Gospel can still claim to be the eyewitness account.

While modern scholarship is unable to solve all the problems of the authorship of the Johannine writings, it is well united in denying that either John the son of Zebedee or John the Elder wrote Revelation or the Fourth Gospel. The three Epistles may come from John the Elder; but many scholars hold that the hand which wrote the First Epistle of John is not the same hand which wrote the Second and the Third. For our purposes it suffices to say little more than that tradition groups together some writings, and that modern scholarship has strong reservations about the tradition.

The First Epistle of John is written in a mild and paternal tone, and in large measure it conceals the bitterness of a schism which occasioned its writing. Certain members of the church, holding views different from the rest, have left the church and have become a thorn in the flesh to their former brothers. The subject of the split was this question: Was the Christ Jesus? John answered yes; the schismatics, no.

What does the question mean? In the view of the schismatics, as we know from the denunciation of it, the tradition that the Christ had become the real man Jesus was uncongenial. To hold that the Logos had become the flesh-and-blood man was to ascribe to the Logos material existence and subjection to human frailties, such as sensual faculties and the demands of physical existence. The schismatics did not deny that the Christ had been manifested in Jesus; they denied that Jesus was an actual man. Jesus only "seemed" to be human. The "orthodox" view, both in this Epistle and in the later church, was to insist equally on the actual humanity of Jesus and on his divinity.

We do not know which of the possible "docetic" forms the heresy alluded to here was. But the Epistle makes it clear that the schismatics not only left the church, but also tried to influence others to leave and to join them. Naturally, they contended that their views were the truth; and undoubtedly they used various devices, including scorn, to attract the undecided and the wavering. The schism and its resultant claims and counterclaims upset the even tenor of the church; and the controversies threatened to destroy the unity of fellowship in the church.

The schism was probably not limited to the single issue of the humanity of Jesus. Overtones in the Epistle indicate that the heretics were "spirituals," that is, their insistence that they were no longer subject to their bodies led them to scorn the usual standards of right and wrong. By denying the reality of physical existence they found a justification for the enjoyment of whatever physical entertainment they encountered. Since they reckoned themselves as already "saved," their actions could not logically be termed sin, for they could reason that inasmuch as Christ's atonement had removed their sin, they were eternally sinless. This, indeed, is the accusation which the Epistle levels against them. The Epistle does not charge them with any specific sin, but with lying in declaring themselves sinless. Moreover, it calls their claims to "prophecy" false. (It is likely that the schismatics had comparable epithets for the orthodox).

The writer denounces the schismatics both as "sons of the devil" and as the "anti-Christ." In the face of the threat from them, he urges the church to be steadfast in its faith. Yet the tone of the Epistle is not that of bitter attack, but rather of solicitude for the church in the light of the schism. The Epistle urges unity, fellowship, mutual love, and fidelity to the doctrines that Jesus was the Christ and that through his death he brought atonement. Denunciation of schismatics is only background and incidental; the primary motifs of the Epistle are its fatherly exhortations.

The Epistle attests to the restlessness, diversity, and doctrinal variations of the growing church. Out of such variety was to emerge the recognition of the need for regulated uniformity in practice. Variety in doctrine led ultimately to the creation of the "creed," that is, the statement of what was proper, orthodox doctrine. First John shows us the effects in the New Testament period of doctrinal differences. It contains one of the strongest affirmations of the view on which the subsequent church was to insist: Jesus was indeed divine, but he was also human.

Unlike First John, the Second and Third Epistles of John each has the form of a letter. They are addressed by the "Elder" to the church. The office of Elder was apparently the same as that which in later times was held by a bishop, though the Greek word "presbyter" yields our English word "priest." Nothing within the Epistles identifies the Elder as "John," except the titles, which come from a later time. A convenient date for the Epistles is 100.

First John had spoken of certain schismatics who went astray on matters of doctrine. Second John warns the church against itinerant preachers who are possibly unsound in doctrine. Third John, addressed to an unidentifiable Gaius, records the Elder's complaint that on a visit made by him to an unspecified place, the local head of the church, Diotrephes, did not allow the Elder to function freely. Diotrephes refused to welcome traveling brethren, and he excommunicated the local people who wanted to welcome them.

In a sense, Third John is a complaint that the advice offered in Second John was taken so seriously that discomfiture to the adviser resulted. The Epistles do not disclose what doctrinal difficulties were at stake, but only the difficulties inherent in the absence of extensive authority, tight organization, and doctrinal uniformity.

# XXII

# Revelation

A PERIOD OF LOCAL PERSECUTIONS by Roman officials in Asia Minor towards the end of the first Christian century led to the compilation of a book of consolation and encouragement. It was dangerous to speak too plainly; an older device of enigmatic utterance (as in Daniel) was utilized. Friends would understand the book and be strengthened; foes would find it a harmless jumble of ecstatic visions.

A library of such enigmatic utterances was already in some circulation among Jews, and it was unnecessary to create completely new specimens; some extant Jewish writings were adapted and edited to serve the more specifically Christian purpose.

The comfort of the Book of Revelation consisted not alone in the general confident assurance of God's solicitude and ultimate vindication of the oppressed church, but more precisely in its claim to have been revealed by God to Jesus, and then in turn disclosed by an angel to a man named John. The book sets forth that however difficult the present lot of the faithful might be, this disclosure of the triumphant future should assuage the sufferings and alleviate the fears of the moment. Through Christ the faithful Christians would ultimately be vindicated. Revelation presents a sequel to the past revelations, and therefore paraphrase and quotation from the Old Testament lend both form and content to the book.

Unhappily, the book is often as dark for modern scholarship as it was for the ancient foes. The allusions in Revelation frequently defy identification. While it is possible to follow the general trend of a long passage, the detailed symbolism is more often than not lost even on the erudite scholar. Symbols whose meaning is uncertain can be interpreted variously, and both scholarship and unscholarly pietism have had no field more fertile for the imagination than Revelation.

John, the author, tells us that he was on the Island of Patmos. There he saw his first vision of what was to come; Jesus appeared to him, and commanded him to write what he had seen to seven churches of Asia Minor. John wrote to each, praising some aspect of its fidelity, or reprimanding it for some minor defections, but encouraging endurance in whatever unhappy lot might lie ahead. We do not know what is referred to in much of the seven "letters" which Revelation reproduces. The presence of the holders of false doctrines is lamented, and persecution by Jews is alluded to (Chapters 1 to 3).

Thereafter comes the body of the revelation. John beheld a vision of God, seated on His throne, surrounded by elders and by four cherubim. In God's hand was a scroll with seven seals. Only the Messiah was worthy of opening it. John then saw a Lamb standing near God's throne. (Throughout Revelation the Lamb represents Christ, out of the facile identification of Isaiah 53:7 with Jesus: "He is brought as a lamb to slaughter.") The heavenly host gave honor, glory, and blessing to God and the Lamb. Then the Lamb began to open the seals.

The first four seals, on being opened, led to the sight of four men riding on horses, each horse of a different color. These "four horsemen of the Apocalypse" were given power over the earth to bring sword, famine, pestilence, and wild beasts.

After the opening of the fifth seal, John saw under the heavenly altar the souls of martyrs. These were told to rest a little longer, until the number of their brethren destined also to be martyred should be completed. The sixth seal ushered in the tribulations expected just before the Messiah: earthquake, the darkening of the sun, and the like. Men of both low and high station fled to caves to hide from the wrath of God and the Lamb.

The opening of the seventh seal did not immediately ensue. Instead, the "true Israel" of God had an identifying seal put on their foreheads. The true Israel included 144,000 (that is, 12,000 from each of the twelve tribes of the Jews — symbolic of "Jewish" Christians) and also a multitude beyond numbering from every nation and every tongue — "Gentile" Christians. They all cried out in a loud voice, "Salvation belongs to our God, who sits on the throne, and to the Lamb." This multitude had come out of great tribulation; they had made white the robes which they were wearing by washing them in the blood of the Lamb.

Now the Lamb opened the seventh seal, producing a series of seven trumpet blasts. The first brought a rain of hail and fire, mixed with blood, and a third of the earth was burned up. At the second, a third of the sea became blood, killing a third of the living creatures in it, and destroying a third of the ships. With the third blast, a star named Wormwood fell from heaven and made a third of the rivers and fountains bitter enough so that men who drank their water died. At the fourth blast, a third of the sun, of the moon, and of the stars were stricken, their light being reduced by a third. Then an eagle flew about in mid-heaven, proclaiming to those on earth the woes which would come at the next three blasts.

At the fifth trumpet call, a star named "Destroyer" fell into the bottomless pit. It was its mission to bring the first of three woes upon the men who lacked on their foreheads the seal of God. At the sixth blast, new destruction came, brought by troops from the east. (Does this allude to the Parthians, at that time actively belligerent?) Despite all the destruction, the surviving men did not repent of their idolatry and immoral acts.

It was time for the seventh blast, but, as before, there is an interruption. An angel descended from heaven, bearing a tiny scroll. John heard seven thunders; he was about to write these down, but a heavenly voice forbade him. (The allusion is not clear; commentators differ as to whether or not the ensuing chapters embody the "message" of the seven thunders.) The angel announced that no more delay would postpone the sounding of the seventh trumpet and the fulfillment of the secret plan of God. John asked for and received the tiny scroll; he ate it, and in his mouth it was as sweet as honey, but it made his stomach bitter. (Possibly this is meant to portray the experience of a prophet; the divine message is at first pleasant to him, but what ensues is not.)

The digression from the trumpet blast continues. John was bidden to measure the Temple, the altar, and those who worshipped there. He was told not to measure the outer court because it was given over to the nations to trample on for forty-two months. (The precise allusion is not clear). Two "witnesses" were given power to prophesy during that period. (These are identified sometimes as Moses and Elijah; or as Moses and Enoch; but again as Paul and Peter.) After three and a half days the two witnesses were conquered and slain by the "beast" from the bottomless pit, in a city spoken of as Sodom and Egypt. Their bodies lay unburied for three and a half days, to the joy of those whom they had tormented; but after that time they went up to heaven in a cloud, in the sight of their foes. An earthquake killed a tenth of the inhabitants of the city, and the remainder, in terror, gave glory to God. This was the second of the three woes proclaimed by the eagle.

Now the seventh trumpet was finally sounded. Loud, heavenly voices proclaimed the arrival of the kingdom of God and of His Christ. God's temple in heaven was opened, and the ark of

His covenant was seen, to the accompaniment of lightning, thunder, earthquake, and hail.

Then a sign appeared in heaven: a woman clothed with the sun, crowned with twelve stars, and with the moon under her feet. The woman was with child, and her birth pangs had begun. Then another sign appeared: a great, red dragon. The beast tried to devour the child, a male baby destined to rule all the nations. The baby was caught up into heaven to God, and the woman fled into the wilderness for forty months, to a place prepared by God.

Meanwhile, warfare arose in heaven between the angel Michael and his cohorts, and the dragon and his. The dragon and his followers were defeated, and the dragon, who was Satan, was thrown down to earth. A voice proclaimed that the kingdom of God and the reign of Christ had come, for the brethren had conquered Satan through the blood of the Lamb.

The dragon was now on earth, and there he pursued the woman, so that she fled back to her place in the wilderness. The dragon then went off to make war on the rest of the woman's offspring who keep the commandments of God and bear testimony to Jesus.

Next, John saw arise out of the sea a beast with, among other attributes, seven heads and a blasphemous name on them. One of the heads appeared to have a mortal wound. To the beast the dragon gave power, his throne, and great authority. The beast uttered great blasphemies against God and heaven, and it was allowed to make war on the saints and to conquer them. The authority of the beast extended over every people and tongue, and all worshipped the beast except those whose names had been written down, before the founding of the world, in the book of the Lamb.

A second beast arose, this time from the land. It affirmed the authority of the beast of the sea, whose mortal wound was now healed. The land beast gave breath to an image of the sea beast, so that it spoke, and thereby caused the death of those who did not worship it. The beast had a number — 616 in some manuscripts, 666 in others. *

It is difficult to retrovert the "gematria" into a word, for two reasons. First, the Greek alphabet begins to diverge from its Hebrew counterpart at about the point at which the number 50 is symbolized, so that a word using the latter letters of the alphabet would yield a different gematria in Greek from that which it would yield in Hebrew. That is, we do not know for certain whether 666, or 616, is a Greek gematria or a Hebrew one, since the basic passage may be a translation into Greek. Second, even if we were certain about the language, we would have to bear in mind that there are infinite combinations in either language which could yield a specific gematria, just as twelve, for example, can be the sum of six and three and three, or of five and four and two and one. The word for which 616 or 666 stands is quite elusive today, although the author's contemporaries recognized it immediately. The usual modern solution is to regard it as a Hebrew gematria for the Caesar, Nero, Nero(n) Kesar; the parenthetical "n" adds the fifty necessary to raise 616 to 666. While this explanation is likely, it is far from certain; accordingly, it is not surprising that the beast has become an appropriate device in some Christian circles for any enemy. It has been interpreted, on the basis of the assumed prophetic character of Revelation, both as the Pope and as Martin Luther; as Napoleon, Hitler, or Stalin; and even as Franklin D. Roosevelt.

---

*Among Greeks and Jews, prior to the late use of Arabic numerals, number was expressed by letters of the alphabet; a was 1; b, 2; and so forth. Any word would have a numerical equivalent. Such a number the rabbis call a "gematria," their adaptation of the Greek word geometry.

The mention of the number of the beast is followed by a new interruption which breaks the severity of the vision with some consoling sights. John saw the Lamb on Mount Zion, and with him the 144,000 who had his name and the Father's written on their foreheads. To the accompaniment of harps, these latter sang a new song before God's throne. These had never defiled themselves with women, for they were virgins; they had followed the Lamb wherever he went, and they were the first fruits of the redeemed from among mankind.

John then saw another vision, an angel who had an eternal Gospel to proclaim to every nation, and who announced that the hour of God's judgment had come. A second angel announced that Babylon (Rome) had fallen. A third angel promised divine wrath and the torment of fire and of brimstone to all who worshipped the beast. John saw another vision of Christ, revealing that the hour of the harvest (the End) had come, and he saw the vision swing his sickle on earth, so that the earth was reaped. Still another angel came out of the heavenly temple and gathered ripe grapes into the wine press of the wrath of God.* Blood flowed from the wine press in a stream as high as a horse's bridle to all quarters of the earth.

Next, John saw a sea of glass mingled with fire, and by it were standing those who had conquered the beast. They had harps in their hands, and they sang both the Song of Moses and the Song of the Lamb. Then the heavenly tabernacle opened, and from it came seven angels with seven plagues, each contained in a golden bowl which was full of the wrath of God. A loud voice told the angels to pour out onto earth the contents of the bowls. The first brought foul and evil sores to

---

*One recalls the Battle Hymn of the Republic: "Mine eyes have seen the glory of the coming of the Lord, He is trampling out the vintage where the grapes of wrath are stored."

the worshipers of the "image." The second killed every living thing in the sea. The third turned rivers into blood. The fourth, poured out onto the sun, led it to scorch men with fire. Men cursed God for the plagues, but they did not repent.

The fifth angel poured out his bowl onto the throne of the beast, and its kingdom became all darkness. Still men did not repent. The sixth poured out his bowl upon the Euphrates, drying up that river to prepare the way for invading kings from the east. From the mouth of the dragon and the beast there issued three false spirits, like frogs, which went out to assemble the kings of the whole world for the battle on God's judgment day. They were assembled at a place called Armageddon (usually, though uncertainly, identified as Megiddo in the plain of Esdraelon; the "Ar" of the word seems to mean "hill," but that plain has no suitable eminence). The seventh angel poured his bowl into the air, and out of the temple there came a voice from the throne saying, "It is done." A storm arose, and an unparalleled earthquake split the city of Babylon into three parts. Islands fled away, and no mountain was found.

Next, one of the seven angels showed John the judgment administered to the "great harlot" who sat on the blasphemous beast and on whose forehead was written her name, "Babylon, the great, mother of harlots and of earth's abominations." The wicked woman was drunk with the blood of the saints and of the martyrs of Jesus. Ruling over the seven hills (which recall vividly the site of Rome) was a series of seven kings, of whom the sixth was still reigning, with the seventh yet to come. There was still, indeed, to be an eighth king, and then a series of ten more kings, these latter each of short reign. All these kings would make war on the Lamb, but he would conquer them. Indeed, the ten kings were the ten horns of the beast, and they would make war on the harlot and destroy her.

John saw another angel, who proclaimed a dirge over the fallen Babylon. Still another angel sang a song of triumph over the oppressor's fall. Kings, merchants, and seafarers who had profited from the great city sang a lament. Another angel threw a great millstone into the sea, and just in that way the wicked Babylon would be thrown down.

John then heard a great song of triumph in heaven, the rejoicing of those invited to the marriage of the Lamb and his Bride.

He saw next the Logos of God astride a white horse, followed by the armies of heaven. These battled against the beast; they captured it and also the "false prophet" who had worked deceiving signs for it. (This may be an allusion to priests of the official imperial cult.) The beast and the prophet were thrown into the lake of fire which burns with brimstone; their followers were likewise slain.

From heaven came an angel who opened the door to the bottomless pit. He seized Satan, bound him "for a thousand years," and threw him into the bottomless pit, which was then shut up and sealed. * A resurrection was not to come for a thousand years. After the thousand years, Satan will be released from his prison, to deceive the nations of the world, who are symbolized by Gog and Magog of Ezekiel 37 to 39; the nations would be moved to battle against the saints. (The change of tenses in this paraphrase reproduces the capricious changes in the text itself.)

These armies were beaten, however, for fire came down from heaven to consume them. Satan himself was thrown into the

---

*Chiliasts (from the Greek word meaning "thousand") in the second century believed that a visible reign of Christ on earth for a thousand years would precede the final End. Millenarians (from the Latin word for "thousand") believe somewhat similarly, and these are heard from in our day from time to time.

lake of fire and brimstone into which the beast and its false prophet had already been cast. They were to be tormented day and night, forever.

John saw a series of three visions of triumph. First, he saw the dead standing before the throne of God. The "book of life," containing the names and deeds of Christians, was opened, and another book, that of death, contained the names of others. All were judged, for life or for death, by what they had done. Then, after Death and Hades had given up their dead for judgment, they were themselves thrown into the lake of fire.

Second, he saw a new heaven and a new earth, for the old had passed away and the sea was no more.

Third, he saw the holy city, the New Jerusalem, come down out of heaven from God, for God's dwelling is with men. The New Jerusalem was the Bride, the wife of the Lamb. On the gates were inscribed the names of the twelve tribes of Israel, and on the walls the names of the twelve apostles. The city was rich in all manner of precious stones and furnishings. There was no temple in it, for its temple was God and the Lamb. From the throne of God there flowed the river of (eternal) life, flanked on each side by the tree of life, which yielded fruit every month. The throne of God and the Lamb were there for worship by the faithful. There would no longer be night, for the faithful, having God as their light, would need neither lamp nor sun.

And, finally, the angel told John that the words of the revelation were trustworthy. John wanted to worship the angel, but the angel forbade him, for he, too, was a fellow servant with those who worship God. John was bidden to worship not that angel, but God. He should not, continued the angel, seal up the words of prophecy in his book, but proclaim them, since the time was near. Somewhat abruptly, the angel is replaced by Jesus, who announced his imminent return. Then the book closes with a stern warning against adding to or subtracting from the book of this prophecy.

The above account, for all that it contains, may possibly conceal some of the peculiarities of Revelation. A careful reading of the text, rather than a paraphrase, discloses what a scholar, James Moffatt, has described as "incongruities and vacillations in the symbolism, isolated allusions, unrelated predictions left side by side" — and ruptures of context and of logical sequence. Scholarship has attributed these anomalies to the various sources used by the compiler and to an imperfect blending of them.

Nevertheless, there is an unmistakable unity which the search for sources has tended to obscure. The author was more interested in the content of his message than in the logical and even airtight consistency which the modern mind demands. Not living in a vacuum, he of course drew on existing patterns of apocalyptic utterance, to which he added his own. The assumption that Revelation was written for all time has produced monstrosities of naïve interpretation, just as a preoccupation with source background has produced some monstrosities of scholarship, in the form of the arrogance of some of the claims of having successfully identified every detail. It needs to be repeated that many of the allusions are far too cryptic for modern recovery.

The Greek of Revelation is replete with "bad" grammar. It has many "Semitic" constructions, which might point to its being a translation of a Hebrew or Aramaic work. I am more inclined to attribute the bad grammar to the relatively poor education of the author, and the Semitic constructions to the influence of the Greek Bible and to the milieu which transported the Semitic folk myths into the Greek world. Semitic sources do lie behind Revelation, but the book as a unit was, in my judgment, composed in Greek.

There are a number of passages in Revelation which can give the student of the history of Christian worship an insight into the prayers or hymns of the early church:

"Holy, holy, holy, is the Lord God Almighty,
who was and is and is to come!"

Again:

"We give thanks to Thee, Lord God almighty, who art
and who wast, that Thou hast taken Thy great
power and begun to reign.
The nations raged, but Thy wrath came,
and the time for the dead to be judged.
For rewarding Thy servants, the prophets and saints,
and those who fear Thy name, both small and great,
And for destroying the destroyers of the earth.

Virtually alone of the twenty-seven books in the New Testament, Revelation is known to have had no immediate universal appeal. The distaste which Martin Luther felt for it in the sixteenth century was anticipated in the centuries long before him. Admission to the "canon" was slow and unenthusiastic, especially among churchmen in the eastern Mediterranean. They had continued to use Greek as their living language, and to them the deficiencies of Revelation were readily apparent. In the West, the translation of the book into Latin smoothed out some of the stylistic shortcomings, and acceptance was somewhat earlier and somewhat readier.

Yet it is likely that even in the West the acceptance of Revelation into the New Testament was mostly for a negative reason. Other such apocalyptic books were in circulation, and they, like Revelation, lent themselves readily to irresponsible interpretation. To counteract and nullify the utility of the many books, no step could have been more influential than to make a single one official. The others, thereby deprived of high standing, would not be so frequently copied, and would tend to disappear. Some scholars hold that the purpose in accepting Revelation into the canon was to undermine the wider apocalyptic literature. The notion that the John of the Fourth Gospel had written also Revelation, even though distinguished early churchmen anticipated modern scholarship in denying the common authorship, lent this book an eminence of a supposed authorship which commended it above the other apocalyptic books.

For some Christians, Revelation still has a religious message, and it still discloses the unborn future. For most liberal Christians, Revelation seems to have little more interest than the historical backgrounds of the time when the book was produced. Revelation is the reflection of how a segment of the church responded to persecution at the hands of Roman officials.

# XXIII

# Acts of the Apostles

THE CLEAREST MARK of the steady growth of the church was the need which it came to feel for relating its history. Out of the internal diversities, the issues of false and true doctrine, and the personal rivalries and the regional emphases on aspects of the tradition, the manifest necessity for greater unity gave impetus to the assertion of some firm bases for guidance and for decisions. These bases were not new; they had been a part of the church virtually from its beginning. But at the time of the writing of the Acts of the Apostles, the events of the beginning were remote enough so that accurate memory of them had begun to fade. So much time had passed since the early days that perspective on the events and on their meaning seemed quite as important as the events themselves.

Acts of the Apostles is a history of the early church. It is a continuation of the Gospel According to Luke. The Gospel dealt with Part One, the significance of Jesus; Acts deals with Part Two, the church after the time of Jesus.

Before, when we looked at Luke, it was to set forth the relationship of the three Synoptic Gospels to each other. We need now, in addition, to look at Luke as part of a connected, two-volume history, written by one man from a single viewpoint, and with a purpose common to both parts. The literary style of the two volumes is the same, the presuppositions are the same, and the deftness of the artistry is the same.

When we looked at the relationship of Luke to Mark and Matthew, we noted that almost all the content of Luke was obtainable from the other two Gospels; had Luke not been preserved, we should still possess in the other two Gospels almost as great a quantity of material as the three Gospels furnish, for the significance of Luke was less in what he told than in how he told it.

The situation is quite different for Acts; if it had not been preserved, we should lack any connected history of the early church, and we should have to piece our information together from what Paul's Epistles reveal obliquely, or from what the "higher criticism" of the Gospels might tell us. Acts is important not alone for its content, but also for its uniqueness among the New Testament books. Accordingly, the historical validity of the account in Acts needs careful and balanced assessment.

Disagreement among scholars on the historical reliability of Acts is sharper than elsewhere in New Testament scholarship. Conservatives, who regard all the books of the New Testament as sharing equally in divine inspiration, seem to have few doubts about the credibility of Acts. Liberal scholarship, however, in its study of the Gospel According to Luke, has revealed a large measure of partisan editorializing and special pleading in support of the thesis that Christianity was the true continuity of Judaism, and that the Jews, not the Romans, were the cause of any difficulties which the church had encountered. Liberals agree that this freedom with which "Luke" uses his Gospel materials is reflected in Acts, but they do not agree on the extent to which the freedom affects the trustworthiness of Acts.

Although we do not have for Acts the ready elements for contrast and comparison which Mark and Matthew provide for the Gospel of Luke, we are not totally bereft; the second half of Acts deals primarily with Paul. Acts and the Pauline Epistles cross each other at many points, and there is a sense in which the Epistles are to Acts the same sort of factual check which, in a broader way, Mark and Matthew are to Luke's Gospel.

When Paul's Epistle to the Galatians is set against the narration of the similar matters in Acts, we cannot help but see discrepancies, not of minor details, but of major and of directly antithetical substance. In Galatians, Paul asserts that prior to his "conversion" he had been unknown in Judea; in Acts, he is present there, indeed, at the lynching of Stephen. In Galatians, Paul refused to have his aide, Titus, circumcised; in Acts, Paul acceded to the circumcision of another aide, Timothy. In Galatians, Paul was defiant of the Jerusalem church; in Acts, he docilely abided by its decisions. In Galatians, Paul and Peter (Cephas) are exponents of contradictory interpretations of the validity of the Law of Moses; in Acts, they are in glorious harmony.

These examples may be sufficient to indicate that Luke's motives and editorial purposes are so compelling to him that they override whatever an acquaintance with Paul and Paul's letters would yield in the way of accurate knowledge. "Luke" purports to have been a traveling companion of Paul, but it would be hard to imagine greater discrepancies between Luke's report of incidents and Paul's report of them. Conservative scholarship often tries ingeniously to harmonize the difficulties, but the effort is quite a vain one.

Some motifs in Acts reflect the almost unbounded freedom of Luke's literary methods. It is in Acts that we are told that Paul was a student of Gamaliel at Jerusalem — that is, Paul is made representative of the very center of Palestinian Judaism. The study of Paul's Epistles reveals that his Bible is the Greek version, and there is no indication in Paul's writings that he knew Hebrew; in Acts, however, Paul is able to converse in Hebrew. It is Acts, not the Epistles, which provides Paul with the Jewish name Saul. Moreover, it is Acts which equips Paul with a highly dubious possession, Roman citizenship.

The Paul of the Epistles is a highly individualistic, colorful man of sturdy and independent judgment. The Paul of Acts is not decisively different from other apostles, like Philip or Peter, all of whom are so tranquil towards each other that no hint of deep friction is discernible. Paul's eminence in the Epistles rests on the formulation of a basis of Judaism which is new and profound, even if to Jews it is uncongenial. Paul's eminence in Acts rests on little more than the extensiveness of the journeys which he made in the interest of a rather stereotyped and conformist religious approach. Acts, in short, deprives Paul of his stature and makes him no more than just another missionary.

The division in liberal scholarship arises after the recognition of the difference between the Epistles and Acts. One viewpoint concludes that in this light, Acts is *in toto* untrustworthy. The cost in this viewpoint is that it thereby rejects the most extensive source for the history of the church between Jesus and Paul. Another viewpoint, unwilling to pay this price, seeks to find in Acts some literary sources to which Luke supposedly had access, and to place some reliability on whatever literary analysis indicates these sources to be.

In my own view, "Luke" was not a historian, but an artist. Acts is not a work of history, but rather a freely composed set of vignettes about the growth of the church. The dimness in which possible written or oral sources are discernible indicates that these were, at their best, no more than points of departure for Luke, and he did not hesitate to depart. Scholars, indeed, differ on whether or not Luke had sources at his disposal; if he did, he has blended them into his account so skillfully that they seem quite beyond any useful recovery.

In Acts, the logic of the growth of Christianity is never ruffled by any human foible or human genius. As the Gospel fell into the geographical sections of Galilee, Samaria, Judea, and Jerusalem, so Acts falls into orderly geography. The earliest followers of Jesus are, in the beginning of Acts, in Jerusalem; Jesus has remained with them after the resurrection for forty days — whether at intervals or continuously is not clear. Jesus has enjoined them to be his witnesses in Jerusalem, in all Judea, in Samaria, and to the ends of the earth; Acts goes on to show the spread of Christianity in precisely those steps.

In Jerusalem, the eleven disciples, and those joined with them, lived in close fidelity to the Temple. (Acts, like the Gospel of Luke, has no allusion to a resurrection appearance in Galilee.) The election of one Matthias, in place of the false Judas, restored their number to twelve. At Pentecost (Shabuoth), the Holy Spirit was "poured out" upon three thousand new adherents, some of whom were Palestinian Jews and others were Jews of the dispersion. Sporadic conflicts with Temple authorities arose, and minor repressions were suffered, but no less a man than the eminent Pharisee Gamaliel defended the right of the church to carry on its activities.

Growth required that the twelve be relieved of some of their duties. Seven men were selected for certain minor functions. One of these, Stephen, became a martyr at the hands of Temple officials and the mob. At his lynching there was present a man named Saul. The incident of Stephen elicited some wider repressions, so that the faithful had to flee from Jerusalem — thereby taking Christianity outside of the Holy City. Philip, one of the seven, made converts in Samaria and Philistia; indeed, he converted an Ethiopian eunuch.

Saul sought and obtained permission to go to Damascus to extradite some of the members of the church who had fled there. On the road Saul himself became a convert after seeing a vision of Jesus. Acts does not tell us who it was who founded the church in Damascus.

The apostle Peter went to Philistia. There a dream led him to reject the Jewish dietary laws and to convert a Roman captain, named Cornelius. On Peter's return to Jerusalem the mother church, over some objection, approved both the rejection of the dietary laws and the reception of Gentile converts.

Other apostles, unnamed by Acts, went to Phoenicia, to the Island of Cyprus, and to Antioch in Syria. At Antioch the conversion of a good many Gentiles prompted the mother church to send an investigator, Barnabas. Barnabas approved of what he saw in Antioch.

From Antioch, Barnabas went on a missionary journey, accompanied by Saul, thereafter known as Paul. They went first to the Island of Cyprus and then to the mainland of Asia Minor. A typical experience was that at Perga. There Paul preached in a synagogue on one Sabbath, and on the next Sabbath the whole city gathered to hear him. The Jews agitated so against Paul and Barnabas that they had to leave Perga. (The Gospel, it is suggested, was offered first to Jews and only thereafter to Gentiles.) In another city, Lystra, the cure of a lame man elicited the pagan opinion that Paul and Barnabas were Hermes and Zeus. Jews again made trouble — usually Acts brings them from a distance for that purpose — and the apostles were stoned and left for dead. Thereafter, however, they returned to Antioch in Syria.

At Antioch, conflict between Jewish Christians from Judea and local Gentile Christians arose over the question of circumcision. Paul and Barnabas were sent, with others, to Jerusalem to get a decision from the mother church. A compromise between those who insisted on preserving the Mosaic Law and those who wished to abolish it was proposed by James, the brother of

Jesus: Gentile converts need not observe the whole Law, but only three items. These were abstinence from food offered to idols, abstinence from adultery, and abstinence from "blood." (These prohibitions are vague enough so that subsequent interpretation, and varying texts, defined their substance in quite different ways.)

The compromise proposed by James was embodied in an apostolic decree. The chief spokesman against the Mosaic Law was Peter.

The remainder of Acts deals with Paul, or, rather, with Paul and his various companions. A second journey began, like the first, to Asia Minor, though omitting Cyprus. A route, uncertain in the text (and yielding literally millions of words of conjecture, in dispute over a "north" or "south" Galatian route), brought Paul to the southwest corner of the peninsula.

At this point in Acts there begins the first of four sections in the first person as if by a traveling companion of Paul. Disputes have been natural about their odd and abrupt introduction. In my judgment, the "we-passages" are not the eyewitness report which they pretend to be; they are a literary device to give the narrative greater vividness and verisimilitude.

Paul crossed over to the mainland of Europe. He founded churches at Philippi, Thessalonica, and Beroea. As usual, the Jews were recalcitrant and the pagans compliant; and it was the Jews invariably who were the cause of troubles which arose.

From Beroea, Paul went to Athens, where he spoke before the council on Mars Hill. He evoked jeers from some of the Athenians, but he persuaded some of them. Next, he went to Corinth, where his successes again brought trouble from the Jews. During his long stay in Corinth, agitation by the Jews resulted in an uproar; the participants were brought before the governor, one Gallio. Here Luke puts into the mouth of Gallio a viewpoint which he sets forth both in the Gospel and elsewhere in Acts: that the difficulties between the Christians and the Jews were only internal "theological" differences, in which the governor had no desire to intervene.

Paul next set sail for Syria, stopping off briefly in Ephesus; he went on to Antioch, but then returned to Ephesus. There an Alexandrian Jew, named Apollos, had been set straight, by some associates of Paul, on some matters affecting baptism; and Apollos had set off for Greece. But Paul found in Ephesus that some of the members of the church had never heard of the Holy Spirit; by laying his hands on these and rebaptizing them, this time "in the name of the Lord Jesus," Paul conferred the Holy Spirit upon them. A stay of three months yielded more conflicts with the Jews, but also more converts. Indeed, the Gentile craftsmen of Ephesus were annoyed at Paul, because his opposition to idolatry was reducing the market for their wares. They raised a hubbub, in which the Jews joined. Paul then departed for Macedonia and Greece.

The rest of Acts describes Paul's return to Palestine and his experiences there. Paul had intended to go directly to Syria, but a plot by the Jews impelled him to retrace his way through Macedonia; crossing then to Asia Minor, he met his companions at Troas. They sailed by an indirect route to Tyre. During the trip Paul wrote a letter to Ephesus, saying that he knew through the Holy Spirit that prison and affliction awaited him in Jerusalem. In his land journey, he sojourned at Caesarea; there a prophet foretold that Paul would be bound and turned over to Gentiles.

Paul went with his company to Jerusalem. He reported to James and the others about his work among the Gentiles. He learned that he was under suspicion of undermining the Jewish Law, and that he could allay such suspicion by an overt act of obedience. Accordingly, on the next day Paul went to the Temple to perform some rites of purification, which lasted for seven days. When this period was almost over, Jews from Asia Minor recognized him and stirred up the mob against him. The Roman garrison, on hearing the noise of the riot, intervened to save Paul from lynching; this they accomplished by arresting Paul.

Paul requested permission from the Roman police to address the crowd. This he did in the Hebrew language. He gave a résumé of his Jewish ancestry and education, and a recital of his early persecution of the church and his later conversion to it. The mob was the more angered. The police wanted to scourge Paul and to find out the source of the mob's wrath against him. Paul protested that he was a Roman citizen, by birth and not by the purchase of the privilege, and he reminded his arresters that it was unlawful to scourge a citizen without previously convicting him at a trial.

The garrison commander, wishing to know the real reason why the Jews had accused Paul, ordered the chief priests and the council to meet the next day. He brought Paul before them, and Paul was allowed to speak. Noting that there were both Sadducees and Pharisees before him, Paul cleverly precipitated a grand quarrel between these on resurrection, by himself espousing the Pharisaic view. It would seem to the Roman commander that Paul was merely a partisan in a well-worn inner dispute; indeed, Acts consistently presents Paul as ascribing his difficulties to his stand on resurrection; in so exculpating him, Acts not only reduces Paul to the role of a quibbler, but a mendacious quibbler at that. The Paul of Acts is never more remote from the Paul of Galatians than in the infelicitous scene before the chief priests and the council.

Thereafter Paul was tried in succession by the Roman governor, Felix, and by his successor, Festus, and even by the Jewish king, Agrippa. There was never sufficient evidence by which to convict him of any misdeed, and the authorities were unwilling to punish him for what were only matters of theology. Accordingly, they acceded to his desire to be sent to Rome for trial.

The journey was a grueling experience, what with storms and shipwrecks; the untoward was relieved by some miracles. Ultimately Paul reached Rome, where he was greeted by the local leaders of the Jews. Paul assured them of his complete fidelity to Judaism, and on an appointed day they came to his lodging to hear him give an exposition of his views, in support of which he cited to them both the Law of Moses and the prophets. Some of the Jews were convinced by what he said, but others were not. Thereupon Paul told them that salvation was henceforth sent to Gentiles, rather than to the unperceptive Jews. For two years he lived there, "preaching the kingdom of God and teaching about the Lord Jesus Christ quite openly and unhindered."

At this point Acts ends, without any word about the outcome of Paul's trial. Some have conjectured that "Luke" died before he could finish Acts; while others have thought that a third volume was written and has been lost, or at a minimum planned but never carried out. At any rate, Acts lacks the sequel which we are led to expect.

A frequent opinion holds that Acts ends where it was intended to end: Paul's vindication is so certain that no specific mention of it was needed. Church tradition at a later time told of Paul's martyrdom in Rome. Such traditions are usually first recorded long after the events described, and they are not very reliable, for a usual way to aggrandize an ancient worthy was to conceive of him as a martyr.

A letter by a Roman governor, Pliny, written about 112,

tells that there was uncertainty in his province on how to deal with Christians. Though he had little reluctance to punish them, he had determined to send to Rome for higher authorities to handle those who chanced to be Roman citizens. The motif of Paul as a Roman citizen probably rests on the historical procedures which Pliny describes; the predicament of the time at which Acts was written was attributed to a hero of the past. I believe that Acts was written well after 115. In Acts, Paul is thus presented as the model to emulate, not only in his steadfastness, but also in his insistence on his right to trial at Rome.

The verdict that Acts is not a source of solid historical material need not necessarily rest on excessive incredulity. Even should a reader accept as fact the mélange of legend, fancy, and repeated miracles which constitutes Acts, and then add up what he has, he would find that quantitatively it amounts to very little. And when the patently fanciful is subtracted, and allowance is made for the author's clear tendentiousness, then the residuum is even smaller. Long and laborious speeches are put into the mouths of the characters; these are not remotely akin to stenographic reports. They are the usual device of the times, for in those days the historian wrote the speeches which he thought his characters should have made. When the speeches are subtracted from Acts, the account, and the possible historical substance, are shortened materially.

In sum, even if one accepts the entire narrative in Acts as historically reliable, one still has only scanty information about early Christianity.

Some scholars, though not so skeptical about Acts as I confess that I am, distinguish between the Epistles of Paul, which they call a primary source for Paul, and Acts, which they call a less trustworthy but secondary source. My own opinion inclines

263

towards the handful of scholars who do not see in Acts any weighty, reliable information about Paul.

Acts, however, is very valuable as a reflection of the church in the early decades of the second century. It is important to see how at that time the church looked at its past. A growing tendency towards bringing about uniformity in doctrine and practice made it natural to read some uniformity and concord into the past. The major issues which were burning brightly over a half century earlier had receded so completely that it was now possible to look upon antitheses as though they were harmonious supplements to each other.

For Acts is not aimlessly recapitulating the past. Its aim in describing the ancient concord and the obedience to the proper authorities is to commend such concord and such obedience for its own time.

Moreover, Acts makes it compellingly true to whom this concerted obedience is due. Proper officials are not alone those selected by the members of the church, but those confirmed divinely, by the Holy Spirit. To the choice of human beings there must be added the legitimacy of divine sanction as the crowning and validating credentials. Accordingly, the emphasis on the Holy Spirit in Acts, exceeding the emphasis elsewhere in the New Testament, is hardly incidental; it is, indeed, central to Luke-Acts.

There is, though obliquely, still another emphasis in Acts, in consequence of the authority conferred by the Holy Spirit. In the early church, Acts suggests, doctrinal differences were minor; but when these arose, they were promptly settled, as the council of Jerusalem settled the dietary laws. Since proper men, filled with the Holy Spirit, offered the solutions, their solutions were eternally valid. In the past, according to Acts, disputants did not rebel against established authority in the interest of some special view of their own. They were quite willing to submit their disputes, and to accept humbly the authorized decisions. In such incidental but pointed touches Acts provides the church with a respected precedent and a contemporary position for "orthodoxy," and suggests the already established mechanism for determining it.

Moreover, it gives the care of this orthodoxy into the hands of church leaders who could trace their spiritual lineage through appropriate apostles back to Jesus himself.

Colossians and Ephesians had given one aspect of the theory of the church as a mystic body of believers. Acts goes further. It gives the church its supposed history and legitimacy.

Acts presents, as an idealized history of early Christianity, the unity, harmony, and obedience to the authority of divinely appointed men which it desired for its own time and for the future. With the composition of the Acts of the Apostles we stand at the threshold of the formation of the early Catholic Church.

# XXIV

# The Gospel According to John

We have seen glimpses here and there of the paradox central to Christianity, that is, its insistence that the Christ was both human and, simultaneously, divine. These glimpses have been but oblique angles of the paradox, the reflections of opposition to views which carried the divinity to the point of excluding the humanity, or, more rarely, views which carried the humanity almost to the point of excluding the divinity.

To hold the two views in a well-counterbalanced proportion was difficult. It was even more difficult to give a lucid and consistent exposition of the paradox. The danger seemed always to lurk that the assertion of the humanity of Jesus might appear to be a denial of his divinity, or vice versa; indeed, merely to linger over the aspect either of divinity or of humanity could seem to amount to an implicit denial of the other.

The exposition of the divine nature of the Christ, as it is reflected in the genuine Epistles of Paul and in Colossians and Ephesians, was abstract to the point of being difficult to comprehend; this verdict, to repeat, is found within the New Testament in its latest writing, Second Peter. The "metaphysical" Christ of Paul was a subject of preoccupation primarily for the more erudite or sophisticated mind.

On the other hand, the Synoptic Gospels, in an age before an acquired antiquity hallowed them into Scripture, appealed readily to the mass mind. But the advantage in the mass appeal was offset by the reduced usefulness for the sophisticated seeker.

Although the emphasis on the humanity of Jesus was important, providing, as it did, an exemplar for the earnest believer to emulate, the excessive humanity of Jesus in Mark was objected to in Matthew, through the device of omitting or changing the adjectives and verbs of the earlier Gospel; and, in turn, Luke further eliminated many human touches.

But however the progressive Gospel process eliminated the cruder details, they still present primarily the details of a human career. However carefully Matthew and Luke pruned away some of the infelicitously overhuman touches of Mark, their tie to Mark inevitably made their Gospels the record of the humanity of Jesus and only secondarily the record of his divinity.

How could one reconcile the divinity of Jesus with his baptism at the hands of John? Or with the temptation, or with his agony at Gethsemane? Of what use is a human genealogy, as in Luke and Matthew, for a being believed to be divine? How persuasive could the miracle of the virgin birth be, in compromising divinity by including a human mother?

The Fourth Gospel comes from the circles which objected to the excessive humanity portrayed in the Synoptic Gospels. John does not go so far as the docetics, a heretical group mentioned before, who denied totally the humanity of Jesus, but he turns away also from the Synoptists' concentration on humanly attainable talent, such as skill in parables and epigrams, which seemed irrelevant to the essential divinity of the spirit made into man. In its drawing away from anecdotes and parables, the Gospel is indeed actually an effort — though never successful — to supplant the Synoptic Gospels with a spiritual history of Jesus.

John has little concern for the abundance of narrative details in the Synoptics; he needed only a few to express his advanced views of the divine nature of Christ. Indeed, the details which John gives us differ so markedly from the Synoptics that it is extremely unlikely that he used the already written Gospels in writing his own. The details which he uses he must have drawn from oral materials similar to those on which Mark had drawn; it is likely, too, that in his interest in the divinity of the Christ he adapted some pre-Christian or non-Christian hymns to the "Logos" of God by the device of applying them to Jesus.

The keynote of the Fourth Gospel is that the Logos of God became the historical Jesus. As in Paul, the abstraction of the philosophers became personal. Although the humanity of Jesus is not entirely absent from the Fourth Gospel, Jesus is almost always something other than human. John either rejects or totally recasts such Synoptic materials as the birth of Jesus, the temptation, his baptism, the recognition at Caesarea-Philippi, the transfiguration, and the suffering before the crucifixion.

Where the Synoptic Gospels permit of speculation concerning the point in his career (birth, baptism, or resurrection) at which Jesus had become the Logos-Christ, in the Fourth Gospel it is set forth that Jesus always was the Logos. While John does speak of Jesus as weary, thirsty, sad, happy, or indignant, these matters are glossed over, and there is in the Fourth Gospel a notable absence of the homeliness and warmth of a human personality. The Jesus of the Fourth Gospel is less a person who did and said certain things and more an embodied entity which spoke like an oracle. Pithy sayings and parables are totally absent. * John used only a bare minimum of incidents. These he joined together by elaborate and lengthy discourses of a meditative and rhetorical nature. The discourses are not from the

---

* An exception might seem to be justified on the basis of the story of the woman taken in adultery, about whom Jesus said: "Let him who is without sin among you be the first to throw a stone at her," but the story is missing from many of the ancient manuscripts of the Fourth Gospel; while in other manuscripts it is found not in John, but in Luke. The story circulated independently of the Gospels; its irresistible beauty led to its interpolation into some texts, but less than uniformly.

historic Jesus; the evangelist is following a custom of ancient historians in making Jesus say what the occasion would call for.

The discourses are of a uniform tenor and nearly identical in form. The mention of water, of bread, or of food in the narrative yields elaborate expositions which emphasize the difference between water and "spiritual water," bread and "spiritual bread," and food and "spiritual food." The "true" water, bread, or food is Jesus. A device by means of which the "spiritual" can be the more readily discoursed about is to portray some hearers, usually "the Jews," as obtuse and befuddled; their stupid misunderstanding of what should be (and is) plain elicits more elaboration of the "spiritual" matters than might otherwise have been needed.

In the Fourth Gospel the opponents of Jesus are no longer the Pharisees and Sadducees and the chief priests and the council, but simply "the Jews." One might suppose that the cumbersomeness of listing these categories over and over again led to the use of "the Jews" as a kind of abbreviation. But Jesus is portrayed as speaking to the Jews of "your law," as though it was not his; indeed, the conflicts are no longer matters of internal sects and groupings. Rather, a more direct cleavage is indicated. Jesus is portrayed as though not a Jew, and thus the group from which he is here fully dissociated can bear the brunt of the animosity which has been kept more subdued in the Synoptic Gospels. In its utility for later Jew-haters, the Fourth Gospel is pre-eminent among the New Testament writings.

The peculiar bent of the discourses, and the relative absence of narrative details, have led to the calling of the Fourth Gospel the "Spiritual Gospel." An early church father spoke of the Synoptics as accounts of Jesus' body, and of John as an account of Jesus' spirit. There is universally a disposition to regard the spiritual as of greater value than the "material."

Moreover, the Fourth Gospel claims to have been written by "the disciple whom Jesus loved" (21:24). The "spiritual" content, when blended with eyewitness eminence, has made the Fourth Gospel the favorite of Fundamentalist and Conservative Christians. For many readers, a selective focusing on some of the passages which are truly majestic has invested the whole Gospel, portions of which are not exalted, with the elevation of some of it.

Modern scholarship does not accept the tradition of an eyewitness, or even the proposed compromise of an eyewitness and his secretary or redactor. Indeed, the entire last chapter, containing the eyewitness claim, is uniformly regarded as an appendix designed to tie up some loose threads and to set forth the reliability of the supposed authorship. We have already mentioned, in connection with the Epistles of John, that the author of the Fourth Gospel was not the author of the Epistles or of Revelation.

John retains only the outlines of a Galilean period and of a Jerusalem period in the life of Jesus. Where the Synoptics depicted no visit of Jesus to Jerusalem before Passion Week, John depicts three earlier visits. The "cleansing of the Temple" occurs in the Synoptics in Passion Week, near the end of Jesus' career; in Mark and in Matthew, it serves as the climactic conflict which leads to the arrest and crucifixion. In John, it occurs in the second chapter as only a minor incident. In the Synoptics, Jesus raised several persons from the dead; in John, there is only a single instance, that of Lazarus, an instance not told at all in the Synoptics. (A Lazarus figures in a parable in Luke.) The raisings from the dead in the Synoptics transpire with no comment from the Jews; in John, the raising of Lazarus is the pivot of the final conflict between the Jewish authorities and Jesus.

The single greatest discrepancy between John and the Synoptics is on the date of the crucifixion. We have seen that there were two layers of tradition in the Synoptics; one layer in Mark implied that the crucifixion took place *before* the Passover, but it was overlaid by another, also in Mark, and paralleled in Luke and Matthew, which allocated it *to* the Passover. A theological motive, we said, accounted for the conscious shift in the second layer, out of the desire to equate Jesus with the paschal lamb. In the Fourth Gospel, the date of the crucifixion is clearly *before* the Passover; it is out of accord with the final impression of the Synoptics (for it is only acute analysis which reveals the earlier layer in Mark). In the second century a great controversy existed in the church between the "Quartodecimans" ("Fourteeners") who held that the crucifixion took place on the 14th of Nisan, before the Passover, and those who insisted that it occurred on Passover, the 15th of Nisan.

The unlikelihood of a trial and execution at Passover, as in the Synoptics, has commended the tradition in John to most scholars as the more acceptable. Accordingly, if in such a crucial detail John is more reliable than the Synoptics, it has been argued that in the other details John is equally more reliable. A single visit to Jerusalem is less understandable than several visits, and the age of Jesus at his death (nearly fifty; John 8:57) and a long public career are more persuasive than a short career — less than a year — and death at the age of thirty (Luke 3:23). But Jesus' age in John is probably chosen as symbolic of the Jubilee year, the 49th, with its expectation of "release" in the fiftieth year. The three Temple visits in John are opportunities to contrast Jewish institutions and Jesus; and they seem to fit conveniently as symbols for such contrasting in a Gospel replete with symbol and allegory. It would appear that only in the matter of the date of the crucifixion is John possibly more reliable than the Synoptics; but it is my judgment that John's date of the crucifixion is a theological item, not a better historical one.

There are a number of minor matters of interest in the Fourth Gospel. At the time of its writing the followers of John the Baptizer were still a distinct group; the Gospel goes to great lengths to subordinate John to Jesus. The Baptizer is given no function to perform nor task to do beyond that of asserting, over and over again, his inferiority to Jesus.

The view known as docetism is contended against through the device of presenting a doubter, Thomas, who, on being persuaded to touch Jesus, discerned an unmistakable physical nature. Also, unlike the Synoptics, in which Jesus was portrayed in direct relationship only with Jews or Palestinians, John describes a visit of Greeks to Jesus.

But over and beyond matters of detail, major or minor, the chief interest in the Fourth Gospel is the conception of the nature, function, and significance of the Christ. For John, the Christ was always in existence; it was Jesus, not the Christ, who came into being. The Christ is eternal; Jesus was but an incident in the Christ's eternity.

A prologue sets forth this view, which pervades the entire Gospel. "In the beginning was the Logos, and the Logos was with God, and the Logos was divine. He was in the beginning with God; all things were made through him, and without him was not anything made that was made." The Gospel of John deals not with the divine qualities of a man, but with the brief interval in which God's Logos took on human form.

John's view of the Logos-Christ is close to that of Paul: God Himself is remote from this world and not discernible to the

senses. The Logos-Christ is that "offshoot" of God which functions in this world. Only in the prologue does John use the word
Logos; thereafter he uses the synonym, "Son of God."

I have preferred, both here and elsewhere, not to translate
the Greek word Logos. Its usual rendering, "Word," gives a
wrong impression, and it tends to conceal the elaborate metaphysics behind the term. Logos, we have said earlier, was God's
wisdom or mind; both a Jewish background and a Greek background furnish the word with a heterogeneous ancestry. Wisdom
had already been personified in the Old Testament Book of
Proverbs. The Greek translation of the Bible led to the identification of the personified Wisdom with the Grecian Logos.

The word Logos at its base means "speech"; in many places
in the Old Testament God is depicted as "speaking," and not
unnaturally there were those who explained how God could
speak by suggesting that His "Logos" spoke. The content of
God's speech was "revelation," and certainly in the Fourth
Gospel "Logos" carries the overtones of "revelation" in the very
word. Some scholars have wanted to limit the "Logos" to
"revelation," and they would translate the prologue as "In the
beginning was the Torah . . . ." Still others, from another side,
would limit the word to some Greek speculative meaning, and
would exclude any Jewish overtone from it. Both extreme views
seem to me to be too narrow. Logos partakes both of the Jewish
conception of revelation and also of the Greek metaphysical
entity. The Logos in the Fourth Gospel and the Logos in Philo
have some notable similarities; indeed, the Fourth Gospel
reflects many moods and trends of a Philonic character.

The divine nature of the Logos is the theme of John's first
chapter, a divinity sharply contrasted with the human character
of John the Baptizer. John was not what the Fourth Gospel calls
"the Light." but his function was to bear witness to the Light.

The True Light, which had created the world, had not been recognized by the world. Though it had come to its own people, they had not accepted it, but others who had accepted it had become "Sons of God." The Logos became flesh (that is, the Christ became Jesus) and dwelled in the World; the term which Christians use to describe the Christ becoming Jesus is "Incarnation."

Previously, Moses had given the Law, God's demand for obedience. But with Jesus Christ there came Grace and Truth — God's love for men who do not need the Law. No man, continues the Gospel, has ever seen God at any time; Christ, however, has made God manifest to man.

The prologue over, the Gospel moves on to specify in some detail what has now been foreshadowed. It moves rapidly from Galilee to Jerusalem, and back. Some incidents are begun but not finished, especially when a discourse interrupts the narratives; at other times an interrupted narrative is abruptly recollected and then resumed, either to completion or to an additional interruption.

Since the incidents serve mostly as the preludes to discourses, it is not necessary here to trace them in detail. A sample of incident, of special interest to Jews, may, however, illustrate the haphazard and disconnected manner of the narrative sections. The scene is the Temple. Some Jews, who had once believed in him, are told by Jesus: "If you believe and are my disciples, you will know the truth and the truth will set you free." They answered him: "We are descendants of Abraham, and have never been in bondage to anyone. How is it that you say, 'You will be made free'?"

Jesus answered them: "Truly, truly, I say to you, every one who commits sin is a slave to sin. The slave does not continue in the house forever; the son continues forever. So if the son makes you free, you will be free indeed. I know that you are descendants of Abraham; yet you seek to kill me, because my word finds no place in you. I speak of what I have seen with my Father, and you do what you have heard from your father."

They answered him: "Abraham is our father." Jesus said to them: "If you were Abraham's children, you would do what Abraham did, but now you seek to kill me, a man who has told you the truth which I heard from God; this is not what Abraham did. You do what your father did."

They said to him: "We were not born of fornication; we have one Father, even God." Jesus said to them: "If God were your Father, you would love me, for I proceeded and came forth from God. I came here not of my own accord, but He sent me. Why do you not understand what I say? It is because you cannot bear to hear my word. You are of your father the devil, and your will is to do your father's desires. He was a murderer from the beginning, and has nothing to do with the truth, because there is no truth in him. When he lies, he speaks according to his own nature, for he is a liar and the father of lies . . . ."

The Jews answered him: "Are we not right in saying that you are a Samaritan and have a demon?"

Jesus answered: "I have not a demon; I honor my Father, and you dishonor me. Yet I do not seek my own glory; there is One who seeks it and He will be the judge. Truly, truly, I say to you, if any one keeps my word, he will never see death."

The Jews said to him: "Now we know that you have a demon. Abraham died, as did the prophets; and you said, 'If any one keeps my word, he will never taste death.' Are you greater than our father Abraham, who died? And the prophets died! Whom do you make yourself to be?"

Jesus answered: "If I glorify myself, my glory is nothing; it is my Father who glorifies me, of whom you say that He is your

God. But you have not known Him. If I had said, I do not know Him, I should be a liar like you; but I do know Him and I keep His word. Your father Abraham rejoiced that he was to see my day; he saw it and was glad."

The Jews then said to him: "You are not yet fifty years old, and have seen Abraham?" Jesus said to them: "Truly, truly, I say to you, before Abraham was, I am." So they took up stones to throw at him; but Jesus hid himself, and went out of the Temple" (8:31–59).

The contrasts in the discourses, as we have said above, are always between unyielding physical things and the fruitful spiritual counterpart — and that spiritual counterpart is Jesus. He describes himself as the "bread of life," "the only door" to salvation, the "light of the world," the "good shepherd who lays down his life for his flock." He is "the way and the truth and the life."

Two typical passages will illustrate the usual discourse: "I am the true vine, and my Father is the vinedresser. Every branch of mine that bears no fruit He takes away, and every branch that does bear fruit He prunes, that it may bear more fruit . . . . I am the vine, you are the branches. He who abides in me, and I in him, he it is that bears much fruit, for apart from me you can do nothing . . . ." Again, before the raising of Lazarus from the dead — that it is an actual death is accentuated in the account by having the raising take place on the fourth day, after decomposition could have set in and its odor filled the tomb — Martha, the sister, said to Jesus: "Lord, if you had been here, my brother would not have died. And even now I know that whatever you ask from God, God will give you." Jesus said to her: "Your brother will rise again." Martha said to him: "I know that he will rise again in the resurrection at the last day." Jesus said to her: "I am the resurrection and the life; he who believes in me, though he die, yet shall live, and whoever lives and believes in me shall never die . . . ."

It is also consistent with the divine character of Jesus in the Fourth Gospel that the crucifixion is neither a calamity nor a surprise, but simply a scheduled incident; indeed, Jesus gives to the traitor Judas the cue that the proper time for the betrayal has arrived. John accentuates beyond the Synoptics the blame placed upon the Jews for the crucifixion, and he exculpates the Romans to the point that Pilate himself is the vehicle for the benevolent recognition of Jesus as truly the King of the Jews, though in a kingship "not of this world." Neither pathos nor regret appears in the crucifixion account, but only a somewhat mechanical accomplishment of a predestined series of events.

Both the evangelist and an accurate commentator come near to the point of contradiction in this: minor touches are present that vouch for some humanity in the Jesus of the Fourth Gospel, yet Jesus' essential divinity is always present, overriding the humanity. The distinction between God and the Son of God tends to be obliterated in a verse such as "I and the Father are one." We have moved in this Gospel so far along the road of meditation on the Christ and his relationship to God that we get an occasional glimpse of the complete identity which became usual after New Testament times. In the Fourth Gospel there is a clear tendency thus to equate Christ with God, but it is yet only a tendency. Paul had kept the distinction completely clear; John moves us in the direction to which the later church moved in calling Christ the very Godness of God. The Fourth Gospel goes less than that full distance, but it goes further than any other New Testament book.

We are, indeed, on the threshold of the doctrine of the Trinity, that God's components are the Father, the Son, and the Holy Spirit. While the Fourth Gospel does not use the precise phrase, Father, Son, and Holy Spirit — a phrase found in the New Testament only in Matthew — the trinitarian formula is implicit in it. John, more clearly than any other writer, even Luke, gives the Holy Spirit a specific function, and his use of "Holy Spirit" is quite different from that of other New Testament writers. John binds it to his reinterpretation of the End. He refrains from the vivid predictions of Paul and of the Gospels; by the time his Gospel was written, the failure of the End to arrive required some revision of the concept. John does not portray Jesus as ascending to heaven to wait for some appointed time to return; instead, John portrays Jesus as returning to the heaven from which he had come, to abide there forever. In the place of the Second Coming, Jesus in the Fourth Gospel promises for the future that the Holy Spirit will be a perpetual "paraclete." The word is difficult to render, and the usual translations ("counselor," "comforter," or "advocate") miss its meaning; its original sense (as found also in rabbinic texts) is that of a friendly spokesman in a courtroom, there on behalf of a person on trial. Paraclete has the additional connotation of intermediary, and the word is so used by Philo in his description of the Logos.

Before his resurrection Jesus served as the paraclete for his followers; now that he was destined to be crucified, resurrected, and carried to heaven, the Holy Spirit would serve the faithful in that capacity. We must notice that in First John the "paraclete" is the ascended Christ in heaven, there intervening with God on behalf of man; but in the Fourth Gospel the paraclete comes from God into the lives of men.

In the account of the Last Supper, John makes no mention at all of an important matter to the Synoptists, that Jesus had instituted the eucharist as a memorial of himself. Some scholars have assumed from this, mistakenly, in my judgment, that John was not interested in the "sacrament." While it is true that an account of the institution of the eucharist is lacking, the eucharist itself is by no means absent from the Fourth Gospel. It is discoursed upon at some length and with fervor: " 'I am the living bread which came down from heaven; if any one eats of this bread, he will live forever; and the bread which I shall give for the life of the world is my flesh.' The Jews then disputed among themselves, saying: 'How can this man give us his flesh to eat?' So Jesus said to them: 'Truly, truly, I say to you, unless you eat the flesh of the Son of Man and drink his blood, you have no life in you; he who eats my flesh and drinks my blood has eternal life, and I will raise him up at the last day' " (John 6:51–54).

It is probably the intimation that the eucharist was merely a memorial which was uncongenial to the author of the Fourth Gospel. A memorial is a reminder, either of an incident or of a man. The eucharist in the Fourth Gospel transcends a memorial; it is the means of mystic union with the Christ. The pruning away of the memorial aspect removes the "body" of the rite and heightens its sacramental significance. Quite incidentally, but with full clarity, it underlines the divinity of Jesus which is the prime motif of the Gospel.

The nature of monotheism has been the latent but truly basic issue between Christianity and Judaism. The rigidity of the Palestinian Jewish use of "Hear, O Israel, the Lord our God, the Lord is One" permitted neither the conception of some rival god of evil, as in Persian Zoroastrianism, nor that of some intermediary who was in substance an aspect of God, as in Philo's Judaism, in the gnostic sects, and in Christianity. To the ancient rabbinic mind, the Christology of the Fourth Gospel would have appeared as a complete rupture of monotheism. Whatever minor matters might have occasioned some stumbling over, such as a lesser amount of favor for Christian miracles than for those in the Jews' own tradition, the rabbinic mind could hardly read without great resistance that the creation was the work of the Christ, rather than of God.

On the other hand, to the Christian mind, as Jews have seldom if ever understood, the monotheism of the Old Testament was in no wise ruptured either by the conception of Christ or by that of the Trinity. The Christian effort was not pointed at compromising the Jewish monotheism, but rather at depicting its nature. Christians have consistently held that their belief was thoroughly monotheistic. They have resented occasional Jewish aspersions of their formulation of monotheism; and they have considered that their view of the component nature of God was more profound and more perceptive than what they have charged is the barrenness of the Jewish formulation.

But conceptions which arise out of either metaphysical patterns or speculative schemes are quite difficult, if not impossible, for outsiders to penetrate. Jews have not sympathetically understood the Christian insistence on its monotheism; indeed, they have hardly even comprehended it. Partiality for traditional, inherited formulations on both sides has been an obstacle to the meeting of Jewish and Christian minds on this crucial subject. The elaborate and complex thought patterns of the Christians, and their recourse to traditional catch phrases, have rendered Christian apologetics even darker and more obscure, and, to the Jewish mind, thereby self-abortive. Moreover, the unphilosophical character of rabbinic thought could not incline a Jew to the concession that monotheism as he sees it is either implicit or explicit in the Fourth Gospel.

Indeed, the Jewish mind and the Christian mind can hardly be further apart than in the appraisal of the Fourth Gospel. This is borne witness to by the fact that in the past, especially in the Middle Ages, whatever discussion between Jews and Christians occurred was carried on in a framework of mutual hostility such as is recorded in the Fourth Gospel. Still, when one has noted the historical antagonisms, the group loyalties, and the diverse viewpoints on the nature of man and of sin and on the validity of the Law, one yet has not penetrated to the truly divisive factor; for Christians, the Fourth Gospel is their pride and treasure as the deepest insight into the way of God and into His love for mankind, while for Jews the expressed formulation of this insight into monotheism has made a judgment of another tenor almost unavoidable.

In the essential formulation of their monotheism, however identical the monotheisms may have proved to be, the Jewish and Christian formulations are diverse. The Christian mind and heart respond warmly to the words "I am the vine" and "I am the resurrection and the life." For the Christian, these disclose God's intimate nearness to and concern for men. The Jewish mind sees in the words, at best, poetic faith, devoid of the power to elicit assent.

The religious vocabularies of Jews and Christians have been similar, so similar, in fact, that it is the specialist alone who is aware that words common to both faiths have different connotations and emphases — such as sin, righteousness, and repentance. However different the sense in which the religious words are used, Christians and Jews use an overlapping vocabulary.

The Fourth Gospel portrays, in a Christian way, and through the medium of the Christ, conceptions about God which are paralleled and held as firmly and as warmly in Jewish tradition in the Jewish way. Scholars have pointed out that the rabbinic parallels to the Fourth Gospel consistently assign to God the role which the Gospel assigns to the Christ. Christians have often been unaware that Jews have expressed these conceptions (for the assumption was that such profundity was attainable only in Christian thought); Jews have been unaware that Christians, in ascribing certain properties to the Christ, have been, in effect, formulating conceptions about God.

For Jews — and I suspect for many modern persons of Christian background — the phraseology of the Fourth Gospel is a stumbling block to understanding. Allegory and symbolic language have lost much of their appeal; the literary devices of the Fourth Gospel are frequently incongruous; the mood and the depth of the religious thought are often broken by startling interruptions.

All this must be noted, for only by noting it can the reader pass beyond a preoccupation with the trivial and the incidental and discern the religious message which, often in feeble contexts, is articulated with vigor and with triumph: God exists; He loves mankind. God is man's assurance of eternal life, man's guide, man's security. This essentially Jewish message, found in beautiful and simple formulation on every page of rabbinic literature, is now expressed in the Fourth Gospel through the exaltation of a divine Jesus to almost an equality or identity with God.

The weakness of the Gospel is its partial enslavement to the time and background of its composition (the second-century Greek world), its infelicitous rhetorical figures, and the occasional lameness of the less than skillful authorship. Yet it succeeds time after time in rising above its handicaps, and any one who gives thought to the matter can discern why to Christians it has been the Gospel of Gospels.

For the modern Jew, however, the Fourth Gospel presents the problem that he can respond to a laudatory appraisal of Jesus only to the point at which no special measure or kind of divinity is imputed to him. From the standpoint of traditional Christianity, however lofty might be the words which a Jew would speak about Jesus, the denial of his divinity amounts to embracing what the church has persistently regarded as a heresy. Whatever laudable adjectives a Jew may apply to Jesus as a man, these are insufficient for traditional Christianity.

It is only the Jew who does not know his own heritage who can join in some modern Christian appraisals of Jesus as the greatest of prophets, as the greatest of the rabbis, or as the greatest teacher. Were all the statements attributed to Jesus in the Gospels genuinely his, the fair-minded student, who examined the words without overassessing them because of their presumed source, would find it necessary to avoid an excess of superlatives. It is all too often the premise that the life of Jesus is "the greatest story ever told" which attributes to his words an eminence actually transcending them. It is not that these words, at their best, are poor or base; on the contrary, they are superb. But they are by no means unequaled either in clarity, in vigor, in perception, or in profundity in Jewish literature.

The greatness of the historical Jesus, were that recoverable, would not lie in any single avenue, nor would any single description be accurate. Rabbinists are correct in affirming that the teachings ascribed to him are not unique. Nor was his career unique, whether he was the preacher of some early end of the world or some political rebel against Rome, in either case a martyr to a despotic power. Jesus was not the only man in the history of the Jews who claimed, or for whom the claim was made, of Messiahship; he was not the only martyr at the hands of the Romans; he was not the only man to undergo crucifixion.

Jesus was not unique in any one isolated way. He was unique, however, in that combination of attributes which made him a person of marked individuality. His gift for parable, his aptness as a teacher, his affinity for the standards of the prophets of Israel, his capacity for leadership of men — if we accept for the moment the Gospel report — all these things combine to point to a personality which impressed itself vividly on his followers. Only a Jew whose unique combination of qualities was extraordinary could have been thought by other Jews to have been accorded a special resurrection. We can be certain that the impression which he made was a deep one, even though, to our regret, we must confess that we cannot exactly reconstruct a delineation of what that impact may have been. In the same sense, the search for historical confirmation of the incidents of the Fourth Gospel is useless and wide of the mark. The Fourth Gospel is Christian supernaturalism set forth in striking form. It is a Christian statement of a view of the nature of God's relationship to man expressed in the affirmation of the divinity of Jesus, through whom man can reach God.

Yet it is at this very place at which Christianity and Judaism are at their most irreconcilable that it is relevant to inquire about the significance of the antithesis. From the impartial standpoint of the study of the history of religions, developed Judaism and developed Christianity stem from a common Biblical source. They both hold that they are monotheisms in the chain of a history of divine revelation to a chosen community. Indeed, once Christianity became a separate and discrete entity, it held that to it had been vouchsafed God's revelation, and that that revelation had been taken away from Judaism.

If to the liberal person of either faith a claim to a special and exclusive revelation is in its literal statement uncongenial, then he needs to ask this question: granting that Judaism and Christianity have separate histories, divergent forms, disparate emphases, and discordant calendars: is there some essence in each of them which discloses their common ancestry?

The traditionalist, zealous to justify his partisanship, would tend to emphasize the separation of the two. Such zeal extends in its usual form to measuring the strengths in the one by the weaknesses in the other, of comparing them at those points where judicious selection yields a predetermined conclusion. Thus, for example, Christians have often expressed the amazing judgment that Judaism totally lacks such beliefs as God's grace and love. On the other hand, some Jews have equated Christianity (indeed, as Protestants have Catholicism) with idolatry, with the worship of a man in place of God. Such judgments derive either from direct ill will, or from the usual inability of an outsider to grasp the nuances and subtleties which are within a tradition; these judgments can appear even in what purport to be books of sober and careful scholarship.

The liberal, however, ought surely to be able to transcend such opaqueness. If he needs to abstain from seeing things as better than they are, then he can also see them as no worse than they are.

In the sense that Christianity, although in forms almost totally divergent from Judaism, also expresses a conviction about God and man, it is in substance akin to Judaism. To be akin is not to be identical, nor is it the same as interchangeable. For those minds to which form is the overriding consideration, or which ascribe substance in a literal sense to form, the kindred nature of Judaism and of Christianity is inevitably obscured — by the forms themselves.

The overarching theme of the Fourth Gospel is that Jesus,

eternally divine, briefly endured human form; that in Jesus God became man and went through experiences redemptive for mankind. Thus, the Christian conviction about God is expressed in a form which is forever alien to the Jewish mind and heart. The Jewish conviction, similarly, is shaped by events, dispositions, and emphases which are foreign to the Christian mind and heart. Yet the common motif to be discerned in the essence of Judaism and of Christianity, as expressed in the Fourth Gospel, is the concern of God for man.

# XXV

# The Pastoral Epistles

How FAR the church has moved from its Jewish antecedents is even more clearly to be discerned from its practical problems of organization than from its problems of metaphysics and doctrine. Philosophical exposition can well have been the concern primarily of random individuals or of small groups. The questions of the form of organization and of obedience to the settled authority of officials affected more immediately a wider segment of the church; indeed, it affected the entire church.

The latest writings of the New Testament are not free from anxiety about proper doctrine; that concern, in fact, has abided in the Catholic Church down to our own day. But the novel items in the latest writings are the specific nature of the instructions about church officers, and their duties, privileges, and responsibilities.

Three Epistles, written as though from the hand of Paul, are addressed to his closest lieutenants. Two of these are to Timothy, and one to Titus. They contain instructions about the duties of church leaders, and therefore they are called the Pastoral Epistles. Some wide agreement exists that the order in which they were written was Second Timothy, Titus, and First Timothy. Modern scholarship is uncertain whether these "pastoral" instructions are from the same hand; Catholic scholarship considers them to be genuinely from Paul. It is likely that there are authentic strands in the letters, but in their present form they are to be regarded as having been extensively reworked in the third or fourth decade of the second century.

The initial theme of Second Timothy is encouragement to the faithful in the face of the distress and suffering caused them by the holders of false doctrines. The speculations and godless chatter of these false teachers must be avoided. It is primarily women "burdened by sin and swayed by various impulses who will listen to anybody" who have been captured by them. "Timothy" in particular should have nothing to do with the stupid and senseless prattle. As effective counter measures, gentle reproof may be offered, or perhaps God may grant the people repentance and escape from the devil.

As though in opposition to gnostics who scorned the Old Testament, the Epistle speaks of the validity of "all scripture . . . inspired by God and profitable for teaching, for correction, and for training in righteousness."

Finally, the writing becomes highly personal, as though it is relating Paul's immediate predicaments and a fate which is in the offing: "I am already on the point of being sacrificed; the time of my departure has come. I have fought the good fight, I have finished the race, I have kept the faith." It is such passages which some scholars believe may be genuine fragments from Paul's hand, incorporated into the late Epistle.

The Epistle to Titus supposes that Paul had left Titus in Crete to correct some things which had gone wrong there. Titus is instructed to appoint elders in every town. Such men were to be blameless, and to have been married only once, and their children were to be faithful believers.

The Epistle seems to equate "elder" and "bishop" as though the office was the same and the titles interchangeable. It was expected of such an official that he should not be arrogant, quick-tempered, a drunkard, violent, or greedy for gain. He had to hold firm to sound doctrine, to teach it, and to refute those who contradicted it.

As for the church members, the older men should be serious and sensible, and the older women reverent in behavior, neither slanderers nor slaves to drink. Young women should be chaste, domestic, and submissive to their husbands; young men should be in full control of themselves. Slaves should be submissive to their masters, give satisfaction in every way, and not pilfer.

And, finally, the church should be submissive to civil rulers and authorities. Gentleness and the avoiding of quarrels are highly commendable. Controversies, over genealogies or the Law, are unprofitable and stupid; if a man is factious, he should be admonished once or twice, but thereafter avoided.

Personal greetings — as though from Paul's hand — close the Epistle.

First Timothy purports to have been written to Timothy while Paul was at Ephesus. Its first section enjoins "Timothy" to deter certain persons from teaching a false doctrine. There appear to be two aspects to this false doctrine; it deals with "myths and endless genealogies," and reflects the desire of these erratics "to be teachers of the law, without understanding either what they are saying or the things about which they make assertions."

I would suggest, contrary to the usual view of scholars, that we are dealing here not with some external Jewish activity, but with an internal Christian movement, and that the passage expresses a preference for a "spiritual" Gospel like the Fourth over Gospels like Matthew and Luke which present realistic genealogies as of mortal men, and shackle the figure of the Christ in human details. Similarly, the would-be teachers of the law are to be regarded as Christians, and not as Jews; the pallid restatement of Paul's position on the Law of Moses is directed against a legalizing tendency within the church which would have challenged the ascendancy of "faith."

The Epistle goes on to enjoin prayer on behalf of kings and those in high places, so that the church may lead a quiet and peaceful life and be godly and respectful in every way. It is the men who should do the praying, "lifting holy hands without anger or quarreling." Women are to keep silent, to have no authority over men; they should be properly dressed, avoiding braided hair, gold, and pearls. A woman achieves salvation, if she abides in faith, love, and holiness, through bearing children.

The requirements for the office of bishop, as in Titus, are blamelessness, marriage only a single time, temperance, sound good sense, dignity, hospitality, and an aptness for teaching. To be well qualified to care for God's church, the candidate must first have managed his own children and household well. He may not be a man of recent conversion; he must command the respect of the non-Christians.

The requirements for the office of deacon are less stringent. Honesty and seriousness are necessary, and overaddiction to wine is a disqualification. This office may be held by women, provided that they are temperate and not slanderers.

Next, there ensues a warning against false teachings. It is prefaced, appropriately, by a passage which in the Greek is more readily recognizable than in the English translation as either an early hymn or a short formulation of the essence of the belief about Christ:

> "He was manifested in the flesh,
> Vindicated in the Spirit,
> Seen by the angels,

Preached among the nations,
Believed on in this world,
Taken up in glory."

The word "faith" is used in this Epistle differently from its meaning in the genuine letters of Paul. There "faith" was a profound and vital inner experience; here "faith" is a set of beliefs and principles, inherited from the past and properly to be transmitted to the future.

It is in this latter sense of faith that the Epistle warns that in later times there would be those who would depart from the "faith," for they would have heeded deceitful spirits and the doctrines of demons. These unfaithful ones would listen approvingly to nonsense about forbidden marriages and forbidden foods — even despite the truth that everything created by God is good, and nothing is to be rejected if it is received with thanksgiving. The allusion here is probably to early teachers of celibacy and asceticism, the holders of a "heresy" known from the church fathers as "encratism." Such heretics might have pointed, for the justification of their actions, to Paul's reluctance to endorse marriages, in First Corinthians 7; if so, the Epistle is trying to correct those who took too literally or with over-persuasion what Paul had taught.

The Epistle, continuing, enjoins Timothy to set a good example in speech, in conduct, in love, in faith, and in spirit. He should "attend to the public reading of scripture, to preaching, to teaching."

Old men, advises the Epistle, should be exhorted rather than rebuked, and young men should be treated like brothers, older women like mothers, and younger women like sisters. As for widows, they must be supported by children or grandchildren, if these are able to do so. For such to withhold support is to disown the faith and is even worse than being an unbeliever. No woman can be enrolled for church support as a widow who is under sixty or who has been married more than once; she must be attested to as one who has brought up children, washed the feet of the saints, relieved the afflicted, and devoted herself to doing good in every way. Younger widows must not be enrolled; since they are able of body, they tend to gad from house to house; thus they become not only idlers, but also gossips. They take a pledge — presumably to remain unmarried and to do church work — but promptly they want to be married. Young widows should remarry and bear children.

Elders who function well deserve both honor and recompense. Charges of misconduct against them are admissible only on the evidence of more than one witness. Timothy should not be hasty in "the laying on of hands."

A very odd verse interrupts here: "No longer drink only water, but use a little wine for the sake of your stomach and your frequent ailments." The context of the verse is very puzzling; the usual explanation is that it is an afterthought to be added to the general injunctions given above to avoid asceticism (The verse has served the anti-prohibitionists quite well; prohibitionists have pointed out that the use of wine here sanctioned is hygienic in purpose.)

The next injunctions concern slaves who are Christians. These should serve their pagan masters well "so that the name of God and the teaching may not be defamed." They should not presume on their common faith for advantages if their master is a Christian, but should rather serve all the better.

Divergence from the duties and instructions outlined above means divergence from the sound words of the Lord Jesus Christ. Those who have departed from the instructions have found their falsity a source of material profit. The faithful should avoid the temptations to gain such profits, for "the love of money is the root of all evil." It is this to which the false teachers have succumbed.

Finally, the Epistle enjoins on Timothy, the man of God, the duty of aiming at righteousness, godliness, and other noble qualities. He should guard what has been entrusted to him, and avoid "the godless chatter and the contradictions of what is falsely called knowledge."

The usual analyses of the Pastoral Epistles point to three needs which they tried to meet. First, the dangers from heresy and from schism were real. A heretic of great significance, Marcion, had written a work called "Antitheses," which we might translate as "contradictions." It is this book to which the last words of First Timothy seem to allude. We shall see a little later that Marcion's heresy consisted primarily in his attack on the Old Testament and in his preference for only a segment of the large library of Christian writings which by this time was in circulation.

Second, a mode of organization and distribution of duties within the church had become essential. Though after New Testament times the organization of the Catholic Church is somewhat different from that which is set forth in the Epistles, the division into the ranks of bishop (which means "overseer") and of deacon ("minister") is already well marked.

Third, it is quite likely that First Timothy, in stressing the reading of Scripture, wishes to counter the intention of Marcion to eliminate the Old Testament. The emphasis on the public reading of Scripture shows that the forms of church worship have become stable and more elaborate than in their earlier random and sporadic expressions.

Some scholars would add a fourth need which the Pastorals

served. They argue that the genuine letters of Paul, which the Marcionites cherished, might not have seemed safe for the church since they seem to countenance nonconformity. Such scholars suggest that the Pastoral Epistles, issued in Paul's name, gave to Paul's letters a more orthodox cast which not only made the genuine Epistles agreeable to the church, but also rescued them from exclusive use by the Marcionites. This fourth point is a reasonable conjecture.

The Jewish reader discerns that out of the confusions and discordancies in crosscurrents of Christianity, which were attendant on its break with Judaism and on its enlargement in the Greek world, stable and crystallized organization is developing. The time which produced the Pastoral Epistles is far beyond those early days when Christian-Jewish disputes were internal affairs. It is beyond Paul's time, when Christianity was already no longer simply the synagogue, but not as yet the institutionalized church. The Pastoral Epistles reflect the church in its beginning as a solid, almost uniform, institution.

# XXVI

## Jude and Second Peter

Two LATE BOOKS of the New Testament are closely related to each other, for the shorter of these is incorporated as a single chapter into the longer of the two.

The twenty-five verses of the Epistle of Jude purport to have been written by "the brother of James." It is directed against the teachers of false doctrines who have slipped into the church secretly. Their teachings, of some "docetic" variety, are said to amount to a denial of the only Master and Lord, Jesus. These heretics indulge in the worst kinds of immorality, for which they court the punishment meted out to Sodom and Gomorrah for unnatural sex practices. The Epistle cites the examples of other Old Testament evildoers in proof of the certainty of punishment.

Against heretics marked by both boldness and vice, only the greatest steadfastness can preserve the faith.

Perhaps a generation after Jude was written, it was included within a writing in the form of an Epistle, as though from the hand of Simon Peter. Scholarship considers this book of Second Peter the latest of all the New Testament writings. Neither First Peter nor Second Peter comes from the hand of the Galilean disciple; indeed, two different men composed the two Epistles which bear Peter's name.

The Epistle begins with an affirmation of the salvation which awaits the faithful believer. It proceeds to assert that the writer was an eyewitness of the events of the career of Jesus, and not some merely clever writer of myths. The truth of the traditions of the earthly career of Jesus lies in the accuracy with which his career was predicted by the prophets of Scripture.

Then ensues the substance of Jude; there are some minor changes and variations, but these are without significance.

The third chapter begins with the statement that this is the second letter which the writer is sending; most scholars believe that the reference to an earlier letter is to First Peter, for the purpose of giving the present Epistle a greater claim to authenticity. (A minority of scholars take the allusion to be to some now lost writing, but we need not linger over this or other occasional conjectures.) Both the First and Second Epistles have the same general purpose, according to this passage, of reminding the reader "of the predictions of the holy prophets and the commandment of the Lord and Savior through the apostles." This last phrase is of considerable significance, for it reveals the accumulated authority in the late church traditions which was ascribed to the generation immediately following Jesus. Indeed, the "apostolic" validity must have become by this time a set of invaluable credentials, or there would have been no purpose in recourse to attributing the Epistle to an apostle. In even later times "apostolic succession" was to become an ultimate test of validity or invalidity.

One type of second-century heresy is identifiable rather clearly in Second Peter. We have seen several times above that the Second Coming had undergone reinterpretation, even to the point of its being virtually denied, as in the Fourth Gospel. To counter such "spiritualizing" efforts, Second Peter reaffirms the Second Coming. The author, therefore, feels that he must account for the delay which has given rise to the existing doubts. This delay, he contends, is not an accident, but intentional, so as to give men the opportunity to repent. Besides, "with the Lord one day is as a thousand years and a thousand years as one day." Paul, too, says the Epistle, had written in such a vein about the delay (in First and Second Thessalonians); some things in Paul's Epistles are "hard to understand," and it is to be lamented that "the ignorant and unstable twist them to their own destruction."

One could conjecture that the author of Second Peter would have been quite happy if some of Paul's letters had disappeared. But we immediately encounter unmistakable evidence that by now the letters of Paul have been elevated to an eminence which was unassailable: the twisting of Paul's letters, says the Epistle, is similar to the twisting of other "scriptures."

It is in this incidental bit of information that the greatest importance lies. Christianity has grown to the point where it has not only its own ritual, its own organization, and its own doctrines. In equating Paul's letters with Scripture, Christianity has come to the threshold of possessing also its own Bible.

# PART FIVE

## *THE SIGNIFICANCE OF THE NEW TESTAMENT*

# XXVII

# The Genius of the New Testament Faith

I<small>F</small>, <small>UP TO THIS POINT</small>, we have looked at the various books and writers, the motives and the historical causes, the clear words of doctrine, and the hidden, it is time now to look beyond and above these diversities. The unity of the New Testament, overarching its different components, is like that of a large and loyal family: sisters may quarrel and brothers may tussle; feelings may be bruised and sharp words may be exchanged. But however individualistic this son or that daughter may be, he or she exhibits discernibly the marks of the family background. We have begun, as it was necessary to begin, with the individuals; to stop there, however, is to miss the even greater significance of the whole family.

The books brought together into the New Testament were selected, we have said, out of a considerably larger number available. (Some of those excluded have been preserved in whole or in fragments as the Apocrypha of the New Testament.) The present number of the New Testament books, twenty-seven, does not represent the number which appeared on what was probably the first list; it is, therefore, not an initial selection, but the result of matured judgment.

It is likely, in fact, that the first selection was made on the fringes of the Church, about the year 150, by Marcion, the heretic whom we have already mentioned. Marcion's list appears to have contained only ten of the thirteen letters attributed to Paul, and only one Gospel, either Luke or a version of Luke.*

---

* Perhaps Marcion shortened Luke; or perhaps, as one scholar has tried to show, the present Luke is a lengthened version of what Marcion had.

From his attributing authority exclusively to the small number of books then in circulation, scholars reason that Marcion's list confronted the Church with the insistent need to assert and defend the validity of many books not listed by Marcion. The more inclusive list was its rebuke to the Marcionites.

The longer and more centrally sanctioned list, technically known as the "canon," expressed the Church judgment against Marcion; as we have said, the heretic was interested in purging Christianity of all its Jewish antecedents, especially the Old Testament. The Church response to Marcion affirmed the validity of not only the Old Testament, but also that of the Christian writings which, by allusion or quotation, made abundant use of it.

The New Testament canon could conceivably be longer than the list of twenty-seven books which it now contains, for there were many writings in circulation. Indeed, the earliest list of acceptable writings, the Muratorian fragment of about the year 175, contains twenty-eight titles, the additional one being the Apocalypse of Peter. Whatever receptivity existed towards that book in 175 faded thereafter, for subsequent lists do not accord it the highest sanction. The Apocalypse of John (Revelation) barely managed, over considerable objection, to be included in the unfolding, approved lists. Countless other books, including additional Gospels, were not considered worthy of inclusion, even though they were precious to some segments of Christendom.

A characteristic common to the excluded books was what in comparison we would call a noticeable extremism. The rejected Gospels, for example, go to naïvely absurd lengths in describing the precociousness of Jesus as a child. Other writings pursue some single phase of the tradition or doctrine too one-sidedly for universal acclaim. Still others reflect viewpoints which we can recognize as those which elsewhere in the Church were regarded as heretical. The rejected books, whether they were marginal or heretical, have considerable importance in the study of the New Testament period, and it is for this reason that they remain of enduring interest to scholars. Indeed, for the understanding of the New Testament as a whole they are highly important, since it is by means of the notice of what the New Testament might have contained that we are able the better to understand the form which it assumed. The New Testament is a collection of writings which present balanced and counter-balanced doctrines and views. The extreme views which are found in the rejected writings emphasize the fact that the accepted writings constitute a mean among extremes. It is as if the finally accepted New Testament writings are the center of a circle to which the rejected writings are tangents, touching the circle, but only on the outer circumference.

Each writing which was accepted is enhanced in value for inclusion by its supposed direct apostolic origin (such as the Epistles of Paul, John, and Peter); or else because it was very intimately associated with an apostle (such as the supposition that Luke was a traveling companion of Paul, or that Mark was a kind of secretary to Peter). Some writings, such as those by the church father Clement of Rome, are older than the Pastoral Epistles, but lack a sufficiently eminent authorship. Thus, even sound doctrine, when unaccompanied by apostolic rank, was deemed insufficient.

The New Testament, brought together by the Church, was in turn a charter for the Church. It was fashioned by a stable and settled Church; a Church not yet — indeed, not ever — free from internal crosscurrents and external involvements, but a Church which had gone beyond sporadic or random manifestation and had become a collective and organized entity. Prior to the existence of the canon of the New Testament, an individual book was hardly more than one man's, or one group's, opinion. Inclusion in the New Testament transformed the individual opinion into a collective conviction.

We have seen, considering each book separately as a more or less isolated work, how views in one clashed with views in others. That this juxtaposition of differing doctrines, however, occurs in a collection all of which was to be deemed inspired has predisposed the reader through the centuries quite unconsciously to harmonize the discordant views, or, indeed, even to be oblivious of discord. The four Gospels, each of which arose out of dissatisfaction with what preceded, were, when placed together, read as though they supplemented each other harmoniously. In fact, an early Church father, Tatian, was able to weave them together into a single, connected strand.

Similarly, the sharpness of one or another particular view was neutralized by the canon. Paul's Epistles reflect the belief that the End was near; but when they are read in the light of Matthew, of Acts, and of the Pastoral Epistles, Paul could seem to be predicting not an immediate End, but rather some ultimate and remote one.

Neutralization of this kind put a veneer of concord over the writings, but thinly enough so that discordance, when sought for, could be found. The student of Christianity notes how frequently, in the period immediately after the New Testament, the veneer either wore off or was peeled off. Special attention or prominence given to some single passage at the expense of other passages could yield factional views, at variance with the generally held opinion of the Church. Thus, heresies arose, usually in connection with a doctrine touched on or intimated in the New Testament, and elevated by a man or by a group into a decisive eminence. The refutation of such heresies was in part the demonstration that a fuller examination of all the New Testament writings would contradict the special view. For the orthodox person, this neutralization of the divergencies within the New Testament was so satisfactorily accomplished that he was unaware of it, even while he was thoroughly influenced by the harmony produced.

Moreover, the latent divergencies were fertile fields in which the seeds of differing interpretation of the commonly received Scripture could be managed. The Church believed that as the collector of the books into a canon it possessed also the proper interpretation. Passages which through terseness or ambiguity were open to various interpretations began to acquire specific "overmeaning"; that is, an authoritative and official meaning. Thereby the veneer of neutralization was made the more durable.

A trend towards such assertion of authority is seen in Second Peter in its protest against the alleged misreading of Paul's difficult Epistles. In a similar way, the Church developed its traditional interpretation of all the New Testament. Since the authoritative interpretation was capable of resolving the tensions and the clashing opinions in the text, the inference became natural that these tensions were of no great moment — if, indeed, they were present at all. Such tensions could escape the need for resolution for long periods of time; they could be maintained as supplementary facets fitting into a congruent whole. It was, therefore, not always necessary to demonstrate by explicit interpretation the harmony of the range of New Testament doctrines; it was sufficient simply to imply the harmony by pointing to their presence in the canon.

The collection of books which constitutes the New Testament, as Roman Catholics correctly insist, is never assessable as a unit except as a reflection of the Church which collected and canonized it. The individuality of some particular book becomes discernible only when it is successfully isolated from the collective context. When the particular book is unisolated, the individuality is markedly reduced in deference to the whole. Paul's defiance of the Jerusalem Church in Galatians seems less rebellious in the light of Acts. The office of the "prophet" is both praised in the Pauline letters and passed over, as though obsolescent, in the Pastoral Epistles. The heritage of the revelation of God in Christ is, on the one hand, proof of the valid authority of those who held the office of apostle; on the other hand, the warnings against false prophets and their false doctrines limit "revelation" to those whose legitimate apostolic succession is unquestioned. Indeed, precisely in the same way in which late Judaism, applauding its legacy of past prophecy, considered prophecy in the present as an aberration, so the Church delimited prophecy to a bygone period, and it saw itself as the sole arbiter of what had been truly prophetic or truly revealed.

It was difficult, but inescapably necessary, for the Church to steer a middle course between ever-present, or ever reappearing, extremes. Thus, the Judaism of the past was for the Church both the valid set of credentials of its authenticity, and at the same time the invalidated and supplanted precursor. The validity of the past Judaism could not be stressed to the point of extending the validity into the present; but the invalidity of the present Judaism could not be read too completely or too far into the past. Similarly, Jesus was to be regarded as both human and divine. His human character was not to be eliminated for the sake of exalting the divine, nor the divine at the expense of the human.

The ability to maintain a balance or to make a choice in the light of such antitheses and of unresolved tensions indicates the existence of a Church, organized, supervised, self-assured, and authoritative. When, after the New Testament age, the Church was confronted by dissident individuals or groups, it dealt with them on two levels. Temporal power was used to compel obedience; but above and beyond the detail of obedience, official interpretation formulated the proper opinions and doctrines, and refuted the dissenters and their use of the New Testament. Since, as we have noted, diversity in the New Testament doctrines bred heresies, the latency of heresies further underscored the need for incontestable authority.

It was the existence of such matured and acknowledged authority alone that accounts for the phenomenon of the acceptance of some writings and the rejection of others. Furthermore, the accrued authority of a Church, with its proper doctrines and proper practices, is the key which unlocks the meaning of the collected New Testament. The Church, as the "bride of Christ," was in its own eyes not simply a fortuitous aggregate of believers. Confident that it had been founded by Christ, the Church could logically claim to be a divine institution. Therefore, its newly formed Bible could be presented as possessing a special measure of inspiration, transcending, so it was believed, the Old Testament alone.

In preserving the Old Testament for its own possession, the Church buttressed its claim to divine ordination. To have cast the Old Testament overboard, as Marcion proposed, would not only have deprived the Church of a merely expedient claim to antiquity, but also, more profoundly, would have made of its charter, the New Testament, a document lacking the all-important preamble, the statement of the charter's purpose. For the New Testament, despite the bulk of its twenty-seven writings, is by itself a book without an introduction and without a thesis. Without the Old Testament, the New Testament is like a blueprint for individual rooms and halls, which omits the plans for the completed structure.

Jews have not always understood that Christians have regarded the Old Testament as "Christian"; they have often erroneously thought that in Christian eyes the Old Testament was a "Jewish" book. We have had occasion to notice that this inference can arise out of some Christian formulations. But it must be affirmed, strongly, that in the prevailing Christian belief, the Old Testament Scripture is held to be as validly a Christian heritage as, within Judaism, it is claimed to be Jewish. Indeed, the Church insisted that it was the true heir of the Old Testament, and that therefore it was the True Israel. The circumstance that the Christians used the Greek translation and the Jews the Hebrew original led the partisan Church Fathers to explain the occasional differences between the two as the result of malicious Jewish tampering with the Christians' possession. On the other hand, the rabbinic lament that no day was as sad for Israel as the day on which the Old Testament was translated into Greek reflects the Jewish dismay at the thoroughness of Christianity's adoption of the Old Testament as its Scripture.

What the Old Testament supplies to the New Testament is a scheme of God's providence in the world, and the role in that scheme of Israel, the people chosen by God. When Christians have read the Old Testament, it has been in their eyes Christian history which they have been reading. It is true that they relegated the Law of Moses to the reduced stature of a temporary guide; but at the same time, following Paul's lead, they distinguished between the literal and the allegorical to deduce from the Law of Moses itself symbolic meanings relevant to Christian purposes. The Prophets and the Psalms, especially when these were read as predictive of Christ, required little recourse to allegorical meaning, but could be retained just as they were.

The Old Testament provided in many ways the bill of particulars for the ethics, morals, and righteousness of the Christian Church. However Christianity may have modified the bill or added to it, the New Testament is not primarily the statement of these religious goals, but rather an exposition of the method by which they were to be reached. The Old Testament set forth the standards; the New Testament set forth the means of attaining the standards.

The retention of the Old Testament contributed weightily to the implicit modifying of some New Testament affirmations concerning the nearness of the End. The Old Testament, by and large, envisages a continuing world. The view that the world was soon to end hardly encompassed the possibility of an abiding Church. The creation of the Church, on the other hand, underlines a tacit Christian deferment, indefinitely, of the End. The change in meaning within the New Testament of the "Kingdom of God," from some new age replacing the old into a synonym for the Church, emphasizes the function of the New Testament. In its complete form, prefaced by the Old, the New Testament is not a set of warnings or injunctions in advance of an imminent catastrophe. It is now, instead, a formula for living in the ceaseless unfolding of time.

In this sense the New Testament and the rabbinic literature are as identical in purpose as they are antithetical in formula. The rabbis prescribed for ensuing time, as the means of attaining Old Testament goals, a regimen of Law derived, they believed, from Old Testament Law. In order to carry out the Old Testament intent, they evolved, out of their devoted study and deliberations, an exhaustive system of regulations, known to us as Talmudic law, which was designed to buttress and protect the ancient law presented in the Pentateuch. The Prophets, the Psalms, and the other writings, according to the rabbinic view, had the purpose of exhorting men about their attitudes or of stimulating their emotional attitudes, with the result that the execution of the required Law was passionately voluntary, and not coldly obligatory.

In Judaism, authority lay in this required Law, in the rabbinic "tradition" which interpreted the Old Testament. Any learned Jew could turn to it on his own; the tradition was so uniformly available that all Jews who cared to could know the tradition and could articulate its authoritative pronouncements. From time to time there arose certain individual rabbis who were men of such acknowledgedly great learning that their decisions and interpretations of the tradition tended to become authoritative, and in that sense the men themselves became authorities. But such authority was never universal, or immediately gained, and other rabbis could challenge the decisions and interpretations, without ever being subject to the charge of heresy. The authority of the rabbi lay, not in his office, but in the inherited tradition which he taught, and his person was never so authoritative as the traditional literature itself.

The Church way was different from the rabbinic. The Church divided the Old Testament Law into the ceremonial, which it set aside, and the ethical, which it affirmed. Initially, it followed the swing of the pendulum away from legalism into a new exaltation of "faith" and belief. In Christianity, as it developed, authority lay not alone in its tradition of belief, but more immediately in the persons of the Church officials who, through the centuries, succeeded each other to the traditionally accepted role of divinely sanctioned guardians of the faith.

Although, as we have seen, the conception of faith differs

contrastingly within the New Testament, from inner experience, as in Paul, to a set of beliefs, as in the latest writings, the word carries with it strong implications of reasoned assent. And since, in the New Testament phrase, before the word faith there is the all-important adjective "proper," then "proper faith" inescapably demands precise definition and precise articulation. Where, for the rabbis, overt action was considered the expression of a faith which they were content to leave implicit, for the Church the denial of "works" as the decisive norm meant that "faith" needed all the more urgently to be defined and explicit. The rabbis could and did tolerate opposing legalistic opinions, as between the followers of Hillel and those of Shammai; and in ultimately preferring Hillel they could still describe the rejected Shammai as the "voice of the living God." The rabbis were choosing between two forms of overt action, expressive of the same unexpressed, basic conviction.

The Church, however, inclined very naturally to the division of doctrine into the true and the false, not out of zeal for mere division, but out of the direct confrontation by explicit doctrines. For the Church, heresy was a matter of wrong formulation or of wrong accentuation; it could not treat the divergent as the voice of the living God, but only as the deceitful voices of lying prophets.

The questions of what specifically are proper and improper doctrine, however, are only the negative approach to the New Testament. On its positive side the New Testament asserts, through its emphasis on the saving power of faith, that the revealed will of God is knowable and, through the medium of the Church, available to men, and that a man's conformity to God's will rests on his fundamental orientation and attitude. The proper faith is revealed, defined, and mediated by the Church.

Man partakes of that intermediated faith by his own will or by God's grace, and possesses in the Church the sure guide for his individual conduct.

The rabbis and the Church accepted it as axiomatic that God's will had been revealed. On this fundamental they were agreed. But thereafter the program of the rabbis was the result of their asking, with reference to every single aspect of man's existence: "What, specifically, does God demand that man do?" The program of the Church rested on the axiom that on the basis of a proper attitude man would do the required thing, and it asked: "What must a man believe?"

In the light of the fundamental agreement, it is not strange that while the developed ritual of Christianity and that of Judaism have lost all but tiny remnants of a common background, the ethical standards remained largely congruent and even strikingly identical. The rabbis prescribed the specific conduct in social situations which the Church, abstaining from specifications, inevitably suggested. Ritual, theology, and exceedingly diverse historical backgrounds are among the items which hide from Jews and Christians their large areas of congruency; but a penetrating Confucian or a man from Mars, studying the two, would notice the similarities more immediately than the differences. Roman pagans, we may recall, found it quite difficult to distinguish between Jews and Christians.

Some Jewish analysts, who have addressed themselves only to facets of the New Testament, have noticed, correctly, how sharply individual items differ from comparable Jewish views. For example, rabbinic Judaism offers almost nothing comparable to Paul's advice to shun marriage. On such a basis, some analysts attribute to all the New Testament, or to all Christianity, the attitude of Paul. The neutralizing factor about which I have spoken above escapes the notice of these scholars. Had the

Church followed Paul slavishly, as such analysts suppose, it would simply have banned marriage. The Church, however, has not only sanctioned it, but has considered it an institution ordained by God; and, to repeat, it labeled as heresy the "encratism" which would have prohibited marriage.

The New Testament view on any single matter is more than the single view of an isolated passage. The differences between the rabbis and the total New Testament are not nearly so extreme as partisan scholarship, on both sides, has supposed. For example, the Greek pessimism, so strong in Paul, is counterbalanced, or, indeed, overbalanced, not only in other parts of the New Testament, but in the Jewish optimism of the retained Old Testament.

The differences, although not so sharp as they are usually thought to be, are by no means absent. They are, indeed, emphasized by the assumption in the New Testament that it contains both a different and a better approach to God than the Jews had. It is very easy for a Jew to have his perspective on the New Testament determined totally by this infelicitous motif; he can, understandably in the light of subsequent history, equate this incidental theme with the entire or primary motif of the New Testament. Indeed, sober Christian scholarship until rather recent times considered the assumption of New Testament superiority interchangeable with established fact. Contrasts were drawn, uniformly unfavorable to Judaism, and a curious by-product of such scholarly partisanship was the fantastic corollary that every applaudable sentiment in the New Testament had in the rabbinic literature some parallel of despicable content. It was comforting to suppose that what Jesus criticized was not the traits universal among men, but the traits specifically of Jews. The New Testament, we were told by these scholars, was universalistic, but Judaism was tribalistic. God in the New Testament was close to men; the Jewish God was remote from man's world, and cruel. Christianity dealt with internals, Judaism with externals. Christianity was earnestness, and Judaism was hypocrisy. The context in which I speak, it is to be recalled, is that of scholars, * not of random Christians.

Yet the presence of the pronounced anti-Jewish motif in the New Testament ought not to blind a Jew who wants to appraise Christianity in the same way that it has often blinded Christians about Judaism. Jews may possibly be unaware that there exists a growing but already large literature in which modern Christians both deplore the intrusion of anti-Jewish sentiment in the New Testament, and describe it as no longer tenable. The "anti-Semitism" in the New Testament or derivable from it is certainly less than the primary motif of the New Testament.

The true genius of the New Testament is that, like the rabbinic halaka, it sets forth an interpretation of the will of God. Like the Old Testament and rabbinic law, it envisages an Israel, a body of believers, a Church. The distinctiveness of the New Testament is its commitment to "faith," faith which is not alone an expression of personal conviction, or a set of beliefs, but "faith" as it is mediated by the Church, which collected and preserved the writings and canonized them.

The exaltation of faith is both the strength of the New Testament, and also its exposure to weakness. At its best, the New Testament is able powerfully to elicit from man the profound search of himself and of his universe for meaning; it can move a man to set himself in a context in which the most fundamental questions of existence, rather than extrinsic and trivial ones, confront him.

---

* An even fuller bill of particulars about this scholarship is to be found in an essay by George Foot Moore, called "Christian Writers on Judaism," in the *Harvard Theological Review* of 1921

But, on the other hand, the pitfall in the concentration on the proper faith is an overalertness to the potentially improper. While the rabbis could, and did, tolerate heterodoxy in thought, for the Church the axiom that some form of faith was proper meant that some other form was improper, and heterodoxy necessarily seemed to be heresy.

The Church officials, exercising their temporal powers, could coerce to orthodoxy anyone who rebelled in doctrine against the constituted authorities. The refinements of details of the Christian doctrine increased the number of possibilities of heresy, with the result that much of the history of Christianity is the history of the successful or unsuccessful experience with such heretical rebels. The march of events, as the world expanded beyond the Mediterranean in geography and beyond Ptolemy in astronomy, brought it about that accrued differences of nationalisms and regionalisms within the Church increased the Church concern for fidelity to the proper faith. Inevitably, faith came to be the commitment not to God alone, but to the Church formulation of that commitment.

The Catholic experience with Galileo and the Protestant Fundamentalist opposition to the doctrine of evolution are logical sequels of this New Testament premise that there is one proper faith, and that it is the office of the Church alone to determine what this faith is. Protestants of our day, who have broken both with Catholic authority and with Catholic doctrine, and who propose, instead, to revert to the New Testament as authoritative have often failed to discern that the collected New Testament is the Scripture not of some vacuum, but of the emerging Catholic Church. Such oversight is surely the result of reading the New Testament selectively. When Protestantism speaks of its return to the "New Testament faith," it does not mean the collective aspects of the New Testament, but rather the free expression of religious conviction, as found *within* the New Testament; Protestantism does not, and cannot, revert to the New Testament as a united body of thought, but only to the formative process out of which subsequently an entity emerged.

Protestantism has become subdivided into almost 275 denominations, not despite the New Testament, but because of it. The enshrinement of the Epistles of Paul in Scripture has exalted the example of the man who broke with the established church. It was Paul whom Luther imitated; it is Paul who serves as the justification for any Protestant group which in its own day sees in its mother church a conformity and legalism which, it holds, stifle personal liberty or mystic or ecstatic experience. Inspired by Paul, Protestants have directed towards Catholics exactly those arguments which the early church fathers directed towards Judaism. Yet, so long as the "unity" of the New Testament was unbroken, the neutralization of Paul in the New Testament was effective. When the renaissance and humanism, by encouraging the lay study of the classics and of Scripture, led to the close scrutiny of the component parts of the New Testament, the individuality of the various books began to transcend the neutralization. Once changed political circumstances made it possible for the holder of a heterodox view to be physically protected, he could set forth a view, based on a part of the New Testament, which was at variance with the Catholic view.

Significantly, the individual, or the group, who selected some particular aspect of the New Testament for special emphasis, and who had reservations about details in the traditional doctrine, was, before the Protestant Reformation, coerced into conformity, or, after it, was obliged to found his own church. The Catholic Church, as the creator of the New Testament, could hardly tolerate within itself any overt or latent challenge to its authority as the guardian of the New Testament.

In its more exact title of the New Covenant, the New Testament, at the time when it was fashioned into a unit, was not simply the outpouring of the souls of individual men. It was the product of a Church, the reflection of a Church. It offers not a general or universal salvation, but a particular plan of salvation for particular people in a particular way.

There is, accordingly, a deep divergency in Christendom. The Catholic Church which produced the New Testament has remained in its own eyes dominant over it; Protestantism, on the other hand, has taken hold of the New Testament as its supreme authority, and it has denied the authority of the Catholic Church. It is traditional in Protestantism that salvation lies in the Bible; it is firmly established in Catholicism that salvation lies in the Church. There is the paradox that the New Testament, fashioned by the Catholic Church, is the supreme authority for Protestants, while the Catholic Church does not elevate the New Testament which it fashioned to the place of sole supremacy which the Protestants do.

Protestantism is, understandably, not able to re-create for our day and time the conditions which existed when the literature of the New Testament was being created. Protestantism, however, can be described as a "New Testament church" in a way which does not truly describe the Catholic Church. Indeed, some scattered Protestant sects make the sincere effort to live by the authority of the New Testament alone, without any form of added doctrine, organization, or liturgy beyond what the New Testament seems to prescribe.

Without the rising Catholic Church there would have been no New Testament. Without Protestantism, the New Testament would have become, in Western society, a remote authority instead of the vivid and near authority which it is for so many.

The genius of the New Testament religion is that the faith

**317**

which it exalted as the highest principle of man's relation to God
was not the tentative faith of the questing individual, but the
confidence of a Church, both in God and in itself.

When the early Church fashioned the twenty-seven writings
into a New Testament, it made its break with Judaism complete
and final.

# XXVIII

## Epilogue

THE HISTORIAN DOES NOT discharge his obligation if his account ends in the past and if he fails to indicate some directions for the future. In a study such as this, however, these indications must be broad and general. In a sense, their range is as great as the complicated field of relationships between persons motivated by differences which are deeply important to them. In a more fortunate sense, their range is as small as the lot which joins neighbor to neighbor. Out of the many comments which present themselves to mind, some few specific ones seem especially cogent.

History has brought us to the point where in the American tradition it is well known that religion is a matter of the private conscience. Religious amity in the United States can be abetted and made more truly attainable only when there is genuine respect, supported by knowledge, for the conscience of one's neighbor.

Beyond the relations of individuals of different faiths, Christians and Jews collectively have made some worthy efforts to find areas of co-operation and bases of reciprocal understanding. These are to be applauded, especially regarding their intent. What reservations one may have can come from noticing an unhappy by-product. It is a zeal on the part of some for glossing over the genuine differences in religious faiths; and if earlier generations were blind to the elements which are common to Judaism and Christianity, many in our day are blind to motifs and convictions which are distinctive. Genuine good will cannot prevail unless it is founded on a recognition of realities. Good will is scarcely authentic if it can emerge only when those who are expected to exhibit it must first disclaim their own individuality. In part Judaism and Christianity do overlap, as in the heritage of the Old Testament and its moral law, but in part they diverge. It is incorrect to call them identical, or apologetically to talk away the divergencies. Religious understanding should never presuppose identity, but rather a respect for acknowledged differences.

When Judaism and Christianity are compared with each other, the sense of their diversity from each other is a natural conclusion. It is as if they were on opposite sides of a fence. Yet when they are seen in the light of a third element, such as Nazism or Communism, the impression changes quickly, and Judaism and Christianity are seen rather as being on the same side of the fence.

How Judaism and Christianity can live together in the fullest amity, but with dignity and adherence to principle, is a quest imposed by modern democracy. It needs to be recognized that the wish for them to live amicably contradicts what was their history for almost seventeen hundred years. I have mentioned several times the anti-Jewish sentiments found in the New Testament. Jewish life in the Middle Ages was largely one persecution after another. Yet it would be unreasonable for modern American Jews to regard our American Christian neighbors as the perpetrators of those medieval misfortunes. The sad history of the Jews in Europe makes it difficult still today in America to steer a middle course between condescension and obsequiousness. Yet it must be recalled that Nazism was virtually as hostile to Christianity as to Judaism. The course of harmony based on deep understanding must steer carefully past the perpetuation of old grievances, however justified in the past, and the partial perception of modern difficulties. It will need more than simply good intentions. It will need also comprehension and wider horizons.

For American Jews to understand the New Testament as scholars do is only the beginning of understanding. A further step is to learn what one's usual Christian neighbor or friend sees in it. Much of what is distinctive in the religious observances of the Christians comes from a period after the New Testament. This is the case, for example, with the observance of Christmas and with the office of the Pope. Understanding the New Testament sympathetically falls short of understanding Christianity.

For Jews, the New Testament is not and cannot be a literature sacred to us. But the sacred literatures of others can be enlightening and broadening to us, even giving us fresh perspectives on our own belief, if we try to understand sympathetically the profound perplexities and deep aspirations which human beings have been inspired to express, and how the lives of our contemporaries are moved by those ideals and institutions which embody them.

The New Testament, although it is not ours, is closer to us than any other sacred literature which is not our own. It shares in a legacy which is eternally precious to us. For American Jews it is the Scripture of our neighbors — and, happily, of fellow citizens and friends.

# BIBLIOGRAPHY

*The New English Bible,* Reader's Edition (New York: Oxford University Press), to appear in 1975.

*The Oxford Annotated Bible, Revised Standard Version,* eds., Herbert G. May and Bruce M. Metzger (New York: Oxford University Press), 1962.

*Gospel Parallels,* RSV, Burton H. Throckmorton, Jr. (New York: Thomas Nelson & Sons), 1949.

Buttrick, George A., ed., *The Interpreter's Dictionary of the Bible,* 4 vols. (New York: Abingdon Press), 1962.

May, H. G., and Hamilton, R. W., eds., *Oxford Bible Atlas* (New York: Oxford University Press), 1962.

*The Interpreter's One-Volume Commentary on the Bible,* ed. by Charles M. Laymon (Nashville and New York: Abingdon Press), 1971.

*Jerome Biblical Commentary,* ed. by Raymond E. Brown, S.S., Joseph A. Fitzmyer, S.J., Roland E. Murphy, O. Carm. (London: Geoffrey Chapman), 1968.

Buttrick, George A., ed. *The Interpreter's Bible* (New York: Abingdon Press), 1951.

Enslin, Morton Scott, *Christian Beginnings* (New York: Harper & Row), 1938.

Fuller, R. H., *The New Testament in Current Study* (New York: Charles Scribner's Sons), 1962.

Grant, R.M., *A Short History of the Interpretation of the Bible* (New York: The Macmillan Company), 1958.

Grant, R. M., *A Historical Introduction to the New Testament* (New York: Harper & Row), 1963.

Kümmel, W. G., tr. by A. J. Mattill, Jr., *Introduction to the New Testament* (New York: Abingdon Press), 1966.

Grant, F. C., *An Introduction to New Testament Thought* (New York: Abingdon Press), 1950.

Moffatt, James, *An Introduction to the Literature of the New Testament* (New York: Charles Scribner's Sons), 1911.

Selby, Donald J., *Introduction to the New Testament* (New York: Macmillan Company), 1971.

Bultmann, Rudolf, *Primitive Christianity,* tr. by R. H. Fuller (New York: Meridian Books), 1957.

Goguel, Maurice, *The Birth of Christianity* (New York: The Macmillan Company), 1954.

Grant, F. C., *Roman Hellenism and the New Testament* (New York: Charles Scribner's Sons), 1962.

Jonas, Hans, *The Gnostic Religion* (Boston: Beacon Press), 1963.

Parker, Pierson, *The Gospel Before Mark* (Chicago: The University of Chicago Press), 1953.

Dibelius, Martin, tr. by Bertram Woolf, *From Tradition to Gospel,* 2nd ed. rev. (New York: Charles Scribner's Sons) n.d.

Bultmann, Rudolf, *The History of the Synoptic Tradition,* tr. by John Marsh (Oxford: Basil Blackwell), 1963.

Robinson, James M., *A New Quest of the Historical Jesus,* Studies in Biblical Theology No. 25 (Naperville: Alec R. Allenson, Inc.), 1959.

Davies, W. D., *Christian Origins and Judaism* (Philadelphia: Westminster Press), 1962.

Bultmann, Rudolf, *Theology of the New Testament,* tr. by Kendrick Grobel (New York: Charles Scribner's Sons), 1955.

Grant, F. C., *The Earliest Gospel* (New York: Abingdon Press), 1943.

Bornkamm, Günther, Barth, Gerhard, and Held, Heinz Joachim, *Tradition and Interpretation in Matthew* (Philadelphia: Westminster Press), 1963.

Cadbury, Henry J., *The Making of Luke-Acts* (New York: The Macmillan Company), 1927.

Martyn, J. Louis, *History and Theology in the Fourth Gospel* (New York: Harper & Row), 1968.

Brown, Raymond E., S.S., *The Gospel According to John* (2 vols), *The Anchor Bible* (Garden City, N. Y.: Doubleday & Co., Inc.), 1966.

Titus, Eric Lane, *The Message of the Fourth Gospel* (New York: Abingdon Press), 1957.

Bornkamm, Günther, *Jesus of Nazareth,* tr. by Irene and Frazer McLuskey with J. M. Robinson (New York: Harper & Row), 1960.

Enslin, Morton Scott, *The Prophet from Nazareth* (New York: Schocken Books), 1968.

Branscomb, Harvie, *The Teaching of Jesus* (New York: Abingdon Press), 1931.

Sandmel, Samuel, *We Jews and Jesus* (New York: Oxford University Press), 1965.

Sloyan, Gerald, *Jesus on Trial* (Philadelphia: Fortress Press), 1973.

Vermes, Geza, *Jesus the Jew* (London: William Collins Sons & Co. Ltd.), 1973.

Cadbury, Henry J., *The Book of Acts in History* (New York: Harper & Row), 1955.

Foakes Jackson, F. J., and Lake, Kirsopp, *The Beginnings of Christianity,* 5 vols. (London: Macmillan & Co.), 1933.

Deissmann, Adolph, *Paul,* tr. by W. E. Wilson (New York: Harper Torchbook), 1957.

Knox, John, *Chapters in a Life of Paul* (New York: Abingdon Press), 1950.

Selby, Donald J., *Toward the Understanding of St. Paul* (Englewood Cliffs, N. J.: Prentice-Hall, Inc.), 1962.

Sandmel, Samuel, *The Genius of Paul* (New York: Schocken Books), 1970.

Barrett, C. K., *The Pastoral Epistles in the New English Bible* (Oxford: Oxford University Press), 1963.

Manson, W., *The Epistle to the Hebrews* (London: Hodder and Stoughton), 1951.

Scott, E. F., *The Epistle to the Hebrews* (Edinburgh: T. & T. Clark), 1922.

Beare, F. W., *The First Epistle of Peter* (Oxford: Blackwell), 1947.

Charles, R. H., *The Revelation of St. John,* 2 vols. (CC), (New York: Charles Scribner's Sons), 1920.

# Index of Passages

# Index of Subjects and Persons

Midrash, haggada, 23; halaka, 24.
Missionaries, rules for, 153–154.
Moffatt, James, 250.
Montefiore, Claude Goldsmith, xiii–xiv.
Monotheism, in Christianity, 279–282.
Moore, George Foot, 25, 314n.
Mosaic Law, *see* Law of Moses.
Mother Church, at Jerusalem, 40; and Law of Moses, 40.
Muratorian fragment, 302.
Mystery religions, 98–101.

Nazism, 320.
New Testament, 3–6, 301–318; anti-Jewish feeling, 10, 203–205, 313–314; attitudes of Jews towards, xi–xviii, 312–313; authority, 307; canon, 3, 302; charter for the Church, 303–304; discordances and neutralizations, 34, 303–307; Hellenistic background, 18–19; "Higher Criticism", 11; language, 13–14; "manuscript" method of copying, 14; and Old, 3, 307–310; rejected writings, 302–303; Testament means covenant, 3.

Oaths, prohibition of, 149.
"Old" Testament, Church view of, 302–310; important to New Testament, 101, 307–310; interpreted as foreshadowing Christianity, 228–234; Jews call the Bible, 3; Pauline view, 88–89; rabbinic view, 309–310; as "record" of Christ's activity, 217.
Onesimus, 79.
Oral Law, and the Pharisees, 25–26.
Oral tradition, preservative factor in, 108–112.

Palestine, background of New Testament, 18–19; Christian beginnings, 13.
Parable, function of, 23, 126.

Parousia, 72, 74, 132, 189–190. *See* "End."
Passover, in Philo, 100; transformation of, in Paul, 76; crucifixion, 128–129; Passover eve, 271; Luke, 184, 188; Mark, 128–129; Matthew, 162.
Pastoral Epistles, 5, 287–289; *see also* individual Epistles.
Paul
  I. Doctrine of: on advantages of Jews, 93; attraction of his doctrine, 102–104; baptism, 60; the Christ, 51, 53, 266; the Church, 61–63; Crucifixion, 57–58, 83; the "End," 72–75, 81–82; "eucharist," 60, 86; faith, 69, 91–92, 291; freedom, 70–71; the Gentiles, 94; in Greek world, 101–104; the need of Christian law, 166–167; Law of Moses, 56–57, 67–70, 88–89, 91–93; love, 86–87; marriage, 73, 85; mystery religions, 99–101; rediscovery of his doctrine, 205–206; rejection of Jews, 63; Resurrection, 57–59, 85; salvation, 51, 57, 69, 91–92; sin, 59; and traditional Judaism, 37–38; *see also* individual Epistles.
  II. The Man: in Acts of the Apostles, 255–256, 261–264; apostle from God, 89–90; background, 44–45, 56–57; break with Judaism, 41; "conversion," 47–48, 55; foremost missionary, 37; inconsistencies, 46–47; independence of Jerusalem church, 89–90, 306; inspiration to Protestants, 316; journeys, 258–260; Judaism of, 57, 63–64; literary style, 46; message of, 37; missionary method, 107–108; and Pastoral Epistles, 287–290; personality, 45; and Peter, 88, 159–160; and Philo, 48–51; revelations, 55, 89–90; in Rome, 262; Roman citizen, 261, 263; "Saul", 257–258.
Pauline Epistles, 5, 37–38; Acts con-

# About SKYLIGHT PATHS Publishing

SkyLight Paths Publishing is creating a place where people of different spiritual traditions come together for challenge and inspiration, a place where we can help each other understand the mystery that lies at the heart of our existence.

Through spirituality, our religious beliefs are increasingly becoming a part of our lives—rather than *apart* from our lives. While many of us may be more interested than ever in spiritual growth, we may be less firmly planted in traditional religion. Yet, we do want to deepen our relationship to the sacred, to learn from our own as well as from other faith traditions, and to practice in new ways.

SkyLight Paths sees both believers and seekers as a community that increasingly transcends traditional boundaries of religion and denomination—people wanting to learn from each other, *walking together, finding the way*.

We at SkyLight Paths take great care to produce beautiful books that present meaningful spiritual content in a form that reflects the art of making high quality books.

# About Jewish Lights

People of all faiths and backgrounds yearn for books that attract, engage, educate, and spiritually inspire.

Our principal goal is to stimulate thought and help all people learn about who the Jewish People are, where they come from, and what the future can be made to hold. While people of our diverse Jewish heritage are the primary audience, our books speak to people in the Christian world as well and will broaden their understanding of Judaism and the roots of their own faith.

We bring to you authors who are at the forefront of spiritual thought and experience. While each has something different to say, they all say it in a voice that you can hear.

Our books are designed to welcome you and then to engage, stimulate, and inspire. We judge our success not only by whether or not our books are beautiful and commercially successful, but by whether or not they make a difference in your life.

Stuart M. Matlins, Publisher

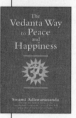

# Kabbalah from Jewish Lights Publishing

**Awakening to Kabbalah:** The Guiding Light of Spiritual Fulfillment
*by Rav Michael Laitman, PhD* 6 x 9, 192 pp, HC, 978-1-58023-264-7 **$21.99**

**Cast in God's Image:** Discover Your Personality Type Using the Enneagram and Kabbalah
*by Rabbi Howard A. Addison* 7 x 9, 176 pp, Quality PB, 978-1-58023-124-4 **$16.95**

**Ehyeh:** A Kabbalah for Tomorrow *by Dr. Arthur Green*
6 x 9, 224 pp, Quality PB, 978-1-58023-213-5 **$16.99**

**The Enneagram and Kabbalah, 2nd Edition:** Reading Your Soul
*by Rabbi Howard A. Addison* 6 x 9, 192 pp, Quality PB, 978-1-58023-229-6 **$16.99**

**Finding Joy:** A Practical Spiritual Guide to Happiness *by Dannel I. Schwartz with Mark Hass*
6 x 9, 192 pp, Quality PB, 978-1-58023-009-4 **$14.95**

**The Gift of Kabbalah:** Discovering the Secrets of Heaven, Renewing Your Life on Earth
*by Tamar Frankiel, PhD* 6 x 9, 256 pp, Quality PB, 978-1-58023-141-1 **$16.95**

**Honey from the Rock: An Easy Introduction to Jewish Mysticism**
*by Lawrence Kushner* 6 x 9, 176 pp, Quality PB, 978-1-58023-073-5 **$16.95**

**Kabbalah:** A Brief Introduction for Christians
*by Tamar Frankiel, PhD* 5½ x 8½, 176 pp, Quality PB, 978-1-58023-303-3 **$16.99**

**Zohar:** Annotated & Explained *Translation and Annotation by Dr. Daniel C. Matt*
Foreword by Andrew Harvey 5½ x 8½, 176 pp, Quality PB, 978-1-893361-51-5 **$15.99**

# Judaism / Christianity

**The Jewish Connection to Israel, the Promised Land**
A Brief Introduction for Christians *by Rabbi Eugene Korn, PhD*
Guides Christians and Jews through the essential meanings of Israel for the Jewish
People and for the world. 5½ x 8½, 192 pp, Quality PB, 978-1-58023-318-7 **$14.99**

**Christians and Jews in Dialogue:** Learning in the Presence of the Other
*by Mary C. Boys and Sara S. Lee; Foreword by Dorothy C. Bass*
Explains the transformative work of creating environments for Jews and Christians
to study together and enter the dynamism of the other's religious tradition.
6 x 9, 240 pp, HC, 978-1-59473-144-0 **$21.99**

**Healing the Jewish-Christian Rift:** Growing Beyond Our Wounded History
*by Ron Miller and Laura Bernstein; Foreword by Dr. Beatrice Bruteau*
6 x 9, 288 pp, Quality PB, 978-1-59473-139-6 **$18.99**

**Introducing My Faith and My Community**
The Jewish Outreach Institute Guide for the Christian in a Jewish Interfaith Relationship
*by Rabbi Kerry M. Olitzky* 6 x 9, 176 pp, Quality PB, 978-1-58023-192-3 **$16.99** *(a Jewish Lights book)*

**The Jewish Approach to God:** A Brief Introduction for Christians
*by Rabbi Neil Gillman* 5½ x 8½, 192 pp, Quality PB, 978-1-58023-190-9 **$16.95** *(a Jewish Lights book)*

**Jewish Holidays:** A Brief Introduction for Christians
*by Rabbi Kerry M. Olitzky and Rabbi Daniel Judson*
5½ x 8½, 176 pp, Quality PB, 978-1-58023-302-6 **$16.99** *(a Jewish Lights book)*

**Jewish Ritual:** A Brief Introduction for Christians
*by Rabbi Kerry M. Olitzky and Rabbi Daniel Judson*
5½ x 8½, 144 pp, Quality PB, 978-1-58023-210-4 **$14.99** *(a Jewish Lights book)*

**Jewish Spirituality:** A Brief Introduction for Christians
*by Rabbi Lawrence Kushner*
5½ x 8½, 112 pp, Quality PB, 978-1-58023-150-3 **$12.95** *(a Jewish Lights book)*

**A Jewish Understanding of the New Testament**
*by Rabbi Samuel Sandmel; new Preface by Rabbi David Sandmel*
5½ x 8½, 368 pp, Quality PB, 978-1-59473-048-1 **$19.99**

**We Jews and Jesus:** Exploring Theological Differences for Mutual
Understanding *by Rabbi Samuel Sandmel; new Preface by Rabbi David Sandmel* A
Classic Reprint Written in a non-technical way for the layperson, this candid and
forthright look at the what and why of the Jewish attitude toward Jesus is a
clear and forceful exposition that guides both Christians and Jews in relevant
discussion. 6 x 9, 192 pp, Quality PB, 978-1-59473-208-9 **$16.99**

# Spirituality

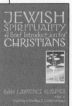

**Jewish Spirituality:** A Brief Introduction for Christians  *by Lawrence Kushner*
5½ x 8½, 112 pp, Quality PB, 978-1-58023-150-3  **$12.95**  *(a Jewish Lights book)*

**Journeys of Simplicity:** Traveling Light with Thomas Merton, Bashō, Edward Abbey, Annie Dillard & Others  *by Philip Harnden*  5 x 7¼, 144 pp, Quality PB, 978-1-59473-181-5  **$12.99**  128 pp, HC, 978-1-893361-76-8  **$16.95**

**Keeping Spiritual Balance As We Grow Older:** More than 65 Creative Ways to Use Purpose, Prayer, and the Power of Spirit to Build a Meaningful Retirement  *by Molly and Bernie Srode*  8 x 8, 224 pp, Quality PB, 978-1-59473-042-9  **$16.99**

**The Monks of Mount Athos:** A Western Monk's Extraordinary Spiritual Journey on Eastern Holy Ground  *by M. Basil Pennington, ocso; Foreword by Archimandrite Dionysios*  6 x 9, 256 pp, 10+ b/w line drawings, Quality PB, 978-1-893361-78-2  **$18.95**

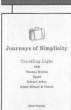

**One God Clapping:** The Spiritual Path of a Zen Rabbi  *by Alan Lew with Sherrill Jaffe*  5½ x 8½, 336 pp, Quality PB, 978-1-58023-115-2  **$16.95**  *(a Jewish Lights book)*

**Prayer for People Who Think Too Much:** A Guide to Everyday, Anywhere Prayer from the World's Faith Traditions  *by Mitch Finley*  5½ x 8½, 224 pp, Quality PB, 978-1-893361-21-8  **$16.99**; HC, 978-1-893361-00-3  **$21.95**

**Show Me Your Way:** The Complete Guide to Exploring Interfaith Spiritual Direction  *by Howard A. Addison*  5½ x 8½, 240 pp, Quality PB, 978-1-893361-41-6  **$16.95**

**Spirituality 101:** The Indispensable Guide to Keeping—or Finding—Your Spiritual Life on Campus  *by Harriet L. Schwartz, with contributions from college students at nearly thirty campuses across the United States*  6 x 9, 272 pp, Quality PB, 978-1-59473-000-9  **$16.99**

**Spiritually Incorrect:** Finding God in All the Wrong Places  *by Dan Wakefield; Illus. by Marian DelVecchio*  5½ x 8½, 192 pp, b/w illus., Quality PB, 978-1-59473-137-2  **$15.99**

**Spiritual Manifestos:** Visions for Renewed Religious Life in America from Young Spiritual Leaders of Many Faiths  *Edited by Niles Elliot Goldstein; Preface by Martin E. Marty*  6 x 9, 256 pp, HC, 978-1-893361-09-6  **$21.95**

**A Walk with Four Spiritual Guides:** Krishna, Buddha, Jesus, and Ramakrishna  *by Andrew Harvey*  5½ x 8½, 192 pp, 10 b/w photos & illus., Quality PB, 978-1-59473-138-9  **$15.99**

**What Matters:** Spiritual Nourishment for Head and Heart  *by Frederick Franck*  5 x 7¼, 128 pp, 50+ b/w illus., HC, 978-1-59473-013-9  **$16.99**

**Who Is My God?, 2nd Edition:** An Innovative Guide to Finding Your Spiritual Identity  *Created by the Editors at SkyLight Paths*  6 x 9, 160 pp, Quality PB, 978-1-59473-014-6  **$15.99**

# Spirituality—A Week Inside

## Come and Sit: A Week Inside Meditation Centers
*by Marcia Z. Nelson; Foreword by Wayne Teasdale*
The insider's guide to meditation in a variety of different spiritual traditions—Buddhist, Hindu, Christian, Jewish, and Sufi traditions.
6 x 9, 224 pp, b/w photos, Quality PB, 978-1-893361-35-5  **$16.95**

## Lighting the Lamp of Wisdom: A Week Inside a Yoga Ashram
*by John Ittner; Foreword by Dr. David Frawley*
This insider's guide to Hindu spiritual life takes you into a typical week of retreat inside a yoga ashram to demystify the experience and show you what to expect.
6 x 9, 192 pp, 10+ b/w photos, Quality PB, 978-1-893361-52-2  **$15.95**

## Making a Heart for God: A Week Inside a Catholic Monastery
*by Dianne Aprile; Foreword by Brother Patrick Hart, ocso*
Takes you to the Abbey of Gethsemani—the Trappist monastery in Kentucky that was home to author Thomas Merton—to explore the details.
6 x 9, 224 pp, b/w photos, Quality PB, 978-1-893361-49-2  **$16.95**

## Waking Up: A Week Inside a Zen Monastery
*by Jack Maguire; Foreword by John Daido Loori, Roshi*
An essential guide to what it's like to spend a week inside a Zen Buddhist monastery.
6 x 9, 224 pp, b/w photos, Quality PB, 978-1-893361-55-3  **$16.95**
HC, 978-1-893361-13-3  **$21.95**

# Spirituality of the Seasons

**Autumn:** A Spiritual Biography of the Season
*Edited by Gary Schmidt and Susan M. Felch; Illustrations by Mary Azarian*
Rejoice in autumn as a time of preparation and reflection. Includes Wendell Berry, David James Duncan, Robert Frost, A. Bartlett Giamatti, E. B. White, P. D. James, Julian of Norwich, Garret Keizer, Tracy Kidder, Anne Lamott, May Sarton.
6 x 9, 320 pp, 5 b/w illus., Quality PB, 978-1-59473-118-1 **$18.99**
HC, 978-1-59473-005-4 **$22.99**

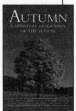

**Spring:** A Spiritual Biography of the Season
*Edited by Gary Schmidt and Susan M. Felch; Illustrations by Mary Azarian*
Explore the gentle unfurling of spring and reflect on how nature celebrates rebirth and renewal. Includes Jane Kenyon, Lucy Larcom, Harry Thurston, Nathaniel Hawthorne, Noel Perrin, Annie Dillard, Martha Ballard, Barbara Kingsolver, Dorothy Wordsworth, Donald Hall, David Brill, Lionel Basney, Isak Dinesen, Paul Laurence Dunbar. 6 x 9, 352 pp, 6 b/w illus., HC, 978-1-59473-114-3 **$21.99**

**Summer:** A Spiritual Biography of the Season
*Edited by Gary Schmidt and Susan M. Felch; Illustrations by Barry Moser*
"A sumptuous banquet.... These selections lift up an exquisite wholeness found within an everyday sophistication."— ★ *Publishers Weekly* starred review
Includes Anne Lamott, Luci Shaw, Ray Bradbury, Richard Selzer, Thomas Lynch, Walt Whitman, Carl Sandburg, Sherman Alexie, Madeleine L'Engle, Jamaica Kincaid.
6 x 9, 304 pp, 5 b/w illus., Quality PB, 978-1-59473-183-9 **$18.99**
HC, 978-1-59473-083-2 **$21.99**

**Winter:** A Spiritual Biography of the Season
*Edited by Gary Schmidt and Susan M. Felch; Illustrations by Barry Moser*
"This outstanding anthology features top-flight nature and spirituality writers on the fierce, inexorable season of winter.... Remarkably lively and warm, despite the icy subject." — ★ *Publishers Weekly* starred review
Includes Will Campbell, Rachel Carson, Annie Dillard, Donald Hall, Ron Hansen, Jane Kenyon, Jamaica Kincaid, Barry Lopez, Kathleen Norris, John Updike, E. B. White.
6 x 9, 288 pp, 6 b/w illus., Deluxe PB w/flaps, 978-1-893361-92-8 **$18.95**
HC, 978-1-893361-53-9 **$21.95**

# Spirituality / Animal Companions

**Blessing the Animals:** Prayers and Ceremonies to Celebrate God's Creatures, Wild and Tame  *Edited by Lynn L. Caruso*  5 x 7¼, 256 pp, HC, 978-1-59473-145-7 **$19.99**

**What Animals Can Teach Us about Spirituality:** Inspiring Lessons from Wild and Tame Creatures  *by Diana L. Guerrero*  6 x 9, 176 pp, Quality PB, 978-1-893361-84-5 **$16.95**

# Spirituality

**Awakening the Spirit, Inspiring the Soul**
30 Stories of Interspiritual Discovery in the Community of Faiths
*Edited by Brother Wayne Teasdale and Martha Howard, MD; Foreword by Joan Borysenko, PhD*
Thirty original spiritual mini-autobiographies showcase the varied ways that people come to faith—and what that means—in today's multi-religious world.
6 x 9, 224 pp, HC, 978-1-59473-039-9 **$21.99**

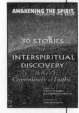

**The Alphabet of Paradise:** An A–Z of Spirituality for Everyday Life
*by Howard Cooper*  5 x 7¼, 224 pp, Quality PB, 978-1-893361-80-5 **$16.95**

**Creating a Spiritual Retirement:** A Guide to the Unseen Possibilities in Our Lives
*by Molly Srode*  6 x 9, 208 pp, b/w photos, Quality PB, 978-1-59473-050-4 **$14.99**
HC, 978-1-893361-75-1 **$19.95**

**Finding Hope:** Cultivating God's Gift of a Hopeful Spirit
*by Marcia Ford*  8 x 8, 200 pp, Quality PB, 978-1-59473-211-9 **$16.99**

**The Geography of Faith:** Underground Conversations on Religious, Political and Social Change  *by Daniel Berrigan and Robert Coles*  6 x 9, 224 pp, Quality PB, 978-1-893361-40-9 **$16.95**

**God Within:** Our Spiritual Future—As Told by Today's New Adults  *Edited by Jon M. Sweeney and the Editors at SkyLight Paths*  6 x 9, 176 pp, Quality PB, 978-1-893361-15-7 **$14.95**

# Meditation / Prayer

### Prayers to an Evolutionary God
*by William Cleary; Afterword by Diarmuid O'Murchu*
How is it possible to pray when God is dislocated from heaven, dispersed all around us, and more of a creative force than an all-knowing father? Inspired by the spiritual and scientific teachings of Diarmuid O'Murchu and Teilhard de Chardin, Cleary reveals that religion and science can be combined to create an expanding view of the universe—an evolutionary faith.
6 x 9, 208 pp, HC, 978-1-59473-006-1 **$21.99**

### Psalms: A Spiritual Commentary
*by M. Basil Pennington, OCSO; Illustrations by Phillip Ratner*
Showing how the Psalms give profound and candid expression to both our highest aspirations and our deepest pain, the late, highly respected Cistercian Abbot M. Basil Pennington shares his reflections on some of the most beloved passages from the Bible's most widely read book.
6 x 9, 176 pp, HC, 24 full-page b/w illus., 978-1-59473-141-9 **$19.99**

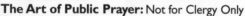

### The Song of Songs: A Spiritual Commentary
*by M. Basil Pennington, OCSO; Illustrations by Phillip Ratner*
Join the late M. Basil Pennington as he ruminates on the Bible's most challenging mystical text. Follow a path into the Songs that weaves through his inspired words and the evocative drawings of Jewish artist Phillip Ratner—a path that reveals your own humanity and leads to the deepest delight of your soul.
6 x 9, 160 pp, Quality PB, 14 b/w illus., 978-1-59473-235-5 **$16.99**; HC, 978-1-59473-004-7 **$19.99**

### Women of Color Pray: Voices of Strength, Faith, Healing, Hope and Courage *Edited and with Introductions by Christal M. Jackson*
Through these prayers, poetry, lyrics, meditations and affirmations, you will share in the strong and undeniable connection women of color share with God. It will challenge you to explore new ways of prayerful expression.
5 x 7¼, 208 pp, Quality PB, 978-1-59473-077-1 **$15.99**

### The Art of Public Prayer: Not for Clergy Only
*by Lawrence A. Hoffman*
An ecumenical resource for all people looking to change hardened worship patterns.
6 x 9, 288 pp, Quality PB, 978-1-893361-06-5 **$18.99**

### Finding Grace at the Center, 3rd Ed.: The Beginning of Centering Prayer
*by M. Basil Pennington, OCSO, Thomas Keating, OCSO, and Thomas E. Clarke, SJ*
*Foreword by Rev. Cynthia Bourgeault, PhD*
5 x 7¼, 128 pp, Quality PB, 978-1-59473-182-2 **$12.99**

### A Heart of Stillness: A Complete Guide to Learning the Art of Meditation
*by David A. Cooper* 5½ x 8½, 272 pp, Quality PB, 978-1-893361-03-4 **$16.95**

### Meditation without Gurus: A Guide to the Heart of Practice
*by Clark Strand* 5½ x 8½, 192 pp, Quality PB, 978-1-893361-93-5 **$16.95**

### Praying with Our Hands: 21 Practices of Embodied Prayer from the World's
Spiritual Traditions *by Jon M. Sweeney; Photographs by Jennifer J. Wilson; Foreword by Mother Tessa Bielecki; Afterword by Taitetsu Unno, PhD*
8 x 8, 96 pp, 22 duotone photos, Quality PB, 978-1-893361-16-4 **$16.95**

### Silence, Simplicity & Solitude: A Complete Guide to Spiritual Retreat at Home
*by David A. Cooper* 5½ x 8½, 336 pp, Quality PB, 978-1-893361-04-1 **$16.95**

### Three Gates to Meditation Practice: A Personal Journey into Sufism, Buddhism,
and Judaism *by David A. Cooper* 5½ x 8½, 240 pp, Quality PB, 978-1-893361-22-5 **$16.95**

### Women Pray: Voices through the Ages, from Many Faiths, Cultures and Traditions
*Edited and with Introductions by Monica Furlong*
5 x 7¼, 256 pp, Quality PB, 978-1-59473-071-9 **$15.99**
Deluxe HC with ribbon marker, 978-1-893361-25-6 **$19.95**

# Spirituality & Crafts

**The Knitting Way:** A Guide to Spiritual Self-Discovery
*by Linda Skolnik and Janice MacDaniels*
7 x 9, 240 pp, Quality PB, b/w photographs, 978-1-59473-079-5 **$16.99**

**The Quilting Path:** A Guide to Spiritual Discovery through Fabric, Thread and Kabbalah
*by Louise Silk*
7 x 9, 192 pp, Quality PB, b/w photographs and illustrations, 978-1-59473-206-5 **$16.99**

**The Scrapbooking Journey:** A Hands-On Guide to Spiritual Discovery
*by Cory Richardson-Lauve; Foreword by Stacy Julian*
7 x 9, 176 pp, Quality PB, 8-page full-color insert, plus b/w photographs
978-1-59473-216-4 **$18.99**

**The Painting Path:** Embodying Spiritual Discovery through Yoga, Brush and
Color  *by Linda Novick; Foreword by Richard Segalman*
Explores the divine connection you can experience through creativity.
7 x 9, 208 pp, 8-page full-color insert, Quality PB, 978-1-59473-226-3 **$18.99**

# Spiritual Practice

**Divining the Body:** Reclaim the Holiness of Your Physical Self
*by Jan Phillips*
A practical and inspiring guidebook for connecting the body and soul in spiritual
practice. Helps you discover your body as a pathway to the Divine.
8 x 8, 256 pp, Quality PB, 978-1-59473-080-1 **$16.99**

**Finding Time for the Timeless:** Spirituality in the Workweek  *by John McQuiston II*
Simple, refreshing stories that provide you with examples of how you can refocus and enrich your daily life using prayer or meditation, ritual and other forms
of spiritual practice. 5½ x 6¾, 208 pp, HC, 978-1-59473-035-1 **$17.99**

**The Gospel of Thomas:** A Guidebook for Spiritual Practice
*by Ron Miller; Translations by Stevan Davies*
An innovative guide to bring a new spiritual classic into daily life.
6 x 9, 160 pp, Quality PB, 978-1-59473-047-4 **$14.99**

**Earth, Water, Fire, and Air:** Essential Ways of Connecting to Spirit
*by Cait Johnson*  6 x 9, 224 pp, HC, 978-1-893361-65-2 **$19.95**

**Labyrinths from the Outside In:** Walking to Spiritual Insight—A Beginner's Guide
*by Donna Schaper and Carole Ann Camp*
6 x 9, 208 pp, b/w illus. and photos, Quality PB, 978-1-893361-18-8 **$16.95**

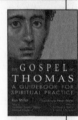

**Practicing the Sacred Art of Listening:** A Guide to Enrich Your Relationships
and Kindle Your Spiritual Life—The Listening Center Workshop
*by Kay Lindahl*  8 x 8, 176 pp, Quality PB, 978-1-893361-85-0 **$16.95**

**Releasing the Creative Spirit:** Unleash the Creativity in Your Life
*by Dan Wakefield*  7 x 10, 256 pp, Quality PB, 978-1-893361-36-2 **$16.95**

**The Sacred Art of Bowing:** Preparing to Practice
*by Andi Young*  5½ x 8½, 128 pp, b/w illus., Quality PB, 978-1-893361-82-9 **$14.95**

**The Sacred Art of Chant:** Preparing to Practice
*by Ana Hernández*  5½ x 8½, 192 pp, Quality PB, 978-1-59473-036-8 **$15.99**

**The Sacred Art of Fasting:** Preparing to Practice
*by Thomas Ryan, CSP*  5½ x 8½, 192 pp, Quality PB, 978-1-59473-078-8 **$15.99**

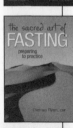

**The Sacred Art of Forgiveness:** Forgiving Ourselves and Others through God's Grace
*by Marcia Ford*  8 x 8, 176 pp, Quality PB, 978-1-59473-175-4 **$16.99**

**The Sacred Art of Listening:** Forty Reflections for Cultivating a Spiritual
Practice  *by Kay Lindahl; Illustrations by Amy Schnapper*
8 x 8, 160 pp, b/w illus., Quality PB, 978-1-893361-44-7 **$16.99**

**The Sacred Art of Lovingkindness:** Preparing to Practice
*by Rabbi Rami Shapiro; Foreword by Marcia Ford*
5½ x 8½, 176 pp, Quality PB, 978-1-59473-151-8 **$16.99**

**Sacred Speech:** A Practical Guide for Keeping Spirit in Your Speech
*by Rev. Donna Schaper*  6 x 9, 176 pp, Quality PB, 978-1-59473-068-9 **$15.99**
HC, 978-1-893361-74-4 **$21.95**

# Sacred Texts—SkyLight Illuminations Series

Offers today's spiritual seeker an accessible entry into the great classic texts of the world's spiritual traditions. Each classic is presented in an accessible translation, with facing pages of guided commentary from experts, giving you the keys you need to understand the history, context and meaning of the text. This series enables you, whatever your background, to experience and understand classic spiritual texts directly, and to make them a part of your life.

## CHRISTIANITY

**The End of Days:** Essential Selections from Apocalyptic Texts— Annotated & Explained  *Annotation by Robert G. Clouse*
Helps you understand the complex Christian visions of the end of the world.
5½ x 8½, 224 pp, Quality PB, 978-1-59473-170-9 **$16.99**

**The Hidden Gospel of Matthew:** Annotated & Explained
*Translation & Annotation by Ron Miller*
Takes you deep into the text cherished around the world to discover the words and events that have the strongest connection to the historical Jesus.
5½ x 8½, 272 pp, Quality PB, 978-1-59473-038-2 **$16.99**

**The Lost Sayings of Jesus:** Teachings from Ancient Christian, Jewish, Gnostic and Islamic Sources—Annotated & Explained
*Translation & Annotation by Andrew Phillip Smith; Foreword by Stephan A. Hoeller*
This collection of more than three hundred sayings depicts Jesus as a Wisdom teacher who speaks to people of all faiths as a mystic and spiritual master.
5½ x 8½, 240 pp, Quality PB, 978-1-59473-172-3 **$16.99**

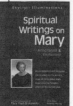

**Philokalia:** The Eastern Christian Spiritual Texts—Selections Annotated & Explained  *Annotation by Allyne Smith; Translation by G. E. H. Palmer, Phillip Sherrard and Bishop Kallistos Ware*
The first approachable introduction to the wisdom of the Philokalia, which is the classic text of Eastern Christian spirituality.
5½ x 8½, 240 pp, Quality PB, 978-1-59473-103-7 **$16.99**

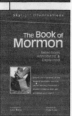

**Spiritual Writings on Mary:** Annotated & Explained
*Annotation by Mary Ford-Grabowsky; Foreword by Andrew Harvey*
Examines the role of Mary, the mother of Jesus, as a source of inspiration in history and in life today.  5½ x 8½, 288 pp, Quality PB, 978-1-59473-001-6 **$16.99**

**The Way of a Pilgrim:** The Jesus Prayer Journey—Annotated & Explained
*Translation & Annotation by Gleb Pokrovsky; Foreword by Andrew Harvey*
This classic of Russian spirituality is the delightful account of one man who sets out to learn the prayer of the heart, also known as the "Jesus prayer."
5½ x 8½, 160 pp, Illus., Quality PB, 978-1-893361-31-7 **$14.95**

## MORMONISM

**The Book of Mormon:** Selections Annotated & Explained
*Annotation by Jana Riess; Foreword by Phyllis Tickle*
Explores the sacred epic that is cherished by more than twelve million members of the LDS church as the keystone of their faith.
5½ x 8½, 272 pp, Quality PB, 978-1-59473-076-4 **$16.99**

## NATIVE AMERICAN

**Native American Stories of the Sacred:** Annotated & Explained
*Retold & Annotated by Evan T. Pritchard*
Intended for more than entertainment, these teaching tales contain elegantly simple illustrations of time-honored truths.
5½ x 8½, 272 pp, Quality PB, 978-1-59473-112-9 **$16.99**

# *Sacred Texts—cont.*

## GNOSTICISM

**The Gospel of Philip:** Annotated & Explained
*Translation & Annotation by Andrew Phillip Smith; Foreword by Stevan Davies*
Reveals otherwise unrecorded sayings of Jesus and fragments of Gnostic mythology.
5½ x 8½, 160 pp, Quality PB, 978-1-59473-111-2 **$16.99**

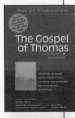

**The Gospel of Thomas:** Annotated & Explained
*Translation & Annotation by Stevan Davies* Sheds new light on the origins of Christianity and
portrays Jesus as a wisdom-loving sage. 5½ x 8½, 192 pp, Quality PB, 978-1-893361-45-4 **$16.99**

**The Secret Book of John:** The Gnostic Gospel—Annotated & Explained
*Translation & Annotation by Stevan Davies* The most significant and influential text of
the ancient Gnostic religion. 5½ x 8½, 208 pp, Quality PB, 978-1-59473-082-5 **$16.99**

## JUDAISM

**The Divine Feminine in Biblical Wisdom Literature**
Selections Annotated & Explained
*Translation & Annotation by Rabbi Rami Shapiro; Foreword by Rev. Cynthia Bourgeault, PhD*
Uses the Hebrew books of Psalms, Proverbs, Song of Songs, Ecclesiastes and Job,
Wisdom literature and the Wisdom of Solomon to clarify who Wisdom is.
5½ x 8½, 240 pp, Quality PB, 978-1-59473-109-9 **$16.99**

**Ethics of the Sages:** *Pirke Avot*—Annotated & Explained
*Translation & Annotation by Rabbi Rami Shapiro* Clarifies the ethical teachings of the
early Rabbis. 5½ x 8½, 192 pp, Quality PB, 978-1-59473-207-2 **$16.99**

**Hasidic Tales:** Annotated & Explained
*Translation & Annotation by Rabbi Rami Shapiro*
Introduces the legendary tales of the impassioned Hasidic rabbis, presenting them as
stories rather than as parables. 5½ x 8½, 240 pp, Quality PB, 978-1-893361-86-7 **$16.95**

**The Hebrew Prophets:** Selections Annotated & Explained
*Translation & Annotation by Rabbi Rami Shapiro; Foreword by Zalman M. Schachter-Shalomi*
Focuses on the central themes covered by all the Hebrew prophets.
5½ x 8½, 224 pp, Quality PB, 978-1-59473-037-5 **$16.99**

**Zohar:** Annotated & Explained *Translation & Annotation by Daniel C. Matt*
The best-selling author of *The Essential Kabbalah* brings together in one place the most
important teachings of the Zohar, the canonical text of Jewish mystical tradition.
5½ x 8½, 176 pp, Quality PB, 978-1-893361-51-5 **$15.99**

## EASTERN RELIGIONS

**Bhagavad Gita:** Annotated & Explained *Translation by Shri Purohit Swami*
*Annotation by Kendra Crossen Burroughs* Explains references and philosophical terms,
shares the interpretations of famous spiritual leaders and scholars, and more.
5½ x 8½, 192 pp, Quality PB, 978-1-893361-28-7 **$16.95**

**Dhammapada:** Annotated & Explained *Translation by Max Müller and revised by*
*Jack Maguire; Annotation by Jack Maguire* Contains all of Buddhism's key teachings.
5½ x 8½, 160 pp, b/w photos, Quality PB, 978-1-893361-42-3 **$14.95**

**Rumi and Islam:** Selections from His Stories, Poems, and Discourses—
Annotated & Explained *Translation & Annotation by Ibrahim Gamard*
Focuses on Rumi's place within the Sufi tradition of Islam, providing insight into
the mystical side of the religion. 5½ x 8½, 240 pp, Quality PB, 978-1-59473-002-3 **$15.99**

**Selections from the Gospel of Sri Ramakrishna:** Annotated & Explained
*Translation by Swami Nikhilananda; Annotation by Kendra Crossen Burroughs*
Introduces the fascinating world of the Indian mystic and the universal appeal
of his message. 5½ x 8½, 240 pp, b/w photos, Quality PB, 978-1-893361-46-1 **$16.95**

**Tao Te Ching:** Annotated & Explained *Translation & Annotation by Derek Lin*
*Foreword by Lama Surya Das* Introduces an Eastern classic in an accessible, poetic
and completely original way. 5½ x 8½, 192 pp, Quality PB, 978-1-59473-204-1 **$16.99**

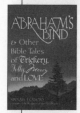